I THOUGHT YOU HAD
A BIGGER DREAM

I THOUGHT YOU HAD A BIGGER DREAM

❧

The Legacy That Built Jacob's House

PENNY ROBICHAUX-KOONTZ

with Claudia Stewart Farrell

Claudia Stewart Farrell

TATE PUBLISHING *& Enterprises*

Published by Tate Publishing & Enterprises, LLC
127 E. Trade Center Terrace | Mustang, Oklahoma 73064 USA
1.888.361.9473 | www.tatepublishing.com

Tate Publishing is committed to excellence in the publishing industry. The company reflects the philosophy established by the founders, based on Psalm 68:11,
"The Lord gave the word and great was the company of those who published it."

Book design copyright © 2011 by Tate Publishing, LLC. All rights reserved.
Cover design by April Marciszewski
Interior design by Chelsea Womble

Published in the United States of America

ISBN: 978-1-61777-387-7
1. Biography & Autobiogrphy, Personal Memoirs
2. Biography & Autobiography, Religious
11.04.25

DEDICATION

To my children, thank you for willingly sharing your mother with hurting people. Thank you for doing it so unselfishly. I want you to know that I know that you did it at great cost. You have been my greatest support and inspiration. It is my prayer that you seize your legacy and run your race fearlessly, with boldness and joy. That you fall in love with God and be filled with His Spirit and a spirit of adventure. That you realize that Jesus said, "Every day has trouble of its own…so you must face each day and each trial as a challenge you are able to conquer. That you call on every memory of God's faithfulness in bringing us through because He is good and we did not quit" (Matthew 6:34, NIV).

QUOTING THEODORE ROOSEVELT'S "MAN IN THE ARENA"

It is not the critic who counts: not the man who points out how the strong man stumbles or where the doer of deeds could have done better. The credit belongs to the man who is actually in the arena, whose face is marred by dust and sweat and blood, who strives valiantly, who errs and comes up short again and again, because there is no effort without error or shortcoming, but who knows the great enthusiasms, the great devotions, who spends himself for a worthy cause; who, at the best, knows, in the end, the triumph of high achievement, and who, at the worst, if he fails, at least he fails while daring greatly, so that his place shall never be with those cold and timid souls who knew neither victory nor defeat.

ACKNOWLEDGMENTS

First, I want to thank my mother, Sally Nelson, who shared her legacy with me and cheered me on through every tough challenge reminding me to never give up, never quit.

To my friend, Claudia Farrell, thank you for taking a manuscript that has evolved over thirty years, the words of my mouth, and the thoughts of my heart and putting it together in book form, wow, what a task. I pray that it is pleasing to God and that it bless those who read it.

To my navy family of the USS *Mispillion* and Chris Munson, who was on the scene in 1952 and continues to be a huge part of my life. To Dick Francisco and the other marine pilots in my father's unit who were dear friends and family for fifty-eight years. Semper Fi

To my fabulous cousins—especially Durm, Hank, and George—and to my friends and sorority sisters, Mary and Tina, for keeping me laughing, humble, and involved through high school, and to Daina Perkins who continued what they began, celebrating life, and standing in faith through some dark days.

To my daughter (in-love), Noreen, who has been a constant source of strength and joy since the day I met you. Thank you for being a child of excellence, motivated by love and having passion for life and for our Lord. Your encouragement has rallied me and your humor, dry as it is, delights me. You are the first child of my heart.

To Eddie and Bessie, how I love you, and all those who came through the Garden, teaching me, stretching my faith, and causing me to laugh from my toes. Your friendship and service still amazes me.

To Joanne King Herring, who seeded our transition when all seemed lost.

To Robert Bauer, Harold, and Barbara Mayfield, gifts from God and first board members and intercessors, thank you for everything all these years.

To Bobbie Hood, dear friend, prayer partner, dinner cooker, and floor scrubber. As iron sharpens iron, the friend that loveth at all times, for this I thank you. A very big thank you for sharing Frank with us all these years, faithful partners…I love you.

To Maria Remy, the steadiest and most faithful woman I know. Thank you for the laughs, for keeping everything adding up, for taking care of my mother until I could convince her to move to Missouri. You were there the first day I inquired about a homeless shelter, and you are still a rock to me today.

To Lynn and Roark Wells for being a bridge between Texas and Missouri, thank you. I am so grateful to my Texas family.

To Becky Kirkland, a special thank you for so many times being my hands and feet at Jacob's House Missouri. We would not be where we are without your gentle devotion and the dedication of your precious time.

To Curt and Kathy Lawrence, from our first meeting on my first day in Branson to today, thank you for your counsel, your friendship, your support and your laughter.

To Greg and Victoria Volich, and Paul and Jill Scribner who believed in my mission and made Jacob's House Missouri a reality through their time, talent, and money, my deepest gratitude. How will I ever thank you? I know, keep changing the lives of children.

To James Garrett, who stayed the course and put it all on the line for Jacob's House on Thunder Ranch, who tells our story to his audiences and loves our children.

To Mr. Paul and Ann Bluto for promoting our cause, believing our dream, and helping us at every turn. Branson IMAX became our second home and command central for ideas and support for our projects. You are the wind beneath our wings.

To Chris, mighty man of God, and Cyndi, my little songbird, thank you for being more than I dreamed of for Jacob's House and everything God promised to me. I love our working together fulfilling the goal of a loving home for every child on this land, and sharing our gifts with each other.

To all our friends and partners in Missouri, too many to name, thank you for your faithfulness. We are so grateful for making us known so the children who need us can find us and then for being part of the supply to raise them. For making a Texan feel right at home.

To the College of the Ozark interns, every one of you have touched our lives and enhanced the experiences of each child who calls Jacob's House home. Thank you for your love and dedication to our cause and to your education. To all our partners and volunteers…thank you.

To my sweet Jeremiah for massaging my shoulders while I typed the manuscript, telling me… "I will be writing books just like you, Mom."

To Haley, the little girl I prayed for more than forty years, for our girls' days out and cuddling in bed watching movies.

To Jacob, dear son, for cooking dinners and bringing me golden nugget happy eggs and for making me laugh in the hard times and reminding me of the good times, I love you.

And to Dan, you had no idea what you were getting into, but you have been faithful holding down the fort while the daunting task of finishing this work was completed. Thank you for never growing weary in well doing. Thank you for waking me up by playing the piano and for crawling through the berry patch and the creek with our kids. I am looking forward to our future, an adventure in faith.

I close with this thank you to John and Dodie Osteen for living their faith in front of me. For sharing their love of family with their congregation—it inspired me. For John's humor and unwavering faith. For Dodie's passion and quiet strength. I thank them for solid teaching and for being touchable, humble, and genuine. Without the grounding they provided, I may never have run my race and certainly would never have discerned the relationship I have with Jesus and may never have come to know my Heavenly Father. As Noreen said recently, "If not for them, this entire family may not have been saved." Thank you, Jesus, for showing Yourself big to me, in them.

TABLE OF CONTENTS

FOREWORD

In 2007, Penny asked me to read a book she was writing about her family. At that time, I read the manuscript suggesting some grammatical and punctuation changes. It was a work in progress, and Penny knew there would be more added as life unfolded before she would attempt to have the book published.

Then three years later, after little contact with Penny due to much travel on my part, I received a beautiful electronic Easter card from her. However, to my deep concern, her daughter Haley's name was not on the card with the other children. I was upset to think Haley was not in Penny's care. I did not realize until that moment how this little girl had captured my heart. Much to my delight, I was soon to learn that all was well with Haley, as Penny told me she was safe by her side.

Was Haley's name missing from the card, or did I just not see it? We will never know because we are unable to retrieve it from cyberspace. What we do know is that at just the right time Penny and I were again in touch. Why? We believe it was divine timing. It was time to publish the book. Penny asked that I once again read the manuscript as she had recorded recent events, completing these chapters of her life. I agreed and received the text via an e-mail–transmitted file.

As I questioned Penny on different aspects of the story, we soon found ourselves working as a team to chronicle her family history. We were able to collaborate in a special way, with her pouring her heart out, sharing her pain, her humor, her joy, and her faith as I hooked up with her vision, adding the commas and breaking up the run-on sentences with laughter and delight for both of us.

It was no longer a cold editing to dot the i's and cross the t's. We camped out together and walked down the road of book writing side-by-side, our skills complementing each other's. As a great storyteller, she recited tales of pain and glory, sadness and humor, effort and triumph, myself expressing and engineering the words into proper format until at last we captured the essence of a story well told, and lives well lived.

We worked from approximately thirty years of written memories, a record of the thoughts, feelings, and oral history of a family to honor the author's mother. The dialogue is, of course, to the best of her memory including actual quotes passed down from mother to daughter.

To write someone else's story, you must not only assimilate the history but also know the heart and character of the person on a level that allows you to express their thoughts in the same way they would. Her story captured my heart as I had the privilege of better learning my friend in all of her external and internal beauty by getting a more complete understanding of the day-to-day molding that made her the amazing woman of strength and virtue she is today.

I am a contemporary of Penny (Nelson) Robichaux-Koontz. We are women born in the same year, reaching maturity 1800 miles apart, who found each other in a small Missouri town, sixty years later. She grew up in the deserts of the western United States and next door to Disneyland, and I on an Iowa dairy farm. We are baby boomer children who faced the scare of the polio epidemic. She contracted the crippling disease at age three. I did not. However, I do remember sensing the great fear of the dread disease in the conversations of my parents and grandparents.

Her life was a series of challenges, both physical and emotional keeping appointments with doctors, therapists, and tutors, sprinkled with adventures and experiences that would delight any child. My childhood was that of a typical Midwestern farm girl enjoying the harmony of nature and family but by comparison uneventful. My memory was tickled by her story and then jogged by my older brother to recall standing in line at a large community building awaiting my turn for the "gun" to be pressed against my upper arm to be inoculated against polio and later sucking on sugar cubes flavored with the polio booster.

I tell this to express the connection she and I made on a level that enabled me to relate her story from her childhood days through her teenage years and young married life and beyond. We are as much the same as we are different by our connection in time, and a common moral compass establishing us as the daughters, mothers, wives, and women we are today.

The purpose of telling this story is to show what a person can accomplish through sheer guts and a never say die attitude. It is also to honor a woman who lost almost everything yet found a string to hold on to until she was able to twist it into a rope that was strong enough to pull herself and her children out of the depths of loss and despair into productive lives that reached outside themselves. Woven into the book are life-lessons, which when applied can alter understanding, shine light on circumstances, and modify behaviors to bring positive changes into the life of the reader.

What can be drawn from this remarkable story is not just a heart breaking and heart touching tale of surviving and virtually overcoming loss but of triumphing in life, through strong character, hard work, and confidence that there is more good in this world than evil.

—Claudia Stewart Farrell

THE KEY

Mother, tonight I am reporter, emotionally set free:
I have to stop and take a breath,
this is of you and me.

Around a table just we two,
sharing, talking as we do,
jotting down notes and things,
remembering the times our lives have seen.

Oh, how revealing, our hopes and our dreams,
from the soft and tender loving times
to the nightmares, pains, and screams.

Shall we tell this? We must I guess,
who could understand the best without the rest.

I started out to honor you for all the special things you do,
to open eyes of passersby, that life is what we make it.
That inside us a power dwells if we do not forsake it.

That prayer is good but not alone,
its works He wants to see,
for at the moment of your birth
the tools were given thee.

When at last I rest my pen
and our story has been told,
what will be the judgment of men,
if I may be so bold?

Will they only understand the parts
like a fairytale,
or will they realize it was the trials
we did not fail.

This one thing I am certain,
for others I cannot plea,
but this has been a great life,
the one you shared with me.

So if this book brings understanding
to just one parent and child,
if it gives hope to one defeated,
or helps one life that has gone wild,
if it makes one single human being

stand up and say "I can,"
then I'm sure we would both be willing
to be judged by any man.

So from the very first page until the very last,
it's your "number one trooper" saying,
"Thanks, Mom, it's been a blast."

THE CRISIS

The night was clear and cool after the heat of another August day. Rolling the window down in her 1950 Cadillac, she took a deep breath, letting it out slowly. She rolled her head back and repeated the measured breathing, taking in the salty smell of the Pacific Ocean. Suddenly, she thought she should drive faster, but the temptation to enjoy these miles along the beautiful coastline tugged at her heart, while worry took control of her mind.

They had been in California just a little over two months, yet it felt like a lifetime since she left Huron, South Dakota. She was waiting for the return of her husband who had shipped out of Long Beach to Korea.

She had been going to the same Catholic church night after night to light a candle for her husband, Forey Nelson, now declared MIA (missing in action). One moment her heart filled with fear, and the next moment she was full of hope. She knew fear had to stop; it was tearing her to pieces, draining her of strength. *He is strong and healthy and had been a guide and hunter in the Black Hills of South Dakota all his adult life. He served six years as a marine. What is wrong with me? He is highly trained for the mission, a fighter pilot; he will fight. He is familiar with the risk and prepared for the possibility of capture, or is he?* Once again, she remembered one of the last conversations they had after his orders came, recalling him to active service.

"My reaction time is ten seconds off, Sally, which is the difference between success and failure of a mission. It is the difference between life and death in war."

Last year at this time, she thought Forey was home for good. The marine was a full-time husband and a father now. His life had changed. He had exchanged planes for a Cadillac, war games and mission strategies for bowling balls and dance halls. Ten seconds in timing just was not an issue outside a "Corsair airplane," then the Korean War, the recall. How long did it take to read the new orders? Ten seconds? *How ironic*, she thought as she brushed away another tear. Coming to herself, she thought, *Hurry, Ella is waiting, and falling apart is not doing Forey or our children any good.*

She realized that she was shaking now. The night air had turned cold as she picked up speed. Reaching to roll up the window, she wondered if she would ever be comfortable again. With one hand, she began gently rubbing her stomach, now swollen in her seventh month of pregnancy. "This has to be hard on you, little one. I hope I can hide my fears and tears from your sister and brother, but your little heart beats with mine."

She put more pressure on the gas pedal wondering and glancing at her watch again, what would Ella think? Ella volunteered to watch the children while she went to church tonight, but Penny wasn't feeling well, and Jon seemed to sense something was wrong. "I can't keep imposing on Ella; she is a newlywed with a husband at sea. They hadn't even had the chance to start their family before he shipped out, and I'm asking her to help raise mine."

The headlights shone on the driveway that led to their trailer park. With both hands, she turned the steering wheel and slowly inched her way to her trailer, trying to be as quiet as possible. It was late. As she opened the car door, a scream pierced the stillness of the night. She froze, and then the scream came again.

Rushing to the trailer door, she knew it was Penny. "My God!" she cried as she opened the door, and then her eyes fell on her three-year-old daughter.

No one was touching her, she hadn't fallen, but the screams continued. Her little arms, until now, had only reached out to hold a doll or hug a parent or her baby brother. Now those arms wrapped around her head. The long platinum curls, so tenderly brushed into ringlets earlier that day, were wet with sweat and lay crushed against her pale, terrified face and the pillow where she lay.

Dropping to her knees, pulling her daughter's body close to her, she said, "My God, you are burning up, Penny. Can you tell Mommy where you hurt?"

Quickly her eyes started looking over the body she had created and taken such delight in watching grow; that perfect little body that was so active just weeks before, running, and dancing was now burning with fever and contorted in pain.

"My head, Mommy, my head," she screamed, crying and pressing her head into her mother's body as if the pressure would ease the pain.

Quietly, out of the shadows, a little boy not two feet tall drew closer. He was afraid of the screams, afraid because his new friend Ella was crying and so was his mom; but it was too hard to be alone in the next room, so he came closer and closer until he stood next to his mother.

Looking over her son's head, she said, "Ella, we need help." The only person she had in town was her brother, Bill. "Ella, will you just stay a minute longer while I go to the payphone to call my brother?"

Ella lifted Jon onto her lap and nodded yes, as she tried to comfort him, rocking slowly back and forth, kissing his head, and brushing away her own tears.

"Penny, I will be right back, honey. I'm going to call your Uncle Bill."

"Will you hurry, Mommy?"

"I'll hurry!"

Running to the payphone, she searched the bottom of her purse for change. She grabbed the receiver, pressed the dime into the slot, waiting for the familiar sound of the coin dropping and the tone that would signal her to dial her brother's number.

"Hello," a woman's voice answered on the second ring.

"Donna, this is Sally. Penny is sick. I need Bill; please put him on the line."

"Bill isn't home, Sally. He's gone to see a play in Los Angeles tonight. I don't know what time he will be back, but I will tell him you called and send him over the minute he comes in." Donna could tell that the line was still open, but it was so quiet that she thought for a moment that the telephone had gone dead. "Sally, are you there?"

"Donna, tell him he has to hurry; we need help. Every doctor that has seen Penny says she just has a virus and she'll be fine. They think I am exaggerating her symptoms or I am hysterical because Forey is missing. They blame my being pregnant as the reason I am getting so emotional about little things; but, Donna, this is not little. If you could hear her screaming… Bill is my only hope right now."

"Sally, I'll tell him just the minute he walks in. I'm sure he will not be much longer," she said, trying to calm her, sensing the panic that was welling up in her sister-in-law. "Let me hang up now, in case he tries calling me before getting on the road, then I'll send him to you right away."

"Thank you, Donna," she said, placing the receiver back on the hook and dropping her head to rest on the hand that could not break the connection completely. "Oh God. Forey, where are you? Why aren't you here with us? I need you; the kids need you!" There was no answer to her question; in fact, there seemed to be no answers at all.

Summoning all her strength, she turned to walk back to the trailer, remembering her promise to Penny that she would hurry. Her legs felt like lead, her stomach cramping, her head throbbing, and her heart pounding so hard it sounded like a drum beating in her ears with every step.

"She just fell asleep. Did you reach your brother?" Ella asked. "Is he coming? Were you able to find a doctor? Sally, are you listening to me?" Jon slipped off Ella's lap and ran to his mother's side, clutching her leg.

"I hear you, Ella. Bill has gone out tonight. You asked if I was able to find a doctor. I have been to so many. One says its bronchitis, another scarlet fever. They give her an antibiotic and then pat me on the back, telling me to go home and everything will be all right. I've been reading about polio in the paper nearly every day. It's an epidemic now, but when I ask them if they think it could be polio, they answer, 'No, Mrs. Nelson.' This has been going on for nearly two weeks now, since Penny's birthday. She was fine in the morning but so sick by evening. She's never sick, and yet whatever this is doesn't seem to end. She just can't shake it."

The screams were intermittent now, as the pain would wake her, mixed with whimpering, then a few minutes of sleep. The two women watched the clock as the minutes ticked by; they seemed like hours and still no sign of Bill and no break in the fever. The room grew quiet and still.

Ella whispered, "Jon has fallen asleep. Should I put him in his bed?"

"Let's not move him right now. I think Penny is waking up again, and I don't want him to hear her from the other room. It's better if he can see us." No sooner than spoken, another scream shattered the eerie peace.

Just then the trailer door opened. Her brother didn't bother to knock, as he heard the scream the moment he stepped out of the car. His sister, sitting on the floor of the small trailer, looked into his gaze. Her brown eyes seemed to consume her face as the dark black circles exaggerated their size until every other feature he knew so well seemed to disappear.

"Bill," she spoke his name and then just stared, holding him captive with those eyes that flashed a look of relief and then instantly filled with tears. For a split second, there was no sound in the trailer. Then, just as quickly, he heard the whimpers and saw the writhing body of his niece. He felt little hands take hold of his leg, pulling on his slacks.

Looking down he found his nephew, whose eyes were as dark as his mother's and as full of fear, brimming, softly crying, "Hold me, Uncle Bill."

Bill tried to smile as he picked up his nephew. "Hi, Jonnie. You're sure up late tonight. Are you being a good boy for your mommy?" He hoped his voice sounded normal.

What a nightmare, he thought to himself.

"Bill, I don't want to hear another doctor tell me I'm crazy or hysterical," she interrupted. "You can see Penny is sick, can't you? You know she's never been like this before. Could you talk to your doctor for me, Bill? Ask him to come and see for himself?"

"How long has she been like this?" He turned his gaze to his niece, as he comforted Jon.

Her small body, so limp, looked as if it had become part of the davenport.

"The fever started again while I was at church tonight. That has been hours ago now. But, Bill, it has never been this high, and she has been sick since her birthday. Please call your doctor."

"I'll go call him now, Sis," he said, putting Jon in Ella's open arms. "I know he'll come right over. Just hold on a little longer, honey. We'll take care of her. "

Walking to the telephone booth he thought, *What more could happen to them? Forey missing, my sister pregnant, and now Penny. How much can one person take? Sally, always the strong one, the one who raised me after Mom and Dad died. No one can be this strong.*

Reaching the telephone booth, he whispered a silent prayer while dialing the number, "Please be available, and please help my sister and niece."

The ringing stopped, and a familiar voice said, "Hello."

"Doctor Sullivan, this is Bill Blatnik. My three-year-old niece is in pain, holding her head, and has a raging fever. I'm telling you, Doctor, she's burning up. Can you please come over right away? I know it's late. I am sorry to wake you, but please help."

"Calm down, Bill, and slow down. Of course, I'll come. Just tell me how to get there, and I'll leave immediately."

The doctor knew exactly where the trailer park was. "I know the place, Bill. I'll be there in twenty minutes."

Bill took a deep breath, squared his shoulders, determined to be the strong one this time. *Always the baby, Sally always taking care of me, but this time, this time I will be there for her.*

"Doctor Sullivan is on his way," he said as he opened the trailer door. "He is a good man and said he would find the answer to this. Try to calm down; it won't be long now."

Bill took the few steps that separated them and knelt down beside his sister, wrapping one arm around her as she laid her head against his chest. Leaning over, he gently placed a kiss on his niece's forehead.

She feels like fire, he thought.

"You will be fine, honey. The doctor will make you all better."

Closing his eyes, he touched her damp hair with his free hand; he bid back the tears that threatened to reveal his own fears.

"Sally," Ella whispered, "I'm going back to my trailer now, but you come and get me if you need me anymore tonight. Do you want me to keep Jonnie until morning?"

"Thank you, Ella, for everything; really, Jon will be fine now that his uncle is here. You have already done so much; how will I ever thank you?"

"Forget it," she said as she closed the door quietly. She didn't want to wake Jon who was curled up in his mom's lap. She knew Sally had made the right decision. He needed his mom, and things would be fine now; surely, everything would be fine.

It seemed like hours when finally they heard the knock they had been waiting for.

Jumping to his feet, taking the single step to the door, "Hi, Doctor," Bill said, opening the door for him. "Sally, this is Doctor Sullivan."

The doctor smiled but quickly made his way past them both to the small body lying on the davenport.

"Thank you for coming, Doctor," she said, trying to keep her emotions under control.

Putting his case on the floor next to the davenport, Dr. Sullivan smiled at the sight of the little boy sleeping on his mother's lap.

"Well, he looks healthy enough," he said, trying to take the obvious edge off the situation. "Has he shown any similar symptoms or been running a fever at all?"

"No," she said, picking Jon up to put him in his bed. "Jon is just fine, a little frightened, but fine."

"Have you been sick, Mrs. Nelson, or any of your daughter's playmates?"

"No, I haven't been sick, and the only children she plays with besides her cousins live in this park. I would have heard if any one of them were sick. Bill, the boys are fine, right?" she asked, suddenly realizing she hadn't asked Donna or Bill about the boys.

"I can't remember the last time the boys were sick," he answered, breathing a sigh of relief, thinking surely they would have shown symptoms by now if this thing were contagious.

The birthday party was nearly two weeks ago, and they had been together all day and into the night.

"Well, then, let me see what is wrong with this little girl. Hello, Penny, may I have a look in your mouth?"

"Uh-huh." She nodded. He gently placed a tongue depressor in her mouth and looked closely at her throat. "Okay, now let me look in those ears. Are there any potatoes growin' in there? No, I can't see any. Penny, will you hold this under your tongue for me and don't bite down on it?"

26

She nodded yes. He placed the thermometer in her mouth; then lifting her arm, he began checking her pulse in silence.

"Okay, honey, just one more thing." Dr. Sullivan took another tongue depressor out of his bag, slowly he drew a line across her stomach, and then another, forming an X. "Does this tickle, Penny?" he asked.

"No," she answered softly.

Dr. Sullivan stood up. "Mrs. Nelson, do you have a telephone I could use?" The look on his face was somber as he met her eyes first and then Bill's. The look softened a moment as he brushed some hair away from the child's face.

"No, Doctor," Bill interrupted, "but there is a phone booth at the front entrance of the trailer park. I'll show you where."

"Why do you need a telephone?" she asked, feeling panic creep back into the pit of her stomach.

"We need to call an ambulance, Mrs. Nelson. Penny needs to be hospitalized immediately."

Her brother drew her closer to his side, taking her hand in his and gently squeezing it, as the word *ambulance* seemed to register in her mind.

"Why, for God's sake, I have a car. Just tell me where to take her to and how to get there. Bill, you can take Jon home with you, and—"

"Mrs. Nelson, listen to me very closely. You will need to follow the ambulance in your car. Your daughter is very ill, and she could be contagious. We really know very little about these cases right now."

"What cases? What do you think it is, Doctor?"

"Mrs. Nelson, I believe your daughter has polio. We can discuss the rest of your questions once we get to the hospital, but right now, I need to use that telephone."

Bill felt the weight of his sister's body sag against him as her legs nearly collapsed under the weight of the doctor's answer.

"Bill, where exactly is that telephone?"

"Right outside the manager's office on the left; you can't miss it. I better stay here with my sister."

Bill could see his nephew coming back into the hall. He could see the fresh tears streaming now as he watched his mother crying in his uncle's arms. Little eyes swollen from interrupted sleep and too many hours of crying. How much could he understand?

"Sally, sit down here by Penny a minute. I'm going to dress Jonnie."

"His shoes are on the kitchen counter. I polished them before I left for church last night. And his clothes are—"

"I'll find everything, honey. Just try to relax a minute. Let's go, Jonnie. We're going to see your cousins and you can spend the night with them tonight, okay?"

The doctor returned, but no one heard the door this time. "The ambulance is on its way, Mrs. Nelson. We'll be taking her to Harbor General Hospital. Once we get her admitted, I'll be able to tell you more about her condition and what treatment will be necessary or even available for her."

"DeeDee sic'?" Jon asked his mother, using the familiar pet name as he and Bill came back into the room.

Kneeling down to kiss her son, she said, "Yes, Jonnie. I'm taking her to the hospital, and you're going to visit Durm and Hank at Uncle Bill's house. Honey, I'll come for you in a little while. Be a good boy."

The sound of a siren in the distance soon started an urgent commotion in the small trailer. The doctor stepped outside to direct the drivers to the correct trailer, and Jonnie started pulling away from his uncle, reaching for his mother.

"Come on, son. Let's get in the car and go see the kids. Sally, do you need me to pick up anything for you after I drop Jon off?"

"No, I can't think of anything right now, Bill. Jonnie, stop taking your shoes off," Sally implored. The frustration in her voice sounded harsh even to her ears. "Let's put your shoes back on," she said, trying to sound gentler now.

"It's time to go, Mrs. Nelson," the doctor said as they placed her daughter on the stretcher. "I think it would be better to let your brother drive you to the hospital."

"I'll follow you," she said, her eyes quickly glancing around the room.

She reached for her scissors and moved toward the stretcher. Quickly she cut off one blonde curl from her daughter's head and slipped it in her pocket. "Okay, I'm ready now."

She hadn't realized how warm it had gotten until she stood outside locking the trailer door. She heard the sound of car doors closing, her son calling her, and then the sirens starting again. Sliding quickly behind the wheel of the car, she kept hearing words over and over that would change her life forever: *missing, polio, contagious.*

Stop thinking, she told herself. *Just follow. It's going to be hotter than hell again today.*

Oh God, what must Jon think? How can he understand what is happening? How did this happen to us?

She was lost in thought as if mulling it over and over would pin point the cause or the beginning of this madness, and then she realized the sirens had stopped. The hospital loomed in front of her, but she couldn't remember turning or even driving past the exit of the trailer park.

Harbor General—all suspected polio cases ended up here. Once the doors opened, it was like walking into a war zone, chaotic. Polio, so little was known about this disease, but it certainly caused panic in everyone. People standing in the halls and sitting in the waiting rooms didn't make eye contact with anyone, almost afraid to see their own fear reflected in the eyes of strangers.

Suddenly thoughts of death and fear flooded her memory as she remembered the headlines: "Husband and Five Children Stricken—Texas." Bodies everywhere on gurneys, there was no indication that this was a childhood problem, as men, women, and children lined the halls, waiting. It was just the beginning of endless waiting.

A nurse had appeared from nowhere holding a facemask and white gown. "What? Are you talking to me?"

"You can see your daughter for a moment, Mrs. Nelson, but you'll need to put these on."

"Yes, just slip this on over your clothes, Mrs. Nelson, and wear this facemask for your own protection. Come with me; she is right down this hall."

"Please, let me take off the mask. I don't want to scare her. She won't know who I am."

"Oh, she'll know you. You must keep the mask on. Just talk to her, Mrs. Nelson. I'm sure she will know your voice."

Once in the room, she couldn't believe so little time had passed, yet such a different child was lying in that sterile white bed. Maybe it was the lighting or that horrible shade of green paint on the walls. She walked to the bed and touched the pale face that was still too hot. Penny was sleeping now, but it wasn't a peaceful normal sleep of a happy, healthy three-year-old child. Instead, it was an uneasy, restless sleep making it all too clear she was still in distress.

"I love you, Penny," she whispered, just as she heard the nurse say it was time to leave. "Leave? I just got here. I won't wake her, but I need to stay with her."

"I'm sorry. You can go to the waiting room just outside. The doctor will come to talk to you, and he may let you spend time with her. Remember, you're pregnant, Mrs. Nelson, and we do not know what your exposure has been or even what it means to your baby. Let's just wait until the doctors come. They'll know more. You must be careful."

Waiting for the doctor was not any easier than watching her daughter slip away from her. How did everything get so hard? She could hear the iron lungs doing the job of pumping air into a body and out.

When did I ever even think about breathing?

She wondered which of the strangers waiting in this ugly green room with her had a loved one in that horrible capsule. Would Penny be the next one? Could she just stop breathing on her own? Some people were standing, some were sitting, some praying, almost all were crying, but no one was making eye contact, no one was talking. Every once in a while, someone new would come in the room, look around until they found a familiar face, and then move toward the person they recognized, embrace them, and then assume that zombie-like state that even now she could feel herself slipping into.

HIDE THIS NUGGET IN YOUR HEART

When the thing you greatly feared is facing you, face your greatest fear.

STRONG STUFF

That is how mother related the story to me so many times over the years. I can't remember the ride to the hospital, but I do remember how my mother looked as I watched her from my hospital bed. The dark circles under her eyes are forever burnt into my memory. I couldn't tell you what she was thinking but I had a clear impression that something was different about her. I seemed to sense her anguish even though she never expressed it in words.

She was in a strange city, and it is true that most of the things that cause us to feel secure were not available to her. She was a determined individual, but somehow all her plans and dreams seemed to be drifting just beyond her reach. Thank God, she came from strong stuff!

My maternal great grandmother, Emma Voelker, had nineteen children, so it is no surprise that she dedicated herself to her home and family. I called her Grandma Gris Mum, which meant grandma-grandma. She didn't speak much English; German was her first language but there was no interpreter needed when it came to drinking tea with her and having a cracker. She instilled in me the love of a *special* tea party.

Grandma Gris Mum's greatest desire was to go to the Vatican. Being a good Catholic she wanted at least one priest out of her brood. When Grandma Gris Mum's children had grown, one was a politician, the other eighteen were hard working businessmen and homemakers but none became a priest. However, her children did fulfill her biggest dream the year they surprised her with a trip to Rome.

Her priority as a mother was to teach her children to be responsible, hard-working, and morally and physically clean citizens. These traits were passed down through her children to her grandchildren. Mother's heritage was hard work, *clean* house, *clean* kids, and *clean* living.

Grandma Gris Mum lived to be ninety-four years old. One day she decided that she was satisfied with life and stopped her newspaper and dairy deliveries and discontinued her telephone service. When her children couldn't reach her, they went to her home and found her lying on her bed with her rosary and prayer book in her hand. Grandma Gris Mum had moved to heaven.

My Grandpa Blatnik, mom's father, came to this country with a fourth grade education. Even though he did not have a formal education, he was fluent in eight languages because of the diverse peoples and languages that surrounded him in Slovenia. He was interested in government, and once he was in America, he took every opportunity to learn the political system. His family were innkeepers in Ohio, so he was exposed to people from all walks of life. It wasn't long before he started acting as an interpreter for other immigrants in his community. He was found trustworthy and was soon introduced to the leader of organized labor, John L Lewis. Grandpa spent the next thirteen years traveling and interpreting for Mr. Lewis as the AFL-CIO developed. Grandpa felt a rush of adrenalin around the action of those early labor days and had the charisma of a masterful speaker as he interpreted Lewis's words for the workers. Grandpa had used the gift he had for languages and forged an admirable career which provided a great life for himself and his family.

On one of those trips, he found himself in Pennsylvania in the home of a very large family. To Grandpa's surprise, he met a 103 pound, roller skating, fair haired, green eyed girl name

Alma and it was love at first sight. Knowing he would be on the road again soon, he courted Alma vigorously and soon they were married. Alma's first husband had died leaving her with one child, Stella. The next Blatnik baby was a son John, then came Margaret, Agnes Sarah (Sally-my mother), Henry (Hank) and the baby William (Bill).

The Blatnik family was one of the affluent families in McKinley Heights, and Grandma made sure her children looked the part, clean and well dressed. Mother learned the golden rule at home, but it wasn't the one most people would think. It was the saying that "cleanliness is next to godliness'. Somehow, I could just see Grandma and my mom very near the throne of God, one with bleach and the other with ammonia.

Grandma was a homemaker. Grandpa was a hard worker by day and a "good ole boy" by night with his cigar and scotch in hand, he entertained some of the biggest men in town in his basement.

The basement was, also, a magic place for my mother. That is where she dreamed her dreams of dancing and found her form perfect. But that passion on the inside of her didn't please Grandma.

"Sally, I sent you for the Hoover, not to daydream; there is work to be done," Grandma shouted firmly.

"Yes, Mother," she answered, grabbing the vacuum and running up the stairs.

"Sally, there is no time for daydreaming. Your father will be home soon expecting dinner, not the sound of you doing your chores. That's what's wrong with those fancy stage dancers. They live loose. Do you hear me, Sally? We live with purpose, and that means we do what is right, when it is right, no matter what."

Nevertheless, when she was in that basement, the room was not made of concrete. It became a ballroom, and Mother was the star. She dreamed of being a professional dancer. She spent all her free time dancing with her shadow. Or was that Fred Astaire?

These were good days, but just around the corner was the Great Depression. Grandpa had managed his money well; his properties and cars were debt free. However, when Mother was in the ninth grade, Grandpa became sick. It was cancer, and death came too soon. Now, not only was the United States in financial turmoil, but the Blatnik home was badly shaken.

Grandma held the family and the store together for the next few years but one day she said, "I'm very tired."

Her daughters knew she hadn't been keeping things up to the standard she had established. "What's going on?" Sally said to her sisters, "This just isn't like her. Mom's a fighter. No matter what happens, she just doesn't give up. I think she needs to see a doctor. Will you talk to her, Stella?"

Even though Grandma Blatnik did see a doctor, he gave no clear diagnosis but suggested exploratory surgery at which time they found cancer. It had progressed too far to do anything for her. She had little time left to get things in order. Knowing this, she prepared her family for their future without her or their father. It was 1939. She decided to sell the store and did some matchmaking to see to it that Stella and Marge were married before she was gone. Hank had met a girl, Emma and married also. This left only mom and Bill. My mother had not given up her dream of being a professional dancer, and Bill was still in high school, too young to live on his own. Grandma had to do something about that.

Soon, Grandma was in the hospital with only days to live. Again, she had a plan. She exacted two promises from my mother. As mother knew, Grandma had a deep seated belief that show business people and professional dancers led wicked lives. She asked mother to promise she would never dance professionally. Feeling the pressure of the circumstances, mother promised. Grandma, also, asked mother to take care of Bill.

HIDE THIS NUGGET IN YOUR HEART

Look around you and see the resources and possibilities you already have at hand. Don't let lack or the things you don't have be a roadblock. Don't forget to dance in the basement. Dream and create your future.

KEEPING PROMISES

After Grandma died, relatives offered to raise Bill, but he wanted to stay with his sister until he graduated and could join the army. Making the promises wasn't hard, but keeping her promises was. She wasn't trying to avoid the responsibility; however, she was young and unskilled for work outside the home.

In 1941 the United States entered into World War II, and as with many women, Mother went to work. Molina Shell Company hired her to make 155-millimeter shells on an assembly line. Many Molina employees formed car pools. One man in her car pool was Tiny Nelson. Tiny told his wife, Arlene, about my mother. Arlene thought she'd be perfect for Tiny's wild marine brother, Forest Nelson. Arlene was sure that Forey only needed the love of a good woman to settle him down. She plotted and planned. Then late in 1942, while Forey was going through cadet training, a meeting was arranged, and the two were about to lay eyes on each other for the first time.

Was he great looking? Oh yes, and he was so cocky and a big tease. However, what interested Mom was, he could dance! Their dark eyes locked, and the dance floor rocked. He'd pick mother up on the dance floor and swing her around. Then she would pick him up and swing him right back. They definitely cleared the floor as others gave them plenty of room to swing. Mom was a star, and this time she wasn't in the basement.

Forey loved being a marine. He had worked hard to get in the corps. He was only five foot seven, and though short, he had a great body and a winning personality. He ate bananas to put weight on until he thought he would hang from a tree. He pumped up and stretched out until he passed the physical and became his dream, a United States Marine.

Grandma had given lots of advice to her daughters about men, but her strongest warning was never get involved with a service man. Sally loved going bowling and dancing with Forey, but she really didn't consider marriage, at least not to this man. So dating was what they did over the next few years while the marine would ship out and then come back in. In 1945, Forey learned that his mother had cancer and came home for good on a hardship leave. He accepted a position to train pilots at a flight school in Huron, South Dakota.

Bill had reached enlistment age and joined the army just as he planned. This left Mother ready to go ahead with her own life. She and Forey had dated for three years. As time passed, Mother knew eventually they would marry but not until he made some changes. She believed that once you married, you stayed home to tend to your home and your husband, and of course, you had a baby. In her mind, Forey needed a more reliable job. In South Dakota, the weather was bad, and half the time he couldn't fly. If he couldn't fly, he wasn't paid.

Now Forey thought he had the world's greatest job, because he loved flying and he loved playing. When he wasn't in the air, he was having a good time. It sounded like a perfect job, right? Not to Mom, but Forey just didn't understand why Mother kept postponing the wedding over a job. After all, he was sure he could earn enough to feed them both and still have money left for a little dancing and bowling. Finally, he got it! Sally wasn't going to marry him until he would "try" to think and live like a stable ex-marine.

Forey loved hunting, dancing, playing practical jokes, and he loved his golden retriever. Oh, did I mention, he loved the girls? As the saying goes, this was before I was "a twinkle in my daddy's eye." From the stories told about those brown roving eyes, there just wasn't room for a twinkle yet.

However, over time, he did sense the wind of change coming his way, and as a good pilot, he understood the effects of the wind. He finally settled down and went to school to be a mechanic. The big day came May 4, 1947, Forest Archie Nelson married Agnes Sarah Blatnik, and my future was not far off.

Mother was Catholic, so Daddy converted. The wedding itself was a total disaster as far as weddings go. I think it was absolutely in line with my parents' personalities. The attendants, Fred and Lois Beck, were very close to Mom and Dad. They not only were to be the witnesses of their union, but they were to play a huge role in the early years of my parents' marriage.

The day finally arrived. The bride meticulous in every detail, the matron of honor on duty and very efficient, pacing themselves perfectly. They heard the chords of the first song notifying them that it was time to walk down the aisle. Mother was a beautiful bride and Daddy so handsome, stood waiting to take her hand and make her his wife. Mother's steps were perfect. After all, she had rhythm and her timing impeccable with each beat of the bridal march. When she arrived at the altar, she turned toward Daddy, and looking into his laughing eyes, she...promptly fainted! The matron of honor came to the rescue, but she, too, fainted. Most of the wedding pictures are of Dad and his best man holding the bridal bouquet and clowning around. It was nearly a marriage by proxy. They were, eventually, pronounced man and wife and did walk back down the aisle together, trying not to make eye contact with their friends who were already having enough trouble holding back the laughter.

Once outside the church, Mother smiled timidly at Dad. She whispered she wasn't sure about going on the honeymoon alone, hinting that Fred and Lois should go along for moral support. I'm sure all—especially the marine—had a great time.

———————————

Home from the honeymoon, Mother was ready to get down to business. She found a huge pickle jar, cleaned it up, and found a picture of a baby that she thought looked just right. She cut it out and glued it to the jar. Under the picture, she printed in bold letters "Penny" and started saving her change to pay the doctor. Mother had beautiful brown eyes and an olive complexion. Dad's eyes were a darker brown, and his complexion was even a darker olive, but Mother's pickle jar baby had blue eyes, blonde hair, and a fair complexion.

Good for his word, Dad continued in school so that soon Mother could quit her job and start being a homemaker. Dad was faithful to his homework as well; however, every month to Mother's dismay, nothing. She still wasn't pregnant.

There could be only one answer to this dilemma, she thought. *God was punishing Mr. Romance for all his philandering.*

In fact, she told Lois that she couldn't stay married to a "rounder" who couldn't have children, under any circumstance!

Lois, who was a good and somewhat sane friend suggested, "Sally, why not make an appointment with my doctor to see if…"

Before she could finish her statement, mother blew up!

"What? You mean my grandmother had nineteen children and my mother six, and you think that I have something wrong with me? Lois, have you lost your mind!"

"Listen, Sally, I'm going to make an appointment for you with my doctor, and I'll go along. What harm can it do?

Lots of newlyweds are under pressure, and there's a lot of reasons women don't get pregnant right away, even if our mothers told us it always happens the first time," she laughed.

To Mother's utter amazement, she did have a problem with her fallopian tubes, and fertility specialists were still decades away. The doctor explained some methods that would optimize her potential for conceiving but explaining them to Dad and getting him to agree to them was another story. I was to learn later, there just wasn't much this woman set her mind to that didn't come about.

Not only was I conceived, but also on Mother's second doctor visit, she presented Dr. Schetter with the pickle jar for his payment. He was a little surprised and told her that it wasn't necessary to bring him all her change. Mother stood her ground, and he accepted the jar. I was born on August 3, 1949, with blue eyes, platinum blonde hair, and a fair complexion, in Huron, South Dakota. My name is Penny, and I was paid in full, of course!

HIDE THIS NUGGET IN YOUR HEART

Keep the promises you make. No excuses. It won't be easy, but it is right.

STICKING HER
NECK OUT

Mother was quick to organize her home. She took care of me and made sure Dad was doing his part in her perfect plan. In case you are wondering, she did have another pickle jar started. They stayed close to Fred and Lois, who had purchased a grocery store and were doing great in business. The weekends found them all out dancing and having fun together.

One afternoon while Mother was buying gas, she got into a conversation with the station owner. He was telling her about the restaurant next door to his gas station. He was a little put out because it was only open on the weekends. Mom knew about the place because they often ate there after dancing. The restaurant served great hamburgers. The station owner was saying how much more business he'd do if the guy would open during the week. Mother with her work ethic couldn't imagine anyone working weekends only.

"So, what does the guy do the rest of the week?"

"Well, he used to be a fighter, and now he just runs that place and drinks," the attendant said, as he finished pumping the gas.

While he washed Mom's windshield, she started daydreaming.

"That does it. Hope to see you around here again real soon."

"You will." She smiled and waved as she pulled out slowly looking back at the restaurant. Days later, Mother was still thinking of all the station owner had said.

I wonder if that ex-fighter would consider selling his place, she thought. *I'm going to call that gas station tomorrow and see if he has a telephone number for his neighbor.*

He had all the information she needed. As soon as she hung up, she came to herself and laughed.

I don't know anything about buying a business. Then, just as quickly, she thought, *but I know someone who does.*

Picking up the telephone, she dialed Lois. Once she had explained her ideas, she asked what Lois could tell her about buying a business. She wanted to know what she was talking about before she spoke to a potentially drunk ex-fighter.

Lois did better than that. She called Fred and asked if he would go with Mom if she could get an appointment with the owner. Somehow, Lois figured that if Mother got the appointment, the man would sell to her, even if he had never considered selling before.

Mother got the owner on the phone, and although he had not seriously considered selling "the joint" as he called it, he was willing to meet with them in a week or so. The date and time were set. She only had to check Fred's schedule since he had so many responsibilities with his store. Fred agreed, and the excitement started stirring in mother's heart.

Fred and Mother arrived a little early and looked around the outside.

"Needs a lot of work, Sally," Fred said and then laughed, thinking that might have made the place even more appealing to her. He heard a car pulling into the parking lot and said, "Let's go around to the front. I think I heard him."

The fighter unlocked the door to the restaurant and quickly walked in talking to no one in particular. It seemed as if he expected the bell to ring signaling the end of a round. Fred and Mom followed him around the small building.

Fred asked, "How much do you want for the restaurant, and what are the terms?"

The owner stopped and said, "I want five thousand dollars, and wha' ya mean, terms?

Mother was thinking things were moving fast, when Fred casually countered his offer with "Four thousand dollars cash." Obviously, Fred was unaware that the big tycoon standing next to him was panic-stricken. Mother was thinking she had no idea it would cost anywhere near that much money, when she heard the guy accept Fred's offer.

"Here's the coolers," he was saying. They were empty and filthy, and Mother was close to that fainting thing she did under pressure.

Fred had seen that look before, and he knew he'd better take Mother outside for some fresh air and find out what was going on in that busy mind of hers.

The minute they were out the door, Mother said, "Fred, what is the matter with you? I don't have that kind of money!"

"What? How much did you plan on paying? How much do you have, Sally?"

"I have fifteen hundred dollars in the bank, but I can't spend that. It's all Forey and I have."

Suddenly Fred understood why Mother had called Lois for business advice. He was feeling the same urge. "Just a minute, I'm going to call Lois. Wait right here for me."

Lois answered the phone on the first ring, knowing that Fred and Sally would be calling any time. "How's it going, honey?" she said when she heard Fred's voice.

"Lois, this nut you sent me with just watched me make a deal with this guy for the restaurant. Then she takes me outside and tells me she hasn't got that kind of money, and the money that she does have, she can't spend."

Lois starting laughing and said, "Well, Fred, what do ya think we should do with her?"

"Well, it's a pretty good deal, and we could enter a partnership with them if they are willing, but we don't have the time to rebuild this place. It's a mess."

Mother was waiting on Fred, wondering how she could just disappear and not have to talk to the ex-fighter. She was a little embarrassed that she hadn't told Fred about their financial status. In fact, they were doing pretty well for a young couple in their day. However, the Depression was not that far behind them, and that didn't make it easy to think about financial risk. She could see Fred strolling back to the car with a half smile on his face.

Relieved, she thought, *At least, he's not angry with me.*

Fred told Mother that if she and Dad could borrow $2,500, he and Lois would add $2,500. This would give them enough to pay cash for the business with a thousand left over to make the repairs and stock the coolers. Mother said she'd give it a shot. Fred went back in the restaurant to let the owner know he'd call next week and bring the offer in writing.

Mother had her first banking experience and was successful in borrowing her portion of the investment. It was a remarkable feat during this time for a woman to get a loan by herself. That night she proudly announced to an unsuspecting husband over dinner that they were co-owners in a rundown restaurant.

Dad looked at her wondering just who knew anything about the restaurant business in this partnership.

He voiced his concern, and Mother answered, "What is there to know, Forey? We cook all the time. It will just be cooking for more people, and Fred and Lois know about ordering food. After all they are doing great in the grocery business."

All the paperwork was complete, the money in place, and the final meeting held to sign off and exchange their money for the keys to their future. The restaurant belonged to them, and they were on the other side of the counter, flipping burgers for their patrons.

Mother took the renovations on with great joy. She cleaned, scrubbed, and polished until it was hard to recognize the place. Fred and Lois ordered the meat, the buns, relish, and everything else necessary to prepare for the grand opening night scheduled on a weekend.

The dance hall let out, and the people poured in. Daddy started making hamburger patties. He didn't realize that the meat would shrink during cooking until his grill area was full of orders and everyone was getting impatient.

Soon the two cute servers went behind the swinging doors demanding their orders. One look told them it would take plenty of personality to pass off hamburgers with patties the size of a quarter, slightly burned! The only reason the evening was a success at all was the four owners had great personalities and were having a ball trying to satisfy a slightly tipsy group of cutups. When the evening ended, the four of them took one look around at the mess, then at each other and started laughing.

The test would be during the week when Mom and Dad had to run the restaurant alone while Fred and Lois ran the grocery store across town. After all, the grand opening was a real experience, but they were about to find out what a group of sober, hungry people would be like.

Truck drivers starting arriving before Mom and Dad were ready for a breakfast crowd. Before the breakfast dishes were cleaned up, the lunch group was coming through the door. Not realizing how fast their food supply would go, they were both surprised when there were still people left to serve and no more food to cook. This was the true test of "Yankee" ingenuity, and Dad was about to prove that cliché true. He quickly went to the store down the street and bought them out of canned stew then returning to the café, announced "Today's Lunch Special, Stew."

It wasn't long before this group of chums got the idea of how to run a café. The hours were long, but they were doing well. Friday and Saturday nights were still the greatest fun because they were all together. Soon the bank loan was fully paid, and they were making a good living.

One day Mom found a little place in Aberdeen that would make another great café. She made her deal and readily planned a chain of cafes. The Aberdeen café did well almost immediately. Mother worked one restaurant, and Daddy the other. Being busy all the time really cut into those intimate times Mom and Dad had with Fred and Lois. Now work took center stage. Their dance hall was reduced to a quick spin to a favorite song on the radio. Fred and Lois's lives were changing too, and they decided to move to the Black Hills of South Dakota. The partners agreed to sell the Huron Café to reduce the stress of trying to operate without the whole team.

Mother made it look like there was nothing to running a house, making sure that I was wearing ruffled panties, hoop skirts, and Shirley Temple–style curls each day, with plenty of time left to run a café and keep Dad on target. The truth was, Mother never took the easy way, nor did she compromise quality for quantity. She chose excellence and expected no less from others. There was a certain order to our life, and it was kept to the letter.

The pickle jar was full again, and as purposed, sixteen months after I was born, the Nelson household increased with a beautiful, bouncing boy with big brown eyes and olive complexion. He was just as Mother said he should be. His name was Jon, and he was the apple of our eyes.

Forey had adjusted beautifully to his new career, husband, father, and provider. He changed from being a handful, to being charmed by his children and settled on his decision to give up being a lifer in the Marine Corps. He still found time to hunt and fish, but now he had to take much more equipment. After all, toddlers required accessories, and he was determined Jon and I would both be marksmen, as well as great fishermen. It is funny to look at family pictures. I was not posed with a stuffed animal, but with a dead duck, or standing over a deer while the hunter unloaded his truck.

HIDE THIS NUGGET IN YOUR HEART

Don't be afraid to try something new. When things aren't working, think about what Albert Einstein said, "Insanity: doing the same thing over and over again and expecting different results."

If you feel you are failing, ask yourself, "How can I repackage myself? Is it time for a change?" Don't be afraid to try something new.

MOVING TOWARD
THE FUTURE

There are those times in life when regardless of how things look on the surface you just have an internal alarm that starts sounding. Dad's alarm kept going off over a period of several months without cause—or so it seemed. Was he longing for the single life? No, in fact, he was hoping that Mother would soon announce they were expecting because he wanted a big family. The business was doing well, but he knew that the world conditions were changing, and somehow knew he would be recalled to active service. The feelings became so strong that he talked to Mother about selling the café in Aberdeen and returning to Huron where his Father lived.

"Sally, this war is likely to change our life and very soon. You can't run the house, take care of the kids and the café alone. I need to know that you are near family in case I am recalled."

"You can't mean sell everything, Forey. After all, you have a family, and you have already paid your dues. I can't believe that you would be recalled."

This time, however, Dad got his way, and plans were made to move. Gone were the carefree days of hunting and fishing with the kids. Gone were the quiet nights at home and the cafés where they worked and played together as a family. At least, for just a little while—they prayed.

Two months after we moved, Dad was called back to active duty, just as he had feared. He was first stationed in Minneapolis,

Minnesota, and felt that this would be his post for some time. It was September, and Mother wanted to be settled in a new house for Christmas. They were diligent in their search for a new home, and they found more than a home; they found a castle. At least, that is what I called it. There was a room shaped in a circle, and on the back two-thirds of the room were windows. Like my mother's basement fantasyland, this room became my special world, where I pretended I was a queen.

Christmas arrived and Santa brought our first television adding a new dimension to that fantasy feeling. Yes, we were cozy and secure. Then Dad's orders changed. Instead of Wold Field, Minneapolis, he was to report to Cherry Point, North Carolina. There was really no time to think about selling my castle. Dad said we needed to rent it out and pack, as he had to leave right away. The hair on the back of Mother's neck stood straight out as she considered the housing we would be living in on base. In fact, there was no telling her that's where she would raise her children. Forey was the marine not her, and he had better come up with a plan.

One afternoon, Dad came home with a picture of a trailer and showed it to Mom. She just stared at it.

"Now, Sally," he started his sales pitch knowing what that look on her face meant. "It has heated floors so the kids will be warm. It's brand new and *spotless*. I got a terrific deal on it!"

Dad had made the deal, and there was no stopping the move. Dad took the trailer to North Carolina while Mom stayed home to rent the house and tie up the loose ends before packing the car and moving us to Cherry Point.

Anytime we were driving somewhere, it was my job to stand by the driver and tell stories or sing silly songs. Just because my parents could dance, I don't want you to get the impression music ran in our family. Mom said I couldn't carry a tune in a bucket, but I had a lot of heart when I sang, and a lot of volume. Like most families, we had our special silly songs. My dad had a favorite, and it still makes me smile when I think about it today.

Take a leg from some ole table
Take an arm from some ole chair
Take a neck from some ole bottle
and from a broom, you'll get some hair.
Then you put it all together
with the aid of string and glue,
And I get more lovin' from a darned ole dummy
Then I'll ever get from you.
Get out and walk.

Written by Lew Brown, Ray Henderson, and Billy Rose

Mom sang her favorite, "Apple Blossom Time." We must have sung a hundred more; we sang all the way to North Carolina. Jon slept the whole way. How, I don't know, but Mother loved every minute. We stayed in Cherry Point until May 1952. We were together, and we were happy, but the war was moving in on us fast.

Daddy's new orders came. He was being shipped overseas from California so it was time to pack up again. Dad thought Mother would be able to stay in California safely with her brothers living there.

This was a hard trip for our family. Dad was concerned about his timing being off, and his concern caused Mother to worry. He wasn't as playful as usual, and it seemed like duck hunting and fishing were things of the past. Jon and I both talked early, and we were physically strong and coordinated. I remember Dad would balance Jon high in the air on his hand, and Mom would balance me. Mother was already grooming her little dancer. While we still had the cafés, Dad and I would play pinball or spin the bar stools at the counter. I still carry a scar on my hand from one of those little games. Now we would only have our memories of performing acrobatic shows for them, doing back bends and the splits. Our lives changed in California, and I was to recognize the greatness in my mother, little by little.

HIDE THIS NUGGET IN YOUR HEART

Be flexible. Change the things you can, and forget the things you can't. If you easily bend, you'll never break.

A LITTLE BLACK CLOUD

On June 21, 1952, Mom, Jon, and I said good-bye to Dad. There were many men getting ready to board that plane, but Daddy kept dragging his feet.

They were yelling, "Come on, Nelson!"

Every man had boarded except Dad and one other. We were crying and waving at Dad, wishing he could come home with us. Mother was standing next to the other marine's wife when Dad went up the steps to board. He came back out of the plane and waved at the three of us again.

The other marine's wife turned to my mom and said, "Oh, he should never have done that. It's bad luck!"

Mother said, "Like he might stub his toe and get to stay home?"

That night Mother turned back the bedspread and found a letter. Dad had written, "If there is any way in this world, I'll be back."

Jon and I went to bed that night with a special prayer in our hearts, "Please bring Daddy home."

The letters started coming, after each mission—one mission in the morning and one in the afternoon, then Daddy would write home. One day I would get a letter telling me he loved me and why he was in Korea and not at home. One day, Jon, just a baby, would get a letter full of love and information about Dad's plane. He told him how much fuel it held and the facts that a son may want to know when he was twenty, but every day Mom got a letter just for her.

My birthday was getting close, and Mother was planning a special day. She started thinking about my last birthday party and smiled. Mom and Dad had invited many of the neighborhood children, and they had planned to have streamers, hats, balloons: the works. Daddy had left the café early that day, promising to return in time to relieve Mom so she could prepare for the party. Time had passed, and Dad hadn't shown up. Mom had been getting really upset, thinking that everything would be a mess and completely disorganized. She hadn't been able to put up the outdoor decorations before work because it had been too windy. As she had waited for Dad's return, her foot had tapped impatiently, then she had started pacing back and forth in front of the window. Much later, Daddy had sauntered in, and she had been ready to lower the boom. Then she had decided it would take too much time, so instead of "cleaning his clock," she had peeled out of the parking lot in a cloud of dust. When she had pulled up to the house she saw that the decorations had been hung all the way from the mailbox to the front door.

"I'm sure the backyard is done, too," she said to herself.

That devil, she thought as she laughed aloud. *He loves to get me started.*

However, that was not going to happen this year, she thought. There was no husband here to be late or plan any pranks and no one to help her. This year she was going to have to plan something extra special because Daddy would not be with us, and there were precious few friends in this new place.

August 3, 1952, was my third birthday. Like any child who has ever had a birthday celebration, I knew this was a special time. After all, the birthday girl gets all the attention, all the presents, and all the favorite activities, plus cake and ice cream.

Mother had invited a few children from the trailer park, my Uncle Bill and Aunt Donna, and my cousins, Durmond and Hank. We were going to the beach. Jon and I loved the beach, the warm sand, the water. It was a great place of exploration. This birthday, however, I wasn't very happy. It was as though a little black cloud hung over me. It was harder and harder to smile as the day went on. When a child notices a "funny feeling" in their body, it's frightening. If I told my mother my tummy hurt, she would ask me if I had gone potty. If my head hurt, she asked if I was hungry. I couldn't explain this funny feeling, and I was getting scared. I was feeling weak all over my body. I was tired, and my head felt better just hanging down. The pictures of this "special" birthday show me unsmiling early in the day, and then slumping against my cousins in the afternoon, and asleep on the beach instead of playing. Something was very wrong. Mom was getting concerned. It wasn't like me not to play with my favorite cousins.

Birthdays are a marker in time, a way to keep track of a life, to mark yesterdays, to challenge tomorrows. I don't think Mother and I will ever forget this marker, nor will we ever have another that so totally sets apart our yesterdays from our tomorrows.

I wanted to sleep on the davenport that night and then every night after that. My mother wasn't feeling very well this birthday either. This time the jar said "Pam."

Over the next few days, Mom took me to see several doctors and not one of them thought my condition was serious. Early one morning, she was helping me get dressed to play and stood me on the table while she went to get my coat. She thought fresh air and sunshine might help me feel better.

As she started to let go, I said, "No, Mommy, don't let go."

"Penny, I'm just getting your coat, honey—stand there, and I'll be right back."

"I can't stand up, Mommy." It was as if my legs couldn't support me, and they seemed to belong to someone else. I couldn't get them to do anything I wanted.

A parent waits a long time to hear their child's first words, take their first steps, then before they know it, its non-stop sentences and chasing after busy feet. This sentence brought no joy to my mother. It was like a knife going through her. I was once again on the davenport, and those all-too-familiar tears were in my mother's eyes. This was only the beginning of our sorrows.

August 7, 1952—Telegram:

Mrs. Forest A. Nelson—

DEEPLY REGRET TO INFORM YOU THAT YOUR HUSBAND FIRST LIEUTENANT FOREST ARCHIE NELSON USMCR IS MISSING IN ACTION SINCE 6 AUGUST 1952 IN THE KOREAN AREA IN THE PERFORMANCE OF HIS DUTY AND SERVICE OF HIS COUNTRY. I REALIZE YOUR GREAT ANXIETY BUT DETAILS NOT AVAILABLE AND DELAY IN RECEIPT THEREOF MUST BE EXPECTED LETTER FOLLOWS.

LEMUEL C. SHEPHERD JR. GENERAL USMC

COMMANDANT OF THE MARINE CORPS

The small troubling feeling that had started with Dad's hesitation to leave began to grow with the apparent illness I couldn't shake. Then this telegram put the troubled feeling in high gear. Mother started her regular trips to the local church, burning a candle for her husband, saying a prayer for strength, asking for help with Jon and me, and wondering if the baby she carried would ever know her daddy.

HIDE THIS NUGGET IN YOUR HEART

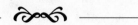

Little black clouds will come. Take cover; guard your heart.

A PUPPY, THREE DOLLS, NO DADDY

All the waiting in Harbor General Hospital was in a small green room. Mother hates green to this day unless it is bright and cheery and in small doses. However, this room was not cheery in the least. It had a small table and hard wooden chairs that didn't offer much comfort, especially for a tired, worried, and very pregnant woman. It was in this room, Mother's life goals changed. She stopped expecting anything. She stopped thinking she needed more. All she wanted was a life, my life.

"All I want is the chance for Penny to have a life," she prayed, as the doctor came through the door.

"Mrs. Nelson, your daughter definitely has polio. Her fevers are so high that if she lives, we believe she will have brain damage. At this time, she's completely paralyzed. You can see her now, if you're ready."

Ready? Who could ever be ready to see their fear manifest, especially in their child? she thought.

Weeks of waiting and watching the weakness take over her little body and now within hours completely paralyzed. This can't be happening.

"God, give her to me, broken if she must be. I'll not ask you for more."

Five minutes later, Mother walked in my room. "Mommy, it has been so hot in here!"

The fever had broken.

I was in isolation, and no one knew how long that would last. Mother was driving twenty-five miles one way in the summer heat to see me. She would stay as long as they would allow, then drive the twenty-five miles back to comfort and care for Jon.

Mentally, she was holding on, but physically all the pressure had taken its toll. She had received no further information about Daddy and asked Bill if he could find something out for her.

It was late in the afternoon when she walked to the payphone at the trailer park to call Bill, hoping he had news about Forey and ready to tell him about my progress. While she was dialing, she started to feel dizzy. She felt something hot running down her legs. Suddenly, she was so dizzy she could no longer read the numbers on the phone. She knew she couldn't look down, and crossed her legs thinking she could continue to stand. Then she fainted.

When Mother was arousing, she heard a woman standing nearby say, "Well, she's drunk."

"Looks like it," said another women.

A man leaning over her pulled her eyelid back. Mother rolled her head. "I'm sick. Can you help me?"

Just then, Ella was coming from the laundry and saw Mother lying in a heap by the telephone booth.

She ran to her trailer to get my uncle's telephone number, yelling to the man, "Please call an ambulance. She's pregnant. Tell them she's pregnant!"

When the ambulance arrived, Mother asked to go to Harbor General. They told her that was impossible due to the polio epidemic and took her to Seaside Hospital instead.

As soon as the ambulance arrived, the attendants were in a rush to stop the bleeding and get Mother stabilized. All the commotion kept her mind occupied. Meanwhile, Uncle Bill had arrived. It took only a few minutes to explain to the nurse what she was going through. His only concern now was what his sister needed. He was anxious to know if she and the baby would be all right. It was then that the doctor drew him aside and explained there was no sign of life. Uncle Bill had the difficult task of getting Mother's signature for the procedure. They needed to draw on an unseen force for the strength to help her through another incredible loss. It was August 15, 1952, and Pam was delivered by Cesarean section at seven months, still born.

Mother certainly needed rest. The physical blow that her body just suffered together with all the tragedy ripping her heart should have made rest mandatory. Uncle Bill had taken up Mother's post at the hospital with me. Jon was staying with Aunt Donna and the boys, but Mother was anxious to leave the hospital and did as soon as she got the doctor to sign her release.

I was to be transferred to Community Hospital, making her daily drive shorter. She only had a few days to settle Jon back in the trailer. Mother realized that the budget wasn't going to stretch far enough to cover everything and she would have to find a job. She knew Douglas Aircraft was hiring and found that a general physical was all that was required. She purchased a rubber girdle and applied for a position. Her application was approved, and a physical was scheduled. She prayed she would not be asked to remove her girdle since she had not completely healed from the surgery. Her prayers were answered. She was hired to work the night shift, doing electrical soldering on airplanes. She was happy to get on nights thinking she could work while we slept and be with us when we needed her attention.

It wasn't long, and the story about our family was circulating around the hospital. One day, a newspaper reporter showed up at

Community Hospital to do a human-interest story about a MIA marine, his wife with a toddler son, and a daughter hospitalized with polio.

As she lies in her bed in the post-polio ward of Community Hospital balloons bob gaily from her bed but she is not entertained by them. She can move her head only slightly, and lift her arms from the elbows. The rest of her body is motionless.

In her hands, she holds a family picture, a father, a mother, boy, and girl. She is the little girl. A troubled frown crosses her forehead. "Why doesn't my daddy write to me?" She asks for the hundredth time. And for the hundredth time, her mother and nurses turn their faces away. To date, no one has summoned the courage to tell Penny Nelson, 3, that her adored daddy 1ˢᵗ Lt. Forest A. Nelson, 34, Marine pilot with a long record of heroic service has fallen, and probably is a prisoner of Communists in Korea.

Her mother, Sally Nelson, 32, hopes that someway someone can be found who can pierce the Red Curtain in Korea and get word from the father to his stricken little girl. This word may help her walk. It may help her live.

The world has crumbled for the Nelsons, a family from Huron, South Dakota, since they came to Long Beach, with their car and trailer, last May, and settled down in the Best Trailer Court, 5602 Long Beach Blvd.

Lt. Nelson was sent overseas June 16. For weeks, a letter came from him airmail every day. He alternated the letters, writing one day to his wife, the next day to his little girl. Occasionally, he interspersed this routine by addressing a letter to his son, Jon, 20 months old.

When Penny was three years old on August 3, she received a birthday letter from her daddy. He wrote, "I hope every day of your life is as happy as it is this minute."

The last letter, written August 5, and addressed to Mrs. Nelson told about the mission he had gone on that morning and the mission he expected to go on that night. (Apparently that night mission was the one from which he crashed.)

He said, in the moving words of a man deeply in love with his wife, "I want to thank you again for being mine and for bringing my children into the world, for waiting for me, and for keeping a home while I'm away. I'll never be able to give you enough love to show you how much I appreciate it, but I'll spend the rest of my life trying."

August 7, 1952, came a telegram that Lt. Nelson had been shot down and was "Missing in action." One week later, August 14, Penny went to Harbor General Hospital with bulbar polio and completely paralyzed. Last Friday she was brought from Harbor General Hospital to Community Hospital post-polio ward, where she had treatments from the adjacent Adelaide Tichenor Orthopedic Clinic. No one knows when or if she will walk again.

Men who served with Lt. Nelson have written Mrs. Nelson that they saw her husband's plane hit, saw him bail out, reach the earth, and with his 'chute under his arm run toward a hill. They quote a British major as saying that looking through his binoculars, he saw a helicopter start for the scene, but before the helicopter could get there, Lt. Nelson was captured by Communists.

"My husband is well and strong," says Mrs. Nelson. "He is used to outdoor life. He was in the service six years before he was called back again last January. He has guided hunters in South Dakota. He played high school football. He is rugged; he can find his way around. He can survive imprisonment, I think. If only someway, we could get word from him to Penny."

Long Beach Independent Press Telegram 1952

In his letter, Daddy promised a "wienie" dog for my birthday. I got polio instead, and no Daddy to kiss it better. Daddy was gone;

Pam, too. Now it was just Jon and I, and Mother was left to care for us alone.

Like her energy, I believe my mother's greatness was a gift in her at birth. It might have lain dormant until now, but within thirty days, her life had completely changed. Her incredible strength was summoned from deep within her soul. The victim role was not her style, and once she caught her breath, she laid out a plan and went into action.

I remember the hallways in the hospital and the clinic. They were lined with parents holding sick children waiting for treatment. I saw children in braces, on crutches, and in wheelchairs. But I never understood if things got better for me that would be my future. You see, I was paralyzed, lying on a gurney so I was not in braces and mentally had not connected with them. I thought it was sad that those poor children were so sick and thought that was why Mom looked so upset when we waited in the hall for my treatment. When I look back at pictures of my mother holding Jon, or with me during this time, she looked so bad. Even then, I was surprised at my mother's eyes being black underneath and looking so sad. Nevertheless, there were the special days too, when her eyes had a sparkle like the day my birthday puppy arrived.

PENNY HAS NEW PUPPY

Penny Nelson has a dog, and Penny can flip over on her stomach. There is no connection between the two facts, but they chronicle today's developments in the case of the little three year old, post polio patient in Community Hospital, whose father, Marine Pilot Forest A. Nelson, is a Red Prisoner in Korea.

The dog, a three and a half month old red dachshund, just arrived from Huron, South Dakota, and the Nelson's hometown. Friends sent it to the child. Penny, who long had wanted a "weenie dog" and had been promised one by her father for her birthday in early August, is enchanted. She looked out the hospital window and saw the dog today as her Mother strolled past it.

To demonstrate that she is gaining strength, the little girl took hold of the sides of her bed and turned over on her tummy. A month ago, she was entirely paralyzed.

Long Beach Independent Press Telegram 1952

Maybe the newspaper didn't think the two were related, but I have an idea that my showing off was just the way Mr. and Mrs. Dennis would have had me say thank you for my puppy and for fulfilling my daddy's promise to me. Since neither my baby brother nor my puppy was allowed in the hospital, I needed something, or should I say *things* to occupy my time.

PENNY HAS

3 DOLLS, NO NOTE FROM DAD....

By Vera Williams

Penny Nelson not only has twin baby dolls—she has triplets. She has named them for herself, for her little brother, Jon, and for a little girl in the adjacent bed in the Community Hospital post-polio ward.

Penny's mother, Mrs. Forest A. Nelson, took the little three year old platinum blonde the original twin dolls, small baby dolls with baby soft skin and painted hair. Then, Wednesday, here came a third doll, the exact duplicate of the others, from Penny's adopted uncle, John Phelps of Burbank who knew Penny's father, Lt. Nelson, when the Marine pilot, was a youth in Huron, South Dakota.

A wardrobe designed for two now hastily has to be stretched over three—but then that has happened to families before this!

63

Happily cuddling her dolls, Penny has named them Penny, Jon and Sandra, for the little girl in the next bed.

Penny also has a handsome dancing doll given her by a photographer—the softy!—who threatened the reporter with mayhem if it was put in the paper.

"I got this dancing doll, and had it wrapped in pink paper and tied it with a big blue ribbon bow and took it out to Penny," he explained. "Gosh, I never saw a kid's eyes shine like hers did when they took the wrappings off and that doll began to dance…It was worth a week's salary just to see her."

Penny, stricken with polio August 14, is responding to hot packs and baths. At first entirely paralyzed, she now turns her head and lifts her arms. She is still in too much pain for therapy.

The child begs for letters from her daddy, and yet has not been told that he was shot down over enemy territory August 5, but is believed to be alive.

Efforts are being made through Senators and Congressmen from California and the Press-Telegram, Washington, D.C. bureau to someway pierce the Red Curtain and get a letter from the father.

Long Beach Independent Press-Telegram 1952

I'm sure I can imagine the joy as the doll danced for me. Even more, I can imagine what my mother was thinking since her dream of dancing was transferred to me, and it didn't look much like *I* would be her dancing doll. That photographer couldn't have known about Mother's dream, but we now had a dancing doll to share and a common dream that one day we'd dance too.

Mom decided my therapy would include the Sister Kenny method of rehabilitation that was controversial as it involved hot packs and exercise. A large portion of the medical community didn't agree with the technique, but Mother did her research and was confident it would help me. I began to respond physically as the therapists worked with me. Their goal was to see their patient whole again and even employed methods that made the establishment raise their eyebrows.

LITTLE PENNY CAN SIT PROUDLY NOW!

By Vera Williams

Penny Nelson can sit in a chair! Smiling with pride, the three year old platinum blonde child proved it in the Adelaide Tichenor Orthopedic Clinic. Brought to the clinic from Community Hospital, next door, where she is a post-polio patient, the little girl was picked up by Alice Clay, physical therapist, and carefully lowered into a tiny white chair in the gymnasium.

Penny caught her breath and her blue eyes widened. After all, only five weeks ago she was entirely paralyzed.

"Look at Penny in the mirror!" coaxed the physical therapist. Attention riveted on her reflection in the triple mirror, Penny sat, only slightly supported by Miss Clay's arm about her neck and shoulders. It was the first time she had sat in a chair since she was stricken by bulbar polio.

Hot packs were begun when Penny became a clinic patient, August 21, and attendants began moving her arms and legs. In a few days, Penny could move her head and could lift her arms from the elbows. Now she can clasp her hands, she can move her legs, she can turn over in bed, and she can sit in a chair.

Long Beach Independent Press-Telegram 1952

SHE'LL WALK

Attendants are certain she will be able to walk, but whether or not she will need crutches or braces still is not known. Penny's mother and brother, Jon, live in a trailer park. Her mother works nights at the Douglas Plant.

Long Beach Independent Press-Telegram 1952

It seemed that everyone agreed I shouldn't know that Daddy wouldn't be coming home right away, for fear I would stop trying to "get better." I had been making extraordinary leaps in recovery. It was a problem shielding me from the truth, yet those important letters that he sent me regularly weren't coming now. However, it wasn't long, and the problem was solved in a big way.

LONG BEACH MARINE CHINA REDS' PRISONER

By Marjorie Driscoll

LONG BEACH, Three-year-old Penny Nelson ill with polio, always said her daddy in Korea would return to her some day.

And her mother, Mrs. Sally Nelson, will not have to tell Penny, as she desperately feared she might, that Daddy Marine Lt. Forest A. Nelson will not come home.

Today Lt. Nelson was named by the Pentagon as a prisoner of the Communists in Korea.

"It was the most wonderful news in the world—the only thing better would be to hear that he has been released," said Mrs. Nelson.

And it will be great news for Sgt Curt Giese of Milwaukee, Marine photographer, and the other men of Nelson's outfit

Long Beach Independent Press-Telegram 1952

Of course, this was wonderful news, at least Mother knew that Daddy was alive, and she believed he was capable of escape if not released, so she expected to hear from him anytime now.

HIDE THIS NUGGET IN YOUR HEART

Focus—Focus is where you put your eye. Purpose is where you put your energy. Hope is the anchor for your mind, your will, and your emotions. Result? You get what you desire.

LOVE, DADDY

Little Penny Nelson, three year old polio victim, is entertaining an important visitor from Korea. The visitor is Marine Sgt. Curt Geise, a friend of her father, Marine Pilot Lt. Forest A. Nelson, a prisoner of war in the Korean fighting.

Sgt. Geise has been playing a game of "pretend" with Penny ever since Penny was stricken with polio. Her father was captured by the Commies. Every day for eight months, the 22 year old sergeant has written "Dear Penny" letters to the little girl and signed them "Daddy."

"If you are a good girl and will do what the doctor says, I will get you a pair of Korean shoes like the little girls in Korea wear. I've decided to name my plane after you darling."

"I pray for you every night and I know you will get better soon, I'm afraid it will be a long time before I get home, but when I do come back to you and Mommy and Jon, you will be a strong, healthy girl again."

Penny's mother, Mrs. Sally Nelson, has been unable to communicate directly with her husband but, thanks to Sgt. Geise, the little girl is unaware of that fact.

Photographs of Lt. Nelson, taken before his capture, have been enclosed in many of the "Dear Penny" letters to help her in her fight against polio.

Sgt. Geise, who served with the public information office of the 1st Marine Air wing in Korea, gave up a chance to be home for Mother's Day to visit with Penny.

"The fellows still attached to the wing want a firsthand report on how Penny's getting along, and I can't disappoint either them or Penny," he explained. He soon will be on his way to join his wife and his Mother in Milwaukee.

When he called at the Nelson home, Sgt. Geise brought with him a Japanese dress for Penny and a handsome Jap robe for her tiny brother, Jon. He also had gifts—stockings and a nightgown—for Penny to give to her mother on Mother's Day.

Penny showed her "Sergeant Curt" all the letters she had received from her "daddy" and told him what was in them.

"He also took me to the beach," she reported proudly.

Tape recordings played an important part during the sergeant's two-day stopover in Long Beach. He gave the family copies of radio programs broadcast overseas and dedicated to Penny. He also put the children's conversation, prayers, and poems on records to present to the father at the first opportunity. In addition, the "Dear Penny" letters? They'll continue until there's no longer a need for them.

Long Beach Independent Press Telegram 1952

As if having my Sgt. Curt had not been good enough, I was soon to inherit forty more daddies—all marines!

40 DADDIES WILL BE GLAD TO KNOW—PENNY NOW CAN CLAP HER HANDS, WIGGLE TOES, LEGS.

Penny Nelson today can move her legs wiggle her toes and clap her hands above her head. She still cannot lift her body from the bed.

Every day she receives an airmail letter signed "Daddy" and presents are beginning to come in from her 40 DADDIES of the 1st Marine Air Wing in Korea.

The little three year old platinum blonde is showing remarkable progress from Mid-August when she was paralyzed completely by polio.

Sgt. Curt Geise, combat photographer in Korea who had photographed and was a friend of her daddy, writes Penny a letter every day, presumably from her daddy. Other members of the wing also write letters signed "Daddy" so Penny has a daily letter even if there is a delay in the arrival of one from Geise.

She has received Korean trinkets from the men, and Major Wiley Green, Nelson's flight leader, has written that a gift is en route from officers and enlisted men. The enlisted men, he wrote, insisted on "chipping in" on the gift for Penny.

PENNY GETS CARDS, CHECK FROM FLIERS...

Penny Nelson, three year old polio patient whose father is a Red prisoner in Korea, Monday received 60 cards and letters and a check for $1,301.30.

The check came from members of Group 12, 1st Marine Air Wing in Korea, with whom her father, Marine Pilot Forest A. Nelson served. The group, which has "adopted" the little girl, writes her daily letters, keeping from her the knowledge that her father is a prisoner.

Lt. Col. M.W. Fletcher, commanding officer of Group 12, enclosed the check in a letter in which he wrote:

Dear Penny, I don't suppose many little girls receive letters from strangers, but we really know so much about you. In fact, Penny, many of us have little girls just like you.

Your daddy is our friend and he is always telling us delightful stories about his beautiful little girl. Just because you are so nice, our colonel said we could name an airplane Penny and that we can fly this plane against the bad men who are fighting Daddy and us.

With our love and prayers,

Daddy's Friends—Marine Air Group 12.

Long Beach Independent Press Telegram 1952

I was holding a picture in my hands of an airplane. There were uniformed men standing by a plane with my name written across the nose, "Miss Penny." I had no idea what that plane was to mean to me in the years to come, but it moved me on the inside like nothing I'd seen before. It was as if Daddy and I were flying that plane, and I felt he was smiling big while he flew his plane with my name on it. I was hoping he could bring it home so all my family and friends could see it and take me for a ride if I were all better.

It must have been encouraging for Mother to read the stories in the newspaper and know that my father's memory was kept in front of people who may be able to help in bringing him home. I know she was happy to see the gifts and cards from so many showing their love by touching our lives in such a tangible way. I loved the attention of strangers who drifted into our lives. But I was still looking for that wonderful familiar face, the face of my father who would kiss me better when he was here.

I loved my father in every different form he took. I loved seeing him in the casual café t-shirt and slacks as he and I played with the stools at the counter, in his fishing clothes, as he would bring home a catch. He was so proud of his skill and his kill. I would listen to his stories as he recounted the day with Mother. However, his dress uniform was my favorite. He looked so important and strong. I felt safe as though nothing could harm me. I needed his comfort now.

Mother was busy keeping us together and making a home while trying to learn all the therapy techniques that would help make me whole again. As if this was not enough, Mother still found time to write to senators, congressmen, the Commandant of the Marine Corps, the Lions Club, and to anyone else who might in some way help bring my daddy home or get help for me medically.

During this time, my mother's faith that Daddy would return was increased because so many of the men serving with him cared and encouraged her with stories of his abilities. Congressional representatives and some senators responded. I even received a letter and mechanical pencil with U.S. Senate on it from Richard Nixon. He told me he was sorry about my daddy not being with me while I was sick, but they were working to get him home.

I know that through Mother's strength and dedication to my therapy, coupled with the prayers of many people, I was happy and showing more progress than anyone expected, except Mom, that is.

There was another doll that would mean the world to me. Most of my dolls shared my quiet whimpers at night, except for one that was of special design and shared my family's living nightmare.

PENNY GETS PAL FOR EXERCISES...

Penny Nelson has a new doll now and it does exercises with her. Reading in the newspapers about the little three year old polio victim whose father, Marine Pilot Forest A. Nelson is a Red prisoner in Korea, Eugene A. Lord carved the foot-long doll from wood, with jointed neck, shoulders, hips, knees, elbows, wrists, and ankles. The doll has a pretty, painted face, yellow braided hair and a yellow and white seersucker dress.

Penny has named it Frances. Side by side, Penny and Frances do the exercises by which it is hoped that Penny will be enabled to walk again.

Long Beach Independent Press-Telegram 1952

Frances was a much better patient than I was because she did whatever exercise my mother helped her with and there was no crying. The exercises looked easy when she did them. Mother would position her in front of me and explain what we were going to do next, and Frances did them. When my turn came, things changed a bit.

My aunt Donna said she would have to leave the room because she couldn't take it when I screamed or begged my mother to stop hurting me. Nevertheless, Mother would continue to push and direct, stretch and pull, bend and straighten my limbs until I was sure she could not possibly love me at all. However, Frances just kept on doing her exercises without screaming one time. Mom always called me her little trooper, but Frances must have looked like a little general. She was just so much tougher than I was. Frances couldn't make the pain go away, but she did help take the fear away. By watching her, I knew what was going to happen next; and somehow that helped me to know that just as sure as the exercises began, they would also end. Frances was my very good friend.

Jon sure could have used a friend like Frances. He couldn't understand why he couldn't come into the hospital to see me. However, I could look out the window and see him in his short pants and cowboy boots, waving at me. He thought I was having all the fun, like riding in ambulances and stuff. Jon had my mother's energy and my daddy's looks. I would find out later that he was full of Daddy's mischief, too. As little as he was, he wanted to be like his daddy and always had an airplane in his hand or close by. He was going to be a marine.

HIDE THIS NUGGET IN YOUR HEART

Don't be afraid to ask for help. Don't be too proud to accept it.

RUB-A-DUB-DUB,
TWO KIDS IN A TUB

One day Mom got a phone call explaining that our family had been chosen to receive special help from a naval support group. Mom was very excited and called Uncle Bill to tell him about it.

"Bill, you won't believe what just happened. I got a phone call telling me that there's a naval ship named the *Mispillion* whose homeport is right here in Long Beach. The caller said the families of the men serving on the ship were a 'support crew.' The support crew finds a community project for the sailors and their families to sponsor. When the captain's wife was looking for someone to help, she was told about Penny having polio, that Forey was missing in action in Korea, and they want to help us. Can you believe it?"

"That's great, Sis. What exactly are they going to do?" Bill asked.

"I'm not sure yet, but we will be meeting them soon. We actually get to board the *Mispillion*. I'm sure I'll find out more then."

Little did I know that Jon and I were going to have a wonderful outing, a special day that would mark my life forever. It wasn't long before Mother got permission from the hospital to take me on a big ship because some nice men had wanted to meet Jon and me.

Near the end of the '51-'52 cruise, the benevolent hearts of the officers and men of the Mispillion opened wide to

74

offer assistance to their new-found "sister," Penny Nelson. Three-year-old Penny, cheery little lass, was a bulbar polio victim and for a time was entirely paralyzed. The crew rallied and raised a "kitty" of $600.00 which went into a trust fund for little Penny and was presented to her when the ship arrived in Long Beach, California, the *Mispillion*'s home port.

USS *Mispillion* Cruise Book 52-53

I didn't get to wear the hoop skirt that day or my ruffled panties, and the ringlets just didn't hold like usual. I was in a nightie with a robe to keep me warm. There was a soft cast on my left foot with my bare toes hanging out. I sure didn't fit Mom's picture for public appearance, but the three of us were together for the first time in a very long time. Jon was excited about the trip but wondered what had happened to his sister. He had to be careful with me now, and I couldn't play with him as before. When we got to the Long Beach dock, we were able to drive out far enough to see a big ship, the USS *Mispillion* just sitting there on the ocean. Before we knew it, there were sailors everywhere, smiling at us as if we were the main attraction. Mom was standing beside the car talking to a sailor, and I thought that maybe he knew my daddy. I wondered if maybe the surprise was that Daddy was there somewhere, maybe on that ship.

"Come on, honey," Mother said, as she maneuvered me out of the car. "Okay, Jon, you're next."

I bet our eyes were as big as silver dollars knowing that we were going to be on that big ship. I felt a sense of wonder, maybe because everyone was smiling at us so much, and a sense of safety.

I was placed in the arms of Captain Munson and was soon to discover he was the boss. Captain Munson said all the men on his ship wanted to meet me and to show Jon and me around. It was overwhelming to us. I was passed from sailor to sailor. They were all so strong, smiling, and laughing. I think doing some tickling, too, because in the pictures I'm smiling bigger than I can remember since going to the hospital.

Some of the men told me they had a little girl at home like me or a little boy like Jon. I told them I had a Daddy too, somewhere. I was hoping he was here with them, but he wasn't. He was in a place called Korea. The sailors told me they were helping to fight that war, too, and that their ship helped get everyone back home faster. Sometimes the sailors cried when they were talking to me, and it reminded me of my Uncle Bill. He cried a lot when we were talking and playing together. I felt that same special feeling with all my new friends that I did with Uncle Bill. I felt I was special to them, but I wished I could make their tears go away.

Captain Munson told us there was going to be a party on his ship soon and for me to keep working hard. I promised I would. I was hoping I was going home but not today, maybe soon. I couldn't wait to be home.

Jon was so active, and yet he never seemed dirty. In fact, as I looked back on our lives, Mother must have had us Scotchgarded at birth because we were just always clean. Mom could really give a great bath, and every inch would be scrubbed clean. When we would get in the tub, we weren't nearly as particular as she was, but then we'd hear, "I'll be in to check you," and here would come that soapy washcloth rubbing us down. I have a memory of the hospital baths, too, and feeling sad because I knew I wouldn't hear, "I will be in to check you."

Some days Mom would come to the hospital, and we would play beauty shop, putting on makeup. Aunt Margie was a beautician and played beauty shop with me before I had polio. She'd put a board across the arms of the shampoo chair, lay my head back, give me a quick bite on the cheek, then the world's greatest shampoo. Aunt Margie was another one who was quick to cry. I would tell her stories, sitting on the sink in her kitchen, saying "and so the big bad wolf did this or that, and so," etc. No matter which story I told Aunt Margie, she would smile and shake her head slowly, cry, squeeze my face, bite my cheek, saying, "You are so good; I could eat you all up." Uncle Bill and Aunt Margie were the world's greatest biters, a kid's bottom or cheek was never safe within arm's reach of either one of them. When my shampoo and new hairdo were finished, it was my turn to do her hair; beauty shop quickly became my favorite game.

Finally, we got some good news. The doctors said they were going to put a brace on my foot that would help it work better, and *if* I promised to wear the brace all day and wear the nighttime brace, I could go home.

"I will," I promised.

"Oh, and one more thing, Penny. We'll need to put a board on your bed to help you stay nice and straight, okay?"

"Okay, Doctor." By now, the disease had begun to twist my body. My spine was curving into an S, technically called a double scoliosis.

POLIO STRICKEN DAUGHTER OF POW MARINE RECOVERING

Penny Nelson is going home Friday. The little three-year-old blonde who was totally paralyzed from polio in August and whose Father is a Red prisoner in Korea will be released Friday from the post polio ward, and will return to the family trailer in Long Beach. Physicians say the child's hands and arms are normal although her body and legs still are weak.

It will be necessary for her to return daily to the Adelaide Tichenor Orthopedic Clinic for treatment.

Her Mother, Mrs. Sally Nelson, who has been working nights at the Douglas plant, will give up her work to stay home and care for the child. Her little brother, Jon, not quite two years old, also awaits her return."

Long Beach Press-Telegram 1952

HIDE THIS NUGGET IN YOUR HEART

Allow the good memories to mark your life. Refuse to let the bad ones destroy it.

MIRROR, MIRROR, ON THE WALL

I can remember returning home and feeling safe. I knew that if I cried in my sleep Mom would come to me, rather than a nurse. I had great nurses, but there is nothing in this world like your mother's comfort. They seem to hold you as if their very life depended on your faith in them. Mother's smell was different from anyone else. There is a certain fit into a mother's body that is better than any fit. A pitch in the voice of a mother that makes the "boogie man" disappear. There is comfort in praying with a mother that no one else can deliver. It was wonderful to be home.

Of course, there were those tiny brown hands, my brother's hands, grasping and touching me as if I were not real. A funny little button nose and his eyes so dark that I could see myself in them. A loud noise that no respectable hospital would allow came from somewhere in his belly. Oh, just to be home.

Mother had been looking for an apartment to rent instead of living in the trailer since we were going to be staying in Long Beach for rehabilitation therapy. Not only did she find a nice little apartment, we had tricycles to ride on the sidewalk.

Just as the doctor had said, there was a board on my bed. It wasn't between the mattresses, no, it was between the sheet and me. Things didn't just seem hard; things were hard even if Mom called me her little trooper. I knew we had a long way to go, and I wasn't feeling much like her trooper most days. Mom couldn't continue to stay off work, so the day came when the normal lifestyle of a single parent set in. Tichenor Clinic was a great help to us. Meg, the driver, of the big woody station wagon would pick me up for therapy and talk to me or, more accurately, listen to me all the way there. She was one very dedicated, cheerful, on time woman who was always there, and I loved her.

Once we arrived at the clinic, Meg would park in the back and out would come a young man with a wheelchair. He would put us in the chair one by one and wheel us up the ramp to a long hall and a waiting room where there was a big box running over with toys. There were also many great books. I could see the *Wizard of Oz* on the highest shelf. This didn't seem like my kind of book, but one day a mother started reading it to a little boy. Dorothy fascinated me, and I hoped this little boy would be back every day, so I could hear more. Dorothy seemed to have bad things happen to her like me. Just when the story got interesting, the double wooden doors would open and a therapist would come for the next child to go to therapy. Whoops, it was my turn.

Leaving the waiting room, we would turn to the right, and there we were, back in that long hallway. The first door on the right was the office. It housed another great woman, Mrs. Neff. I know she was my mother's teacher in how to handle me. They were very much alike, so when their paths crossed, I was their target. Failure did not stand a chance. I loved going to Mrs. Neff's office to visit and to call my Uncle Bill to let him know it was time to pick me up. It is funny what children find interesting. Mrs. Neff had a great big Rolodex on her desk. I'd pretend I forgot Uncle Bill's number so I could watch her work it! I don't think I ever fooled her.

Further down the hall were private therapy rooms. That was where consultations were done and where we rested between sessions. The tables were cold since they were covered in plastic, but they each had a beautiful hand-knit blanket at the foot. There were two therapists I adored, Ms. Clay and Ann. Ann had blond hair and laughing eyes. Mrs. Neff would come to the private therapy room to talk to me and instruct Ann on what to do that day. Concentration is very important to retrain muscle. Now concentration is one thing, but to concentrate, you must first focus. This means to understand what you are trying to do, how you intend to do it and to recognize how you will know when you have accomplished it! Mrs. Neff was the chief in charge of attention getting!

She had a long fingernail that she would drag across my leg and say, "Feel this muscle, Penny. Feel it." Then, *"Now think this muscle, Penny. Think it."* Finally, "Now work this muscle, Penny. Make this muscle work." Feeling it was never a problem with that fingernail digging deep across the muscle, and thinking was not hard either, but making it work was not easy at all. I remember sweating and straining to accomplish my mission.

When I managed to make the muscle work, even a little bit, I would hear, "Good girl!" I would get her big smile as she watched the muscle work, and it was a wonderful reward because no one had a smile like Mrs. Neff. Then she would gently touch me on the leg and say, "Don't forget to work hard."

There were mirrors I worked in front of which showed me the result of the exercises and I would beam at Ann smiling behind me. However, some days, that mirror made me think I was going crazy. It reminded me that I was different than I used to be and different from other children now. I wondered if my dad would be upset that I couldn't stand on his hands anymore, or go fishing with him. I would be alone in the mirror silently giving up, trying to let go of the pain, trying to hold back the tears. I was too tired to think this muscle, too disappointed and frustrated to work hard. Just then Ann or Ms. Clay, or another nameless therapist, would be in the mirror with me, with laughing eyes and a smiling face, with gentle arms to support me or was it a hug?

Then quietly, "Come on, Penny. Shall we try one more time?"

I could feel the tightness swelling in my chest as my heart said, "No more." My mind would pray, "Please no more," but each time my mouth would say, "Yes." Over and over I knew; one more time—one million times—just let me walk!

Looking straight down the long hallway in front of me, there were three doors. First, on the left was the swimming area. This room had tiled floors and a big sparkling pool. A stainless steel table would lift out of the water. They would place me on the table and lower it into the water, supporting my body while the therapist exercised my arms and legs. He would tell me to put my head under the water and hold my breath expecting me to increase the count each time. He said this would help strengthen my lungs and sure enough I could go longer and longer every month. My next goal was getting off the table so I could practice swimming to strengthen the rest of my body. Holding the edges of the table, I would kick my feet while watching my mother on her hands and knees scrubbing the grout between the floor tiles. The poolroom had the cleanest grout in Long Beach, and I thought it was great that my mother could do her favorite thing, clean. My goal was to get off that table and Mom's was getting off that floor. Mother seized every opportunity to make ends meet. There was no task too big or too small that she wouldn't tackle making sure the bills were paid and our future sound.

The second door down that hall turning right was the hot pack anteroom. This was not my favorite place. Actually, I always had to blink to make my imagination stop working. Sometimes going in that door, white uniforms turned black, little caps became pointed, and instead of hearing "Hello, Penny," I heard, "Boil, bubble, toil, and trouble." Therapy in this room began by being put in crib with the sides down. Wearing just my panties, I watched as the nurses pulled wool blankets out of the boiler, twisted them with wooden handles, and then rolled me up in the hot blankets from neck to toes. This was to relax my muscles and keep them from drawing up, becoming deformed and rigid. At three years old, I was sure this was just plain old torture. The sides of the crib would be pulled up and then I waited for the cooling down. This was the hardest part, but a clown would sometimes come to do magic tricks for me, distracting me from the discomfort. Most often, though, someone from my family would come and read to me. My favorite was Uncle Bill. He would read or color pictures for me and try to make me laugh, but when he wiped the sweat off my forehead, I noticed he would have to wipe tears from his eyes. It was confusing to me that everyone told me to be brave when all the grownups around me cried and they weren't even in the hot packs.

Now the third door down that hall was my favorite. It was the back door, and there was Meg waiting on me with a big smile, "Ready to go home, Penny?"

"You bet!"

Once home my mother was faithful to her promise to make sure I did all my exercises on time.

The ones I could do alone, I was reminded to do. "Penny, do 'Trot trot to Boston.' I'll be in to help you with the rest."

Lying on my stomach, I would rock like a rocking horse, head up then feet up, singing, "Trot, trot to Boston to buy a loaf of bread, home again home again, horsy go to bed." Once, twice, three times...thinking, *I remember trot, trot to Boston...*

I remember to tuck my tail feathers in... I remember Mrs. Neff; to think this muscle, over and over—think this muscle.

Why are your eyes so black, Mother? Why does Uncle Bill cry so all the time, Mother? Why am I sick, Mother? When will my daddy be home, Mother? Four, five, six...still no answers, "Trot, trot to Boston to buy a loaf of bread, home again, home again, horsy go to bed."

HIDE THIS NUGGET IN YOUR HEART

Push past the pain. Just as sure as the problem began, there will be an end.

AN UNCOMMON LOVE

I was like a bug on my back. I couldn't get up without help because my stomach muscles didn't work. Once sitting, I could do some things just like before I had polio, but walking wasn't one of them, and I wasn't any good at crawling either. My legs didn't want to do what they were created to do. Polio had rendered my sphincter muscle slow to signal me, so when my bladder was full and stimulated by standing or rocking, I had to get to the bathroom quickly.

"Mom, I need to go potty!"

"You're a big girl, Penny. You can get to the bathroom, and I'll be in there to help you."

Sometimes I didn't know what I was feeling. It felt like anger to me as I fought back the tears. I thought my mother hated me. I didn't like her much at that moment either. I had to drag myself, which increased the urge to go; in fact, it was painful. By the time I got to the bathroom, I didn't want to talk to her, but I'll bet my eyes spoke volumes. It wasn't until later I realized dragging myself to the bathroom was just another way Mother got me to exercise.

Little did I know she was heating the toilet seat to be sure the shock of the cold seat didn't complicate the functioning of the sphincter muscle. I had no way of appreciating this because I didn't know what a cold seat felt like, that is, until I went to school.

One day, while Mom was making dinner and Jon and I were riding our tricycles, we heard Mom open the screen door and tell us to come in. She sounded so excited, we knew something good was happening and it wasn't just time to eat.

"Do you remember our friends on the *Mispillion*?" she asked.

"I do!" I yelled, and Jon said, "Me, too."

"Well, they have asked if we would like to go a party on the ship."

"Today?" we asked.

Laughing, she said "No, not today. Next week."

Oh, boy this was good. We started planning what dress I would wear instead of a nightie, and what Mom and Jon would wear. I almost forgot about how hard my bed was to sleep on all that week. Mom told me Captain Munson and his wife, Mrs. Ann, along with all the men on the ship had invited my friends from the clinic to come to the party, too. Some of the nice newspaper people I met at the hospital would be there with important people from the National Foundation for Infantile Paralysis. I just knew this was going to be a great party.

The big day came at last, and we were ready for the fun. When we arrived at the dock, everyone was waiting and watching for us.

Little Penny came aboard the *Mispillion* to greet her "big brothers." Miss Penny, after receiving a salute worthy of her station, was taken on a tour of the ship so she could see where the men ate, slept and worked. Earlier this year the men of the *Mispillion* joined the "March of Dimes" campaign, and, in the name of Miss Penny Nelson, contributed over $1,650.00 to the Long Beach Branch of the National Foundation for Infantile Paralysis.

Penny continued her recovery from the paralysis but again her struggle for health was jeopardized. This time it was a case of pneumonia that placed her in the Navy hospital at Oceanside, California. Fighting hard the high-spirited

Penny strove to ward off the chest ailment and rebuild her weakened chest muscles.

Back aboard the *Mispillion* the crew members didn't call it "quits" when the "March of Dimes" campaign had ended. Instead, they continued their "Penny Nelson Fund" in order to raise enough money to present the Long Beach Branch of the National Foundation for Infantile Paralysis with a child-size iron lung to be used in other cases such as little Penny's. Upon being advised that the Long Beach area be not in need of an additional iron lung, the crew, not to be thwarted, continued to swell their funds this time for an electromyograph that was direly needed by the foundation.

USS *Mispillion* Cruise Book 52-53

We crossed the gangplank and saw that the sailors were dressed differently this time. They had on their good clothes, too. Mom looked beautiful, and she was smiling bigger than I'd seen her smile since Daddy left for war. I saw Mrs. Neff and others that I loved, but many people I didn't know. This time the sailors lined up behind us. We saw two little boys waiting for us, too. They were Captain Munson's sons, John and Chris. I saw a big machine. It was a little bit scary with things that looked like eyes staring back at me, but everyone seemed so excited about it that I was sure it was good.

Someone brought a chair for me. Everyone was talking about the machine. The captain's son, Chris, stood close behind me listening to every word. His brother was nearby, and his father stood off to the side, smiling.

Someone was explaining the big machine, which was an electromyograph. It was a machine for producing an electromyogram from electrical activity picked up by electrodes inserted into muscle tissue. Mrs. Neff said it would help her and others locate the areas of weakness in me and other little children like me.

I knew she was excited about it, and I could already hear her saying, "Penny, think this muscle." Then I found out that all those wonderful sailors had used their own money to buy that machine and donated it in my name to the Tichenor Clinic.

They found many ways to help us. They had a fundraiser they called "Pennies for Your Thoughts," where they had pennies held out of their paychecks. They even raised money to help Mom by playing bingo. Mom explained to Jon and me how special it was for these young sailors to give their money because many of them had their own families to support. As sailors, they didn't make much money. They were very generous and loving to help us so much.

Many pictures were taken that day. I spent a lot of time looking at those pictures during the little war with polio that I was in. Not only did so many service men sign Daddy on their letters, but also their faces were now so familiar that they became like family in my mind.

All of a sudden, they gave the microphone to me and wanted me to say something. I'd never seen a microphone before and really didn't know what to do, but I did know what I wanted to say. These men made me feel safe and special.

I was sure they could do anything, so I said, "Go win the war, and bring my daddy home." I was sure that ship could do the job, but my new friends knew that was too big an order.

Next, the best thing happened. They made me an official part of the USS *Mispillion*. I was named, "The Queen of the *Mispillion*." I thought that was wonderful because I really liked houses that looked like castles and canopy beds, and now I really was a queen.

It was a great party, one that we didn't want to end. By the time it was over, I was tired but full of hope. Jon just wanted to take a ride on the ship, and Mother, well, she was missing another man in uniform and wondering how much longer before we heard he was coming home.

PENNY GLAD TO SEE MISSING DAD'S PALS...

By Vera Williams

A tiny girl with a pale face and a mop of pale gold hair rode her tricycle up and down the street in front of the little apartment. Behind her trotted a small boy in a yellow suit. A car roared up and two young Marine officers stepped out. "Hello, Wiley...Hello, Bill," said the tiny girl. "Why, hello, Penny!" said one of the officers, a major and picked her up in his arms. "Did you bring my daddy?" "No," he said, "I didn't, Penny. I sure wish I had. But, I came to tell you about him."

It was Maj. Wiley Green, 32, and Capt. William Bizzell, 28, just back from Korea where they had flown with Penny Nelson's daddy, shot down and believed to be a prisoner of the Reds.

Bizzell had flown with Nelson in an uneventful mission in the morning. Green was with him on the disastrous mission in the afternoon.

The two visiting officers chuckled with Sally about Lt. Nelson's foibles—how he liked to sleep late in the morning and grumbled at getting up, unless he was going on a mission. They laughed ruefully about how when they wanted to brag about their own wives and children, they "couldn't get a word in edgewise because Nels was always talking about his."

Penny cannot quite stand or walk, but she can ride her tricycle with her hands and arms supporting her body. She has one small brace on her left foot.

The officers brought Penny a wooly dog and brought her little brother, Jon, a toy gun.

Long Beach Independent Press-Telegram 1953

No, they didn't bring back Daddy; no one could. Daddy would never come home, not Forest Archie Nelson, First Lt. Nelson. He would stay in our hearts. He would have formed a part of each of our lives. He would live in my brother's face, but he would never again live with us in a trailer or in a house I thought was a castle. He would never again work at a restaurant with my mother, or tell her that she had beautiful legs. He would never again swing her on a dance floor, and she would never again swing him right back.

HIDE THIS NUGGET IN YOUR HEART

In a cloud, as in fog, you have no direction and no hope. Pierce through the cloud where there is *always* blue sky.

SCHOOL BELLS,
WEDDING BELLS,
ALARM BELLS

The newspapers said the Nelsons' world had crumbled after the move to California, and I guess that is close to being true. However, the people in our world had not. We had new rules to live by, but our leader was familiar to us. Mother had changed physically some, but we were all together, and the adrenalin started pumping. She took the crumbled pieces, the fragments of our life, went into action, and the pieces started falling into place.

When the doctors told her my legs were very weak and I may never walk, she turned a deaf ear. While I was sorry for the children in hallways, she was planning how she would bring me through those hallways. While I screamed in pain during therapy, she could hear me singing and laughing—walking with other children. She was ready, and because Mother had her goals, Jon and I were ready. So, lead on, Mom.

Mother bought a café on Fourth Street in Long Beach and hung the sign, Sally's Café. Mom having her own business meant Jon and I could be with her. What a great location, a movie theater across the street, a toy store on the corner, and Uncle Hank's shop, Blatnik Custom Hand Controls, around the block. There he designed automobile hand controls for paraplegics and quadriplegics, making it possible for them to drive. The best people came through our doors, and those that became regulars ended up part of the family. Mom would tell us to call them Aunt or Uncle so and so. Jon was tickled, and I was hugged a hundred times a day. I figured out that blood relative's bite but adopted ones tickle and hug.

A tall, blue eyed, dark haired man named Tom became a regular. Boy, could he make Mom laugh. One day he asked her for a date. She was thinking it had been a long time since she'd danced, so she asked, "Can you dance?"

"Dance, of course. I can dance, and I will be glad to show you Saturday night."

She took a lot of time getting ready, and we were happy for her.

The next day Mom told Uncle Bill about her date. "Tom couldn't dance at all, Bill. He has two left feet and stepped all over mine."

"But did you have fun, Sis?"

"Yes." She smiled. "We had fun but no more dancing until he takes lessons. Next weekend we are going skating. He claims he was a champion in his hometown."

Well, Tom had stretched the truth again. He could hardly stay on his feet, knocking people over. Mother couldn't even help him up for laughing.

One afternoon Tom came by the café, and Mother was doing her best to keep up with the customers. Tom asked if she wanted him to come behind the counter and help.

"Can you cook?" she asked.

"Cook, I can cook a little bit."

"Right," she said but expected nothing after those two dates. "Okay, get back here. I do need some help."

By the end of day, Mother saw that Tom really could cook. In fact, he whipped that kitchen in line and had the orders up hot and on time. She found out that Tom was an excellent chef, and he became a regular feature at Sally's Café.

On one of my regular doctor visits, we were told I needed to have foot surgery to correct a drop foot, as the soft cast hadn't worked. By now, it was clear that we were going to stay in Long Beach. Mother found a beautiful house. My therapy would include pool time for many years, but we didn't have the money to put in a pool. Once again, we called on the help of the military. Both the navy and the marines made donations to put a pool in our back-yard. At first, all the children in the neighborhood wanted to be my friend and swim, but as the months wore on, the newness of the pool wore off. There were long, lonely hours of exercising in the pool while my friends were riding bikes or playing at the park.

I had strengthened my lungs with the pool exercises at the clinic so I was able to stay under water for a very long time. I loved to swim near the bottom where my belly nearly touched the floor and slowly travel from the shallow to the deep end. Mother would look out the window and not see me. Trying not to panic, she would rush outside thinking I had drowned.

"You can sure stay under water a long time, Penny," she would say, and then the worried expression would leave her face and a big smile would replace it as I bobbed to the surface.

I was going to start school soon and hoped I would make friends. Mom took me shopping for school clothes and, though I was dif-ficult to fit, bought me beautiful things. One shoulder stuck out, pulling on buttons and zippers in a funny way.

I could hardly wait for the first day of school. The day finally arrived and off I went wearing a blue and red plaid dress with pleats, crutches, and one small brace attached to saddle shoes.

I was all too familiar with medical people staring intently at my body and watching me closely as I tried to maneuver about with my braces and crutches, a cast, and a body that still clearly

93

had a mind of its own. I was not ready for my new school friends to study me so closely.

"Mom, why is everyone staring at me?"

"They may never have seen anyone their age walking on crutches before. Don't worry, honey, they will love you, and the staring will stop."

"Good morning, you must be, Mrs. Nelson, and you must be Penny." I remember newspaper stories about your family," she said, looking at Mother. Then looking down at me, she said, "And I think you have been a very brave little girl, Penny. My name is Mrs. Donovan, and I'm your kindergarten teacher." She had a great smile and kind eyes. I smiled back and forgot about the other children for a minute.

"I am pleased to meet you, Mrs. Donovan." I was concerned for a minute, as Mother had taught me to curtsy when I met someone new, but I just couldn't figure out how to do that on crutches.

Mrs. Donovan said, "This is your desk, Penny. Why don't you sit down while I talk with your mother, and then we'll begin class."

Sitting down, I turned slowly and looking around saw some children smiling at me and others turning away quickly. I smiled back and then faced the big desk in the front of the room. I felt a little funny in my stomach, but maybe the other children were feeling that way too.

Mom leaned down and whispered, "I am going now, Penny. I'll meet you by the sandbox. Have fun, honey."

Class started, and Mrs. Donovan said, "Stand up and put your right hand over your heart. We're going to say the pledge of allegiance.

"I pledge allegiance to the flag of the United States of America, and to the republic for which it stands, one nation, under God, indivisible, with liberty and justice for all."

My eyes stung with tears, but this time they were tears of joy. I thought about my friends on the *Mispillion* and my daddy and all of his friends that were so kind to me. I thought about how lucky I was to be at school and not in the hospital.

"Let's pray. God, bless our country, our families, friends, and school. Amen. Okay, everyone sit down. We are going to tell who we are and a little bit about our favorite things."

There were plenty of giggles, and some children dropped their heads down. Mom would say they were shy. It was my turn.

I said, "My name is Penny Nelson, and my favorite things are Curries ice cream and playing jacks."

There were some whispers and pointing, but just as Mom said, it was changing. After school I sat on the side of the sandbox, watching the children running to the bus and cars lined up at the curb—then I saw Mom. She smiled and waved at me while she was parking the car, then she burst out the door and came running.

"Did you have fun, honey? Did you learn a lot today?" I started laughing and thinking, this was a very good day.

"I said the pledge of allegiance and told the other children I liked playing jacks, and we took a little nap and played outside on recess. I like school, Mom, but I scratched my shoes up and…"

"Bye, Penny!" shouted one child.

"See you tomorrow," said another and waved.

Mom laughed as we got in the car. "I told you they would love you, honey. Now what else did you do today?"

"I said my ABC's, and we counted, and where's my brother?"

"He stayed at the café. I was out shopping and didn't have time to pick him up, but you'll see him at the clinic later, okay?"

"Okay," I said, thinking I had forgotten about my therapy— oh, I could hardly wait to tell Mrs. Neff about my first day. "Mom, do you think my underwear got dirty while I played at school?"

Mrs. Neff was so much like my mom. No holes were allowed in underwear, and they should never be dirty.

Mom would always say, "What if you were in a car accident, and they found you had dirty underwear?"

I didn't know what that meant, but I did know one should never be caught wearing dirty underwear.

"You're fine, Penny. Here we are."

I bet I danced into the waiting room that day, and sure enough, the nurse noticed my pretty dress and big smile.

"Where have you been today, Miss Penny, all dressed up?"

"I go to school now," I said as I sat down waiting my turn. I didn't play with the toys or look at the books. I just sat there with my eyes closed thinking about all that had happened that day.

I like school, I thought. *Maybe I will be a teacher one day.*

The big double doors opened, and there was Mrs. Neff, smiling and saying, "Penny, we're ready."

I chattered all the way to the exercise room.

Mrs. Neff said, "Really, oh my, what a day."

Then it was time to get to work at making me stronger. Off came the brace, down went the crutches, and my pretty dress was hung on a hook. Gentle hands lifted me onto the table, and the stretching and working began.

The week passed quickly. I noticed Mom smiling about a secret she had for me, but every day when she came to pick me up there was no surprise and no telling her secret.

"It must be a pretty big secret," I said to her on the way to the café.

"It is," she answered.

Jon was glad to see me when I was finished with school and the clinic and was always ready for the weekend.

"Let's go get an airplane, DeeDee!" he yelled when he saw me.

"And get a loaf of bread on the way," Mom said as we started out the door.

"Barbara Ann," Jon said over and over, "Barbara Ann bread."

One afternoon, Mother didn't make it to school on time. I was sitting on the sandbox, and everyone else had gone home. I was getting pretty upset. It seemed like I had been sitting out there forever.

Mrs. Donovan came outside and said, "Don't worry, Penny, I know your mom is on her way."

"I'm not worried," I lied, trying to be a good soldier. A few minutes later, I saw Mom as she parked the car.

"Sorry to be late, honey. I was waiting on that big surprise, but now we can go."

I didn't see a big surprise when I got into the car. Then I noticed we weren't going to the clinic or the café.

"Where are we going, Mom?"

"Home. I told you that the surprise is finally here."

When we got home, Mom said, "Follow me."

Just as we got to my bedroom door, she said, "Close your eyes, no peeking."

Mother opened the door and said, "Now, open your eyes."

When I did, I saw the most beautiful canopy bed. It was just what a queen would sleep in. I screamed out for joy. It was a big bed, big enough to have someone sleep with me, and I was very happy.

"I promised you'd have your own room and a special bed if you were a good girl and worked hard to get better. You've been working hard, and you are a very good girl. I'm so glad you like it."

As I got up on the bed, I realized that the board was still there, but it was so beautiful, I really didn't mind at all.

This was a season of surprises, and it was not long that Mom told us she was getting married. Jon and I were happy that Tom was going to be our daddy and not just our Uncle Tom. We were hoping that Mom would be very happy.

Tom's family came to witness the ceremony that not only got us a dad but a grandmother. Tom's family was from Mississippi and talked with a Southern accent. They had funny little sayings and funnier stories to tell about their life in the south.

Tom did most of the cooking at home and at the café; everything he prepared was so good. His sisters told us that he had been a chef in New Orleans, Louisiana, in "The Quarter" which made adults' eyes wider as they nodded their heads. We didn't have a clue what that meant, but we knew it was serious and wonderful. We were beginning to settle in to our new life and our new home. We worked in the yard as a family. Mom had us plant the entire front yard in strawberries. They were oh so good, fresh or frozen. We went to pick cherries as a family. When there were too many to eat, we froze them for later. We went to Santa's Village in the snowy mountains of Big Bear, California, and gave our written Christmas list to the man in red in person. Many times, at places like Santa's Village, special attention was paid to me or I was given a gift and encouraged to get better. Before we left the village that day, my named was called over the loud speaker.

"Penny Nelson, please come to Santa's Workshop."

"What do you think he wants?"

"Let's go see, honey," Mother said as we walked that direction. There was a cute little "helper" dressed in green holding the whitest and softest little bunny I'd ever seen.

"Santa wanted you to have a present early; besides, he didn't want this little bunny to get cold in his sleigh. Will you take care of her and give her a good home?"

"I sure will. If my mom says it's okay. Is it, Mom?"

"Yes, it is, but you will have to take care of it all by yourself."

"I can do that! Thank you, and please tell Santa I said thank you, too."

Jon felt bad about not getting a bunny, so Mom and Dad stopped at a pet shop to get him one, too. Mother was seriously telling Jon how to care for his little rabbit.

"Jon, you must not hold the rabbit too tight. You need to feed it and keep its hutch clean and do not ever, ever, ever let your rabbit's feet get wet. She could get sick and die!"

"Yippee," he said, "I get a rabbit, too."

Mother would tell Jon, laughingly, that if he wasn't a good boy she was going to throw him in the trash. Jon was having trouble with his rabbit. It just would not mind, so he threw the rabbit in the trashcan and put the lid back on tight. Mother, on her way out the door, grabbed the old newspaper and the morning trash to put out. Balancing everything, she took the lid off the trashcan and out flew a rabbit!

"Jon, come and get your rabbit," mother exclaimed, laughing.

The next weekend Mother was washing her car in the driveway. Jon's rabbit scurried under the car, and Jon was on its heels in hot pursuit.

"Do not ever, ever, ever get your rabbits feet wet" came back to his mind. Just then, he gained on his furry pet, snatching it up quickly before Mother could see. He had a plan.

What Mother started she always finished, so car clean, floors washed, yard mowed, pool clean. All that was remaining on her list of chores for the day was laundry. Our garage was not attached to the house. It was at the end of the driveway, and that is where the washer and dryer were located. She started a load in the washer and noticed that the dryer was turning with a thump, thump, thump. Curious to see what Tom had put in the dryer, she opened the door and behold, a dizzy rabbit escaped, hopping at top speed down the driveway. We never saw Jon's rabbit again.

Things were sweet in those early days. We played in the pool and took family vacations. Jon was so strong, healthy, and full of energy with just a touch of mischief. He loved anything that moved and moved fast. One day a surprise came for Jon. It was a "quarter midget" racecar. He named it "the Sputnik." The whole neighborhood came out to play. Jon entered and won competitions in his little white racecar, and did he ever enjoy that. It sure looked like we were going to be very happy, but things are not always as they appear.

———

Mom took a job with General Tel in the yellow page sales division. She was one of the first female sales supervisors in California heading up a team of women who were offered a chance to travel to places like Hawaii.

Sometimes when Mother was out of town, Daddy would come to my bedroom at night to check on me. He would get in my bed, cuddle up real close, and touch me in a different way than Mom or anyone else. He would tell me it was a secret between daddies and their little girls. He said that it was how daddies show their little girls how much they loved them. Things were certainly changing, and some of the changes were confusing me. I learned one thing quickly. Not all secrets were fun.

HIDE THIS NUGGET IN YOUR HEART

When your life crumbles, pick up the pieces; and like working a puzzle, find your corners and dare to dream again.

SEE YA LATER, ALLIGATOR

Playground was not my best subject. I wanted to make friends, so I would let my classmates take my crutches to see if they could walk with them. The only problem was when the bell rang they'd drop the crutches and go to class, leaving me stuck on the playground with the crutches somewhere in the grass. My teacher spoke to Mother about this. I received quick instruction to keep my crutches with me and not allow the children to play with them. My crutches could no longer be used as a friend-making tool.

That was okay. By now, I was in the third grade and able to handle most rejection from my schoolmates. I just kept thinking about how much better I was, how much stronger, and I just knew that one day I'd be free of all the braces and stuff. It was time for the foot surgery, and I was hopeful that afterwards I'd able to play with the other children.

I was more aware of how my clothes were fitting. The twisting and bending of my back had gotten much worse, so the doctors designed a body brace made of canvas and metal stays. It had straps that went over my shoulders and looped through my legs, keeping me very straight. I'd lie down on the brace, and then we buckled up the front tightly around me. They hoped this would cause the hump to go away. I had watched an old black and white movie called *The Hunchback of Notre Dame* and wanted to do whatever it took to keep from looking like that.

For now, my foot was the pressing issue. It was time for surgery. I was admitted, and though I didn't know what to expect, the hospital scene was familiar to me.

When the nurses came for me, Mom said, smiling, "See you later, alligator."

I answered, "After while crocodile."

They rolled me off to surgery. The ceiling lights seemed to be one long light until we stopped at the elevator doors. Minutes later, doctors and nurses were rushing around the room and talking very low. A doctor I didn't know was giving me a shot and asking me if I could count backwards, and before I knew it, sleep fell on me like a shade being pulled over a window, everything went black. When I woke up, the nurses asked me questions and promised I would see my mother in a few minutes, and then Mom walked in. I felt so funny, but seeing my mother made me know that I was going to be fine. They sent me home with a cast halfway up my leg.

I wore the cast for several months, still walking with my crutches. It was finally time to remove the cast and try out my new foot. The dried blood and part of the bandage had fused the cast to the bottom of my foot, but the doctor was not aware of it. He cut the cast in half but it didn't fall away, so he jerked on it. The subsequent pain was excruciating. The jerking action took with it a chunk of flesh from the bottom of my foot. It was such a shock to my system and so painful, I promptly fainted falling back against the table I was sitting on. When I came to myself, I was sick to my stomach and sure I never wanted another operation. I know the doctor felt bad he had caused me more pain. He apologized to me and mother saying he didn't have any way to know the cast was stuck to my foot or he would have done something different. Mother felt bad for me but lightened the mood by saying, "She's just keeping with family tradition by fainting when under pressure."

I was so happy to go home, but before the day was over, I noticed something was different. My left leg was skinny, nothing like the right leg. I asked if it would grow back. Mom acted as if she didn't know the answer, but it did not. I would hear the word atrophy later, which meant I couldn't exercise it back into shape. This was devastating to me because I thought my mother's legs were beautiful and mine had that same nice shape. I felt the surgery had left me disfigured. I was trying to improve my condition, not exchange one bad thing for another. The surgery extended my heel cord as part of the correction, leaving a scar on top of my foot, a small hole on the bottom, and a short scar on the outside of my ankle. There was a longer scar from my heel up my calf. Now I had a skinny leg, a stiff foot, and scars on every side.

There was no more drop foot, but somehow I knew I would never get to wear high heels like my mom, nor would I ever again walk around in her shoes like other little girls, playing dress up.

Polio is called a crippling disease because it marks those who had it with deformity. Sometimes the things that we thought would make me better didn't work out so well, and I wondered if this would be a new reason for children to stare or make fun of me. It seemed that the price for strength was high. No matter what a good girl I was, I was sure I was getting ugly and I thought to myself, *as stiff as that board on my bed*.

At last, my leg braces were gone, and that was good news. I wore saddle shoes that were built up since my left leg was shorter than my right, but at least the steel bars were off my shoes. The body brace and crutches were still part of my life, but I was sure they would be gone one day, too.

Mother, on the other hand, had strong beautiful legs and could she kick her legs and dance. I loved Mom's legs just as my father did. We all had Saturday morning chores. It was cleaning day. We would watch cartoons for a while and then start our jobs, but when it was time to take a break, Mother would put me in the big chair in the den and dance for me. She would do the polka and swing her leg over my head. I was always laughing at her and wanting to do the polka too.

"I wish I could dance with you, Mom," I would say, and she would smile, saying, "Do your exercises, and one day you will." It was years later before I realized Mother never sat down on our breaks. The breaks were a time for me to rest, and she showed her love and devotion by dancing for me. Yes, one day I would be free of the braces, the crutches, and the funny shoes. I would be able to walk on my own and dance but until then, Mother danced for both of us.

Jon and I had our part in family entertainment, too. We both did a good Elvis impersonation. I sang "Love Me Tender" and Jon sang "You Ain't Nothing but a Hound Dog." We would stand on the fireplace hearth and sing with the record playing as loud as it could. Jon could move his hips like Elvis and push his lips doing a great impersonation.

There was more good news for me. I wasn't going to have therapy at the clinic any longer. They had done everything they could. It was bittersweet saying good-bye to Mrs. Neff and all the others who had helped me over the years. My last visit was really to summarize where I started and where I was now.

"Well, Penny, it looks like you've done everything we asked of you and you can do your exercises at home now."

"I will do them all, Mrs. Neff, and I promise to do the swimming exercises too."

"Good, now remember to come to visit us."

I don't remember Mrs. Neff ever getting personal like kissing or hugging me in the past, but that day she kissed my cheek and I told her, "I love you."

Walking out the front doors that day I realized how far I had come. Many of the children I saw every day had not improved as much as I had, and I knew our prayers were being answered.

Since I was not going to the clinic anymore, Mother decided it was time for a change, time for a new life. She wanted to sell the café and house in Long Beach and move to Anaheim.

We moved next door to the Magic Kingdom (Disneyland), and I watched out my window as the construction workers built the Matterhorn. Just a few blocks away was Knott's Berry Farm. It was a wonderful place to visit with the yummy jellies and fried chicken. Still my favorite treat was Mother's pies. I was sure this move was a magic place, and we were getting a fresh start as a family. We had a new house, new school, new jobs, and we were going to make new friends.

Mom did everything she could think of to give us a normal life. We took music and dance lessons. I tried to learn to play the organ, but I didn't like to practice. Jon hated dance class but found his niche, karate, and was he great at it.

I wanted to ride my bike, but I couldn't keep my balance. One day I had an idea. I held onto the door handle on the outside of a neighbor's car. Once I got up on the bike, I pushed hard and the bike started to roll, then I could peddle. Wow, it felt like I was flying. Ouch, well, turning was a challenge, and now there was no way to get home until someone parked their car on the street so I could push off again.

At school, we heard about orphans in another country, and the teacher said the school had a fund you could give money to and they would send it to help those children. John, a classmate, lived down the street from me. We would meet in his backyard and talk about what we wanted to do for the orphans. He had a statue of the Virgin Mary in his yard, and thinking it was safe, we put our change under her until we had enough to adopt an orphan. The money didn't seem to be coming in fast enough so we had a great idea. There was a woman on our street that had the prettiest red flowers in her front yard. She didn't have any children of her own and she was cranky with us when we were walking in front of her house. The flowers were geraniums. We waited until it looked safe and then we picked her flowers. The leaves were big and round, making a perfect corsage. We walked door to door selling our creations, telling everyone the money was for the orphans. Did we ever collect a lot of change! We were so excited, but when we got home, we were in big trouble. The neighbor called our mothers and told them that we ruined her garden. We tried to explain, but she didn't care. We did take the money to school and felt good doing our part for those who needed help. John thought we should ask the Virgin to forgive us for stealing the flowers and making our neighbor so mad, so we did.

HIDE THIS NUGGET IN YOUR HEART

Stay positive in spite of today's troubles. Your attitude today affects tomorrow's outcome. Never forget the seed of your dream is planted in your heart as a child.

NOT THE ONLY CRIPPLE

I was in the fifth grade and feeling good about things regarding my health but not my body. Not only was I not happy about my body, I wasn't happy with my step dad visiting my room at night. I could hear him come in late at night supporting himself by walking his hands down the walls, trying to get to the bathroom or, worse, to my room. Sometimes he smelled like the stuff he drank, and other times he smelled as if he had on too much cologne or something. He never came to my room when he was drunk, nevertheless, I worried he would. This could have been a great time for Dad and Mom, but instead there were fights.

It was getting close to Christmas. Our tree was beautiful. I had asked for a little sewing machine and a doll. The presents were piling high and so was the excitement. Christmas Eve came and it was very hard to fall asleep, but we were trying our best. Mom was quiet that night, and Dad was not home. I must have fallen asleep for a minute when I heard the familiar noises of hands on the walls. Dad was home, and he had been drinking. I heard Tom say he wanted a needle and thread, and then there was a lot of noise. It sounded like things breaking, and I wanted to see what was happening. I crept out of bed to have a look—I couldn't believe my eyes. Tom had walked on our presents, breaking and scattering them across the floor. He was sitting on a chair sewing up a bad cut on his hand. He'd been in a fight and a man fired a gun, grazing his hand. He was bloody, dirty, and smelled awful. In fact, you could smell him all over the house. Christmas was officially over, and Tom was out of the house before morning. We didn't talk about what happened. Mother had cleaned up the mess, but there was my sewing machine, broken, just like my mother's heart.

Dad wasn't gone long and it was a new year, full of promise. We were learning a new sport at school, volleyball. I was happy about this because my arms were strong from walking on crutches, so I could really hit a ball. I just needed someone to help me get it back over the net if there was any footwork required.

After the teacher explained the game and showed us what to do, she chose two captains who would pick the teams from the rest of our class.

One captain would say, "Mary, I'll take you," then the other captain would say "Joseph, I'll take you," and so on.

After everyone was chosen except me, the teacher blew her whistle and everyone ran onto the court. I was standing there feeling sick to my stomach. No one looked at me. In fact, I was invisible. I knew what it was like to be stared at, laughed at, humiliated and teased. Once I remember I asked a boy sitting on the school bus staring at me while I tried to get my heavy shoes, weak legs, and crutches up the steps to take a seat, what he was looking at. His answer was "nothing much." I felt like that many times, nothing much. I never asked that question of anyone again. However, I'd never been invisible until that day. I stood there while they played, which seemed like forever. My stomach ached, and my eyes stung while I tried to hold back the tears. I didn't cry, not then, but when I got home, I went to my mother's room and cried for hours, waiting for her to get home. Jon was worried and kept checking on me. I was not a crier so he thought something terrible was wrong, and it was. I couldn't wait for my mother to get home. I knew she would go to the school and tell that teacher what a mean thing she had done. I knew she would make it better, but the minutes just dragged and the tears wouldn't stop. I was tired, tired of everything. I was tired of exercises, tired of pain, tired of stiff feet, hunched back, crutches, ugly shoes, and hard beds. *Hurry, Mom. I need you.* Then I thought I heard her car. Jon ran to the garage and tried telling her I was crying and had been for a long time. Mother rushed in her room "What is it, Penny? What's the matter? What happened?"

I started telling her the story between sobs. I watched as she turned her back to me and looked out the window. I could tell she was very mad. I continued with what happened, and Mother's back seemed to get stiff and straighter somehow. *Yes*, I thought, *she is going to make them sorry*, but she didn't say a word.

"I'm sick of polio. I don't want to wear ugly shoes anymore, and I don't want to stay in the pool for hours or do 'Trot, trot to Boston.' I hate my crutches and this brace and my body, and I don't ever want to go back to school."

I was empty. I had cried and now I had poured out my heart and I was empty. Mother just stood there with her back to me. My champion was perfectly quiet.

"Well," she said, "I am so glad you let me know you are quitting. You know, Penny, you're not the only cripple in this house. You can't walk fast so we don't walk fast. You can't climb a mountain so we don't climb mountains, and you can't run so we don't run; but we were willing to go at your pace because I thought you had a bigger dream. I thought you wanted to go to your prom in a beautiful dress, finish high school, and celebrate graduation. I thought you wanted to fall in love and walk down the aisle to marry. I thought you wanted to have children. I thought you wanted to dance, but if you quit, we are free to go after our own dreams." Then Mother walked out, closing the door behind her.

I was stunned! This is not what I thought would happen. I sat there, and the tears started again. *No one understands*, I thought, drowning in self-pity. My head hurt from crying but then I thought. I do want to go to prom and graduate and I do want to fall in love, I do want to get married someday. I do want to have children, and I do want to…dance. I got up from Mother's bed and walked out to the kitchen where she was starting to prepare dinner.

"Mom, I do want all those things."

Slowly she turned to look at me with those brown eyes and said, "Then don't quit!"

That night as I lay in my bed, I knew something had changed for both of us. I determined that day that I wouldn't quit, and I was glad to know Mother wasn't quitting either. I had learned a truth, a great truth. Quitting is never an option.

HIDE THIS NUGGET IN YOUR HEART

Throw self-pity out the window; embrace hope and laughter as you refocus on your dream.

CALM BEFORE
THE STORM

We were getting our rhythm now. Mother's job was interesting and challenging for her. Selling advertising was easy, and she really enjoyed being in the business world. She no longer had to wear waitress uniforms and could dress up every day. She wore pretty flowers pinned to her dress or jacket and bows and fancy accents on her shoes. Did she ever love shoes! The stiletto four-inch heels were her favorite, and not just black, brown, or blue; no, she had orange, red, and bright yellow. This could explain why I thought my shoes were so ugly, no fancy accessories and boring colors.

I returned to school with a new attitude. It didn't matter what others thought of me or said about me or even if they looked right through me. What mattered was the next step to achieving my goal.

There was a school talent show coming up. I didn't want to be part of it, but Mother wouldn't hear of that. She got the record player out, and I practiced to "Peg of My Heart" an acrobatic sequence that ended in me doing the splits and laying my head down on the floor. All the exercises and the Sister Kenny treatments had paid off. I was very limber; however, I couldn't get back up once

I was down. This was only a temporary hang-up for Mother. She spoke to the stage crew and informed them that the curtain would be closed until I was in position. Then when my routine was over, the curtain would close again until she could pick me up and give me my crutches, helping me off stage. The show went perfectly; and I know that I looked calm, cool, and collected, but I wasn't. I couldn't think of a worse idea than being a spectacle. At this point, being on stage was the last thing on my favorites list. I stopped looking in mirrors and was bothered about my reflection in windows; that reflected image always caught me off guard. I didn't realize how much of a limp I had developed until I saw my reflection. Things like this took all my strength to ignore.

Tom concocted a great recipe for baked beans. He decided we'd make, package, and prepare for shipping, "Tom's Baked Beans." He found a perfect location, and we were off to a big start—the beans were great and the work fun, at least it was for Jon and me. Tom cooked the beans, and we helped fill the containers, put the lids on, and wiped away any spillage before we attached the labels. Then the big cases were loaded on a pallet waiting for the truck drivers to pick up and deliver to local supermarkets. One day I was allowed to ride in the refrigerated truck to make the delivery. Seeing how our food arrived in stores was great fun and listening to the driver talk to other truckers on the CB radio was great. It was almost like learning a foreign language, like 10-4 and 10-10 and "hammer down."

Jon was competing and winning trophies in karate, and he continued racing his quarter midget. Durm and Hank would go with us to watch Jon compete. I can just see him eating red licorice while waiting for the next race.

Durm, the oldest, was full of compassion, gifted in the arts, and he loved me. Hank was full of mischief and gifted in playing pranks, but he loved me too. However, he had a strange way of showing it, like when we played hide and seek. Before I was walking much, certainly not running, one of the boys would help me by putting me in a wheelbarrow then hide me somewhere. When the coast was clear they would come, get me, and run to the tree while I yelled "oly-oly-oxen free." That was the plan anyway. But not Hank, he would put me in the wheelbarrow, and once he hid me, I could forget coming in. Durm would have to ask, "Where's Penny?" and worse, sometimes he would have to call my name and look for me as Hank and Jon had ran off to play. I guess you could say that Durm kept me safe, and Hank kept me humble.

One Saturday, Mother read an ad for Charlie's Yacht Club at the Salton Sea. This was a desert resort in the Imperial Valley, and she thought it perfect for a vacation. She and Tom bought a boat that summer, and Mother was determined to water ski, so Charlie's Yacht Club sounded like her kind of place. She made reservations, planned our meals, and bought all the necessary equipment for skiing, boating, and camping. She loaded the car and hitched the boat. Yacht club, here we come!

We were so excited on the trip, Jon and I singing, Tom choking us with his big cigar, and Mom talking about all the fun we'd have. Since I couldn't stand up on the ground very well, there was not much chance that I'd be able to stand up on skis, but Mom said I would try it. No matter about the skiing, if that didn't work I could drive the boat.

The drive was hot but nice most of the way. Once we got out of Indio, there was highway, sand and more sand and little else.

"Hummmm," looking at the map, Mom said, "There's Salton Sea, we should be able to see the yacht club by now."

However, we could not. Then a mile or so farther down the road, we saw a little sign Charlie's Yacht Club, at the next turn. Mother's jaw dropped as we turned on to packed sand, followed the previous tracks left by campers, saw a few trash cans and then a tall box with a door on it.

"What's that?" we asked.

Mom put her hand to her heart and said, "That's an outhouse!"

By that time, we had approached a sign that said, *Check in at office*, with an arrow. Just ahead, we saw a shack, a real old, beaten-up, dirty shack and over the door a sign: *Office*. By the look on Mom's face, I thought we might be turning around and going back home. However, she paid the $3.00 fee, and we were directed to our section of sand, thankfully, not too far from the "outhouse."

I didn't manage to get up on the skis, but Mother and Jon were naturals. Jon single skied almost immediately and was great on doubles. Mom, well, you couldn't shake her off those skis. She couldn't swim and was afraid of water, so she was determined not to fall. I was all too familiar with her determination, so I never worried about her drowning. We laughed about ole Charlie's, but it became a favorite weekend trip for our family.

The summer passed too quickly, and I was back to school, but this year was special. I was off the crutches and walking on my own. I still had the body brace and built-up shoes, but I was getting stronger.

We were riding a school bus now so that we could be dropped off with Tom after school. We enjoyed our *after school job* at our "beanery" because there was plenty of action. Most days, Mom was at work, but sometimes she would be off early and come to help us.

One afternoon as I came in from the bus, and I started back to the kitchen, I heard Mom telling someone to, "Put it down," in a strange voice. I opened the door, and there was Tom holding a knife to Mother's throat, pushing her against the sink.

I yelled, "Daddy, stop."

He did. I knew we wouldn't be making any more beans, and Daddy was moving out again.

I was scheduled for a follow-up doctor's visit to see how I was doing without crutches and to discuss the body brace. In my mind, it was going to be a good visit, and I was hoping the doctor would let me go without the brace and get rid of the board on my bed.

Dr. Rowe would come in, check my x-rays, smile, and say, "Walk for me, Penny." I would be in my panties only, no built-up shoes, no braces, and then he would say, "Good, now turn around and walk back to me." He always ran something down my spine, and he would put a hand on either side pressing down on my hip-bones. "Okay, let's get you up on the table." He would stretch out my legs and make a note, rotate my feet, first one way, and then the other. Then he would cross one leg over the other and pop me on the knee with something that looked like the tomahawks at Knott's Berry Farm.

"Mrs. Nelson," he said slowly, "I believe we need to make a decision about the surgical options to correct Penny's spinal curvature. The loss of muscle is advancing the scoliosis. The body brace has not decreased the curvature nor slowed the damaging effects even after all this time. I believe it is only giving her the needed support to walk."

Mom looked at me and smiled, giving her the needed time to take a deep breath before asking, "Well, Doctor, what are you suggesting?"

"Dr. Harrington has been successful with rods and other devices in fusing the spine, and I believe it would be an effective procedure for Penny. It does require a long-term recovery so it needs thought before you schedule. It is best to do it at about age twelve, so we have a little time yet. I have some information here for you to consider and then let's set another appointment to discuss the idea in month or so."

"Okay, Doctor," Mother said as she handed me my clothes. "Here, honey, get dressed."

"Is there anything you wanted to talk to me about, Penny?" he asked as he reached for the doorknob.

"No, Doctor, I was just hoping you would say I didn't have to wear my brace anymore."

"Well, if the fusion does all it is supposed to do, you won't have to wear your brace ever again."

That sounded good to me, but the operation part didn't. "Mom, do you think I will really need to have this operation?"

"I don't know yet, but if you need it, you will have it," she said, sounding very sure. I could almost see the wheels turning in her head, trying to figure out what we would need to do in case surgery was the answer.

In fact, Mother did read everything the doctor gave her. She called the military to find out where this type of surgery was being preformed and was told San Diego, California, at Camp Pendleton.

Mother had been pondering a move for a while because I was having trouble with pneumonia and frequently ended up in the hospital. Tom was coming around, and she was determined to reunite, but in a different location. It was mentioned that a drier climate might help me, so now she was trying to do the "best thing" right.

One weekend we went to a luau on the other side of Salton Sea. Instead of a yacht club like Charlie's side, we were on the country club side where builders and developers were busing people into the area to buy land. It appeared this was going to be a hot spot. We saw a restaurant that was for sale near the highway, right across the street from the only hotel for miles. Since I needed a drier climate and considering all the fun we had in the water, buying this restaurant just seemed like a perfect thing to do.

We bought the restaurant and opened it under the name Hoffbrau Haus serving the food cafeteria style. Tom wore his "whites" with the tall chef hat and carved the meat while working the serving line. I helped Mom at the cash register and with drinks. We learned some tricks of the trade early. Buses would come and fill up the restaurant. Before they were through, the next busload of potential land buyers arrived and had to sit in the heat, hungry. Tom told us to play fast songs like "Ally Oop" or "The Battle of New Orleans" or "Flying Purple People Eater" because people would eat in time to the music and speed up the show. Then when the last buses were in, we would put on slower music so everyone could relax and enjoy their meal. Jon was the bus boy and really had to be on his toes because we were the only restaurant in town.

We had made a new friend. Her name was Kaye—she became Aunt Kaye to us. She was a waitress who carried more dishes on her arms than anyone I'd ever met. She was from Texas and had the biggest laugh and a funny way of talking. Aunt Kaye taught me canasta, and we played each afternoon until the buses came in. However, when the buses hit, everyone was up and busy.

Salton Sea was very hot all year long. We had only two sets of regular playmates, lizards and the customers at the restaurant. Our school was miles away in the Coachella Valley. Even the school bus didn't come far enough into Salton Sea to pick us up, so Mother knew it was time for me to learn to drive. I really wasn't frightened, even though I was only ten years old. Mom always made me think I could do anything with a little practice, so she bought my first car. It was a 1955 Chevy convertible, teal, and white. The road I drove was sand-covered black top with only two or three cars traveling it on a busy day. We were miles and miles from civilization. Mother knew the threat of heat and trying to walk from the house to the bus stop or restaurant were more of a danger to us than driving.

Mother took our organ to the restaurant, and Tom figured out how to play it himself even though he had never taken lessons. He got an eyebrow pencil and wrote the notes on the keys. Then he used a "cheaters" music book and would play music on Tuesday nights for the newly formed "Stein Club." We bought steins in all sizes for members to purchase and then they would leave them in the restaurant for the next time. Beer was cold and popular in that dry desert, and everyone had a good time.

Mom thought I should be learning more about business, so she suggested I open a gift shop at one end of the restaurant. It was up to me to order, stock, price, and then sell all the items in the little corner shop. I was feeling real grown up and enjoyed the atmosphere of the restaurant. I enjoyed people and watching them enjoy themselves. Even though the area didn't develop as planned, the locals liked our Tuesday nights with Mom dancing the polka and our customers singing old funny songs.

One night we had a big windstorm. When there were storms in the desert, sand would get into everything. There was no keeping it out. This night the sand hit the windows so hard that it woke me up. I got out of bed to look out. It wasn't just sand that I saw but a fire in the distance toward the Hoffbrau. The telephone rang, and someone told Mother the restaurant was on fire. They said they had called the fire department and that they would meet her at the Hoffbrau. She and Tom hurried to the restaurant, but it was too late. The A-frame roof caught fire from a spotlight that had turned downward from the high winds causing the wood shingles that were dry from the desert sun to burn quickly. Our fire department was a long way off, and by the time they arrived, the fire was nearly out.

I felt sad as I looked at the mess in the morning. The deer-head gun rack that my father had made when I was a baby was gone. The organ was gone too and all the beautiful steins. All we had left were memories. I had a feeling that we were moving again, and I was right.

HIDE THIS NUGGET IN YOUR HEART

Momma said there'd be days like this. Suck it up and keep going. Adversity is just another opportunity to quit; like water off a duck's back, let it pass you by.

DADDY LIED

We found ourselves in El Cajon at a trailer park with a pool. The routine we had for exercises stayed the same as it was in Long Beach and Anaheim. The city was growing as San Diego residents were overflowing into this rural area. There weren't many children in the trailer park, so I needed to convince Jon to swim with me to help the time go faster. But he wanted to spend his time riding his bike and looking for new playmates. He would play army men with me, and we'd have fun shooting rubber bands knocking them over, but Jon needed to be running and climbing, not hanging out with me.

I spent a lot of time reading. My favorite was Nancy Drew books. Mother would get a new book as soon as I had finished one. I couldn't wait to read them all, and I quickly learned that books would take me places I couldn't otherwise go and let me do things in my mind that I couldn't actually do. They weren't just for education but for fantasy. I thought, *Maybe I'll be a detective when I grow up.*

School was starting again, and those long lazy summer days were nearly over. Aunt Kaye moved with us from Salton Sea and purposely took a night job so she could help take care of us until Mother got home in the afternoon. She started dinner on the days that Tom wasn't home to cook. Her idea of the perfect dinner was half an avocado with mayonnaise and lemon juice. I really tried but just couldn't enjoy it as she did. I wanted to like what she liked. She was my best friend and my confidante.

One day shortly after school started, I came home disturbed and full of questions, feeling like I'd been bad. Aunt Kaye was in the kitchen getting dinner and gave me her big Texas hello, as I came in the trailer. "Hi," I said.

"What's the matter, Penny?" she asked, knowing that something was on my mind.

"Nothin'," I lied and just sat down at the table. I knew I was quiet and that wasn't normal for me with Aunt Kaye, but I didn't know exactly how to tell her what I was thinking. We had watched a movie at school during health class that had talked about our bodies and the changes that we would go through soon. It was called puberty. The movie talked about menstruation and reproduction. As I sat in that dark classroom, I began to know those troubling feelings over the years were true. My stepfather had lied about how daddies show their little girls that they love them. I felt scared and dirty, bad and ashamed—I didn't know what to do, and I was worried about going home. Tom hadn't been in my room for a while, but he was drinking again and I knew things could get bad in a hurry.

I wanted to talk to my mother, but I didn't want her to be mad at me. I especially didn't want to start any fights between her and Tom, so the day just dragged along mostly in a blur as I watched the clock, wondering what I should do.

"What did you learn in school today?" Aunt Kaye asked. "Did you play jacks or two square?"

"No, we had a movie today."

"A movie? What was it about?"

"Health and growing up, you know that kind of stuff," I answered, thinking I should go change my clothes and the subject.

"Oh Lord, girl. I should have guessed that. Are you worried about starting your period? Come back here, honey," she said, pulling out a chair and sitting near me. "Every girl goes through that, and it's nothin' to worry about. Anyway, you know your mom and I are right here, and we'll get you everything you need. In fact, let's go shopping and pick up the right things for you so you'll be ready. Okay?"

"Aunt Kaye," I said, starting to cry, "I think I have done something really bad, and I'm scared."

"Penny, what are you talking about? What do you think you've done?"

I dropped my head down on my arms and said, "Daddy has been coming in my bedroom at night for a long time and doing things that I didn't like. He said all daddies did those things to their little girls to show how much they loved them, but I don't think so, Aunt Kaye, not anymore, and I am afraid to tell my mom."

"You've done nothin' wrong, Penny," she said in a voice I'd never heard her use before. "I'll tell your mother for you first and then you can talk to her." She took me in her arms and rocked me.

I was still scared of what would happen, but I felt better now that Aunt Kaye knew, and I was ready to tell Mom.

"I think you should go down to your friend's trailer until dinner. You just stop worryin' and go play until I call you," she said turning her face from me. "I'll tell your mother about this when she gets home."

I thought it sounded like she was talking through her teeth. Aunt Kaye followed me to the door, but she didn't say anything more. I noticed a very odd look on her face, and her usually rosy complexion had faded to a ghostly white.

I was glad to go. I didn't want to be in the house while she talked to Mom, and I sure didn't want to see Tom right then. I went to my friend's, but I couldn't stop thinking about it and so I waited to hear Aunt Kaye call my name or come by and get me.

"I have a funny record to listen to if you want," my friend said. "This guy named Bill Cosby tells funny stories. Come on, Penny. Let's listen."

"Sure," I said. I didn't want to keep thinking about what I had told Aunt Kaye.

Aunt Kaye didn't come to get me. My mother did. As I came out the door, she picked me up and carried me home. She didn't say a word, but I could tell she had been crying. When we got to the trailer and opened the door, there was Tom standing in the kitchen very unaware of what had happened. My mother set me down and flew at Tom, slapping and yelling and crying—knocking him around until he fell to the floor.

"How dare you touch her!" she screamed. "Get out, get out, I'm calling the police." He did get out, just as fast as he could.

I was sure our world was ending. I just knew it was my fault. I wanted everything to stop. I wanted it to go away, but I was to learn that this was something you couldn't wish away and what had happened was just the beginning.

Mother took me to talk to some men who would prosecute Tom for what he had done. I hated talking to them. They were very nice, but I didn't know them and I didn't want to remember or even say the things I had to say. Afterwards they took me to an office and told me that Mom would be back in a little while, and then they left the room. I felt sick, and I was ashamed of myself. I wondered if I knew it was wrong before now and if I let it happen. I wondered why I kept that secret from her for so long, and I wanted to get away from everyone.

A few minutes later, Mom came back and told me that we were going home. I was glad to leave, but she acted funny and I wondered if I was in trouble with her now. I was quiet in the car and so was Mom. We had both cried, and now we just kept our thoughts to ourselves.

Within a few days, I met a new doctor. He told me he was going to do an examination, but I found out it had nothing to do with polio. I was more ashamed than even talking to those attorneys, and I didn't ever want to have that examination again.

I heard the doctor talking to my mother as I was getting dressed.

"There was no *serious* penetration and no *physical damage* that I can see."

I guess he couldn't see my damaged heart.

"Thank you, Doctor," Mother said as she came in the dressing area, peeking behind the curtain to see if I needed any help. "Are you ready, Penny?"

"Yes," I answered, and boy *was* I ready to get out of there.

We didn't talk on the way home that day either. In fact, we did not speak about this again, at all. I was glad that we didn't have to go to court, but something had changed at the Nelson house, something that no one talked about but was very loud in my heart and head.

HIDE THIS NUGGET IN YOUR HEART

Thank God for big Texans. Everyone needs a friend, so be the kind of friend you need.

THE RACK

Camp Pendleton was a huge marine training base and naval hospital. There were men in uniform everywhere you looked, and I felt right at home. I had always been in a children's ward in the hospital, but now I was in a military hospital and things would be different. I learned new sayings like, "Hurry up and wait!" We did a lot of that in the beginning, but once we got our "orders," things moved right along. I was going to have more surgery, this time on my spine.

First, my new orthopedic surgeon suggested a trial period in a body cast. He explained they would have to do a procedure to see how much correction we could expect and if I could tolerate being in a cast for a long period. He also suggested that I stay in the hospital for a week to have some tests, and then be put in the cast. Mother set the appointment and began packing my bags.

Since I wasn't sick and I wasn't having the surgery right away, I was assigned a duty at the hospital. I went from room to room taking orders for breakfast and turning them in at the nurses' station. That was an easy job for me, after all, I had been in charge of menus before, and I was able to visit with everyone on the floor. There was a big recreation room at the end of the hall where the corpsmen and patients could watch television, read, play cards, do puzzles, and smoke. After a day of x-rays and other tests, the corpsmen would treat me to a movie or bowling on the base. I wasn't able to bowl so they taught me to keep score for them. Wow, I was enjoying being *in the service*.

"Good morning, Penny," said Larry, my favorite corpsmen. "Today we get body armor, I mean your cast. So hurry up, I'll be coming for you in ten minutes."

I was sliding out of bed and thinking about all the doctor had told me. I was short, even shorter because of the curves in my spine. So today, they were going to stretch me out and then put a cast on me to hold that position for three months. I would be coming back to the hospital every month to have everything checked out but wouldn't have surgery until the end of the three months. I brushed my teeth, put on a funny gown, and waited for Larry to come for me.

"Hop on, Penny," he said, pushing a wheelchair through the door, smiling at me.

"Can I eat first, Larry?"

"Not today, but I promise a big lunch if you want when you're done. Now, no more questions; just hold your horses. You might want to cover your eyes because this is going to be a thrill ride." Off we went, swerving and laughing and being silly, while I held tight and laughed with him.

We were the first ones in the room where they were going to put the cast on.

"That's a funny-looking table. How can I lay on that?" The table was really just a metal frame with a long strap like a barber's strap down the middle of it.

"I don't know, sir. It's just my orders to deliver the goods to get plastered!" He laughed again, and I thought he was acting a little peculiar this morning.

"Hi, everyone," another young corpsman said as he came in with Dr. Bingham, who was reading a file. "Hello, Penny. Are you ready to get started?"

"Yes, sir, Dr. Bingham," I said, "but I am wondering how I am going to stay on that strap."

Larry and the other young man wheeled in a table and said, "We have your answer," lifting me up on it and sliding it under the frame.

They placed the strap under the center of my back and then strapped my feet at one end and my head in a device at the other.

I was a little bit uncomfortable and scared, but Larry stood by my head and said, "I'll be right here, Penny."

"Okay, this is what we are going to do. First, we are going to stretch you to straighten out your spine, and then we'll wrap you in a tube-like stocking, then some padding, and then your cast. It'll hurt for a little while, but we'll do it as fast as possible. Once you smell the plaster and feel a little bit damp, you'll know it's almost over. Ready, here we go. I'll come to your room later today and check on you. All right, you can get started.

"Larry, get x-rays before taking her back to her room. I'll want to see the correction," instructed the doctor.

Someone started turning the wheel at the end of the frame, which began the stretching as Dr. Bingham left the room. It wasn't too bad to begin with, but as they increased the stretch, I was sure I was going to be pulled apart. I remembered a torture chamber in a movie I saw with a device called "the rack," and this sure felt like that. The stocking they had placed on me came up over my face like a mask, with only nose and eyeholes cut out. I looked up into Larry's eyes, but they grew blurry through my tears. I wanted to be a good girl and not scream, but this was the worst thing that I'd ever experienced. My tears slid down the sides of my face and fell into my ears making sounds like I was in the ocean. I was feeling faint and hot. So hot and clammy, then I heard crying, sobs through my muffled ears—they were my sobs—but the head piece was so tight I couldn't cry out—it cupped my chin and surrounded my cheeks—in my mind I begged them to stop. I was stretched so taut that even though they had removed the gurney I was suspended within that frame on a strap. The turning stopped suddenly. I felt the stretching stop, and everything seemed frozen in time. I heard someone ask for the felt. Whatever they were wrapping around me came through the stocking made my body itch, but I couldn't ask anyone to scratch me. The doctor was right. I could smell the plaster, and when they started wrapping it around me, it was damp and hot. In fact, it got warmer and warmer reminding me of the hot packs back at the clinic. Time passed so slowly.

I was dizzy even lying down and sick to my stomach—and then I heard someone say they would be back in thirty minutes to remove the strap so Larry could take me to x-ray.

There was a lot going on in the room, but I couldn't see.

Larry was touching my forehead saying, "You're all wet in there, Marine, but I'll break you out of here in a few minutes."

I wanted to tell him I felt sick, but I could not move my mouth much—I grunted a bit.

"Are you trying to tell me something?"

"I'm going to throw up," I muttered.

"Did you say throw up? No, you aren't. You just feel like it. Don't worry; you're not going to throw up."

The voice returned, the one who said he would get me out of the contraption, and he did. Once all the straps were removed, they rolled the top of the stocking down to reveal my face and then I saw the cast. It was enormous, running behind my head, to the back of my ears, then around my chin line, down my neck to the middle of my hips.

My jaw was just a little freer, and I said again, "I'm going to throw up."

"Naw, you're not," he said, laughing, "that is, unless you are cart sick because of my driving."

Off we went in a hurry. When we got to x-ray, I could see people lined in the hallway…yup, it was hurry up and wait again.

"Larry, I'm going to throw up."

"Okay, I'll get you a puke pan, but let's talk about something else and get your mind off that crazy idea. Stay here. I'll be right back. Oh yeah, I forgot, you need me to drive!"

I lay there thinking that the doctor had been right about everything so far. It did hurt. It hurt like nothing ever had, but when they took me off "the rack" (the frame), the pain mostly went away. It did stink and was wet, but the worst was over.

"I'm back," Larry said, "and my buddy in x-ray said you out-rank these other guys, so you are up next. Say, you never mentioned it, but are you married to the president or something? You've got a lot of pull around here."

Yup, I loved Larry. He was twenty-one with a great sense of humor.

"Okay, Penny. This is what we're going to do," said Mike, the x-ray tech. "I'm going to strap you onto this table, and then I'll tilt it until you are almost standing up straight. I'm goin' to take a picture of you under all that plaster so the doctor can make sure we did everything just right. Ready?"

It took a second or less to put me on that table, but as it started to tilt, I muttered, "I'm going to throw up."

"Did you understand what she said?" Mike asked.

"Penny, I couldn't understand what you said," Larry asked, leaning close to me.

"Larry," I said with all the force I could muster, "tell him I'm going to throw up!"

As the two of them walked behind the window, I heard him say, "She thinks she is going to... Oh man, I hate it when this happens."

"Guess you really meant it, huh, Penny?" It was like a projectile.

"Did you eat something behind my back this morning?" Larry kept the chatter lively while they got someone to come with a mop and bucket.

"I tried to tell you, Larry," I said, crying.

"Ah, forget it, honey; this happens all the time around here."

"Okay, Penny, hold your breath while I take the picture," Mike said. "I'll tell you when to breathe—hooooold it! Okay, breathe. Now just one more for good measure—hooooold it. Breathe. That's it; you two can go."

As Larry was pushing the gurney down the aisle, he said, "Listen, I'm going to be off in about an hour, and I have some stuff I need to do, but I'll come back before sack time if you want me to."

"I want you to," I said.

"You know, I'm getting used to the way you talk now. In fact, I can almost understand every word. Here we are, Marine, at your quarters. Now get in that bunk. What? You need a little help?" he said, lifting me off the gurney. "You need a diet, that's what you need. I swear you have put on weight even since this morning." Larry was starting to remind me of my cousin Hank.

I was hungry now and asked Larry, "Am I getting that big lunch you promised me?"

"No food yet, doctor's orders; and besides, Penny, that cast around your chin won't let you open your mouth enough to eat. See you tonight."

He was right. I thought, *What am I going to do without eating for three months?* My troubled thoughts were interrupted when a nurse poked her head in the door and said, "Your mom called. She's on her way."

I hope she is bringing me something I can eat, I thought. It got quiet in my room and before I knew it, I fell asleep.

I woke to the smell of Mexican food and realized mom was there. I was very glad to see her and glad she had brought food from our new favorite restaurant. But one look at me and she knew that sneaking it in was the easy part. Getting it in my mouth would be the problem. Ringing for the nurse, Mom placed a kiss on my forehead and said, "You are going to need some new clothes, Penny. This is a really big cast."

When the nurse came into the room, she explained that Dr. Bingham would be in to see me soon. They were bringing the x-rays for him to see. It looked like I was only going to smell food for a while longer, but my stomach was roaring. I wanted to tell Mom all about what happened, but I couldn't talk much and I really didn't want to think about it anymore. I was going to tell her that I never wanted to do this again so maybe we could forget having the operation. Just the thought of getting another cast put on brought tears to my eyes again, so I closed them, pretending I was asleep.

"Hello, Mrs. Nelson," Dr. Bingham said as he walked in holding the x-rays. "She's having a little nap I see, and I don't blame her. It was a pretty tough morning for her. Now, let's look at the correction we got."

I just continued with my eyes closed willing him to say, "Everything is perfect—no surgery necessary. She can go home with you right now."

"This really looks good, you know, Mrs. Nelson, and we have a four inch gain. Now all I need to do is cut the chin a bit so that she can eat and talk, of course. Then she can have dinner—it's Mexican food by the smell." He laughed.

I was glad he wasn't going to tell the head nurse we had food in the room. I opened my eyes and acted as if I was just waking up.

Dr. Bingham took out a pen and drew a line under my chin where he wanted the cast cut. He also drew around the armholes, enlarging them a bit so they wouldn't rub, and then he asked me, "Can I sign your cast?"

"Sure," I said, looking at Mom. After all, it was white, and she didn't like whites getting dirty, but she smiled, letting me know it was fine with her.

A man with an electric saw came in and trimmed the cast, cleaned the dust off and asked me, "Hey, what's for dinner? Mexican? I can tell you didn't get that at the mess hall."

Everyone left the room, and it was quiet.

"Mom, I'm hungry. Thanks for bringing me my favorite."

"I'll get it," she said, and we both ate in silence. Every once in a while a tear would escape my eyes, and I saw the same thing happening to my mother, but neither one of us spoke a word.

"The doctor said you can go home soon. They just want to make sure you are doing fine first. Did you know that you will be taller now and straighter? We are doing the right thing, Penny. I know it isn't easy, but you'll be so glad you did. Now, if you go potty tonight, they will let me take you home tomorrow."

"I know, Larry told me I needed to have a cup of coffee and prunes so I could go home faster."

"He's a nut," she said, cleaning up our mess. "What do you want me to sneak in next time?"

"A cherry pie!" I answered, smiling so she wouldn't worry about me.

Mom turned around as she opened the door. "See you later, alligator," she said, smiling and waiting for my response.

"After while, crocodile," I said, fighting the tears that rolled down my cheeks as the door closed behind her.

"Okay, I have been thinking about something all evening, and I have a great idea," Larry said, holding a bag in his hand as he came in the door.

"What's in the bag?" I asked, glad to see him.

"Green paint! Like I said, I have been thinking, and it came to me that you look like a turtle. So, let's paint your shell."

"Oh no, my mother would kill me, Larry!"

"Okay, if you think she wouldn't like it...let me see what else I have in here." Opening the bag, he pulled out a long box and card and handed them to me. "This is for you, Marine. You did great today, except for that puking thing."

I opened the box and saw a beautiful bracelet with hearts all around it. Each was a different colored charm dangling from a gold chain. The card said something about hearing I was sick but a little mustard plaster on my chest would help. I didn't understand the card too much, but I knew goodness when I saw it and kindness too. I was sure that men in uniform were the best men in the world, and I was having a "crush" on this one.

"I have to go and hit the sack now, but I'll check in on you tomorrow," he said, knocking on the cast. "Do you need anything before I go?"

I was thinking I would like a hug, but it was going to be three months before I would feel anyone hug me.

"No. Good night, Larry. And thank you for my present. I really like it."

"Lights out, Marine," he said, turning them off and closing the door.

It was dark and quiet. I couldn't turn over or get comfortable. I realized just how stiff and difficult this cast was. Regardless, I was going to have to get used to it. This was just the beginning. Quitting wasn't an option. A nurse opened the door and said she had something to help me sleep. I was happy to hear that, but first I needed some help getting to the bathroom as this was one time I didn't want to wet the bed.

"I don't know how to get up," I said, trying to get off the bed.

"Here, let me put the side up for you. Can you grab hold here?" she said, pointing at the rails.

"Got it," I said, feeling as if I had the keys to the kingdom.

"Just press this button," she said, "and I'll come help you in the night if you need me, Penny."

I took my pill and made it back to bed, climbing up was easier than I thought it would be, and I fell asleep.

I spent the next two days learning how to "live" with the cast—like how we should wash my hair with a dry powder shampoo. I could tell by looking at Mom's face that we were going to figure something else out. I couldn't fit into my clothes, so Mother brought me new ones in order to leave the hospital. We had to cut the top of the pants to pull them up over the cast. The top was pretty, but it looked excessively big to me, sort of like a dress only short. Mother said it was a maternity top, whatever that was. It fit, and we were finally getting ready to go home.

"Can we stop by the Mexican restaurant on the way home, Mom?" I asked as I was putting my bracelet on. "Can you hook this for me? I'm so hungry, and I was thinking about the crisp dessert they make."

"That was my plan," Mother said, hooking my bracelet and putting the suitcase on the bed. "I'll get the car, honey; you wait here."

I looked around the room and thought about the fun I'd had on base and the friends I'd made. Larry came by but could only stay a minute. He had signed my cast and taken me around the base to have other people sign it the day before. They drew funny faces on it and wrote silly sayings then signed their names. Someone dropped a wheelchair off near the door to my room, and I knew it was time to go. I could hear Mom's high heels on the floor as she came down the hall.

"Ready, honey?" she asked as she pushed the wheelchair into the room.

"Did you get my scrapbook and magazines about Sandra Dee and Moon Doggie?"

"I put them in your suitcase. What's a moon doggie?" She laughed.

The doctors were right to give us a chance to try the cast before I needed to be in it for more than a year after the surgery. In order to wash my hair with real soap and water, we had to learn a trick. Mother laid me on the counter on my stomach, then wrapped plastic wrap around the headpiece of the cast while I leaned my head way out (just like that turtle Larry mentioned). Then Mother was able to shampoo my hair without getting the cast wet. I was so tired by the end of each day and thought, *Getting better is exhausting*.

Junior high is an important time in a girl's life, and fashion was certainly close to the top of my list. However, shopping in the cast was unbearable. There weren't many choices in maternity tops. The colors were drab and dark. Certainly not what a girl would enjoy wearing in junior high. There was no telling me I would only have to wear these clothes for a little while because I knew that I was looking at sixteen months all together, and I was only in my second month.

The first day of school, I was surprised how mean kids my age could be. There was something about the clothes and cast that brought a lot of laughter. The teachers went to the principal to discuss the disruptive behavior that they felt was a damaging atmosphere for me. They didn't have to wait long for a solution. With the surgery scheduled for the spinal fusion, I needed a tutor.

I enjoyed the tutor in the beginning, but it was not a full day of school, just a few hours a day, and I ended up with too much free time. I learned to put on makeup, pluck my eyebrows, and spent hours reading books, including a more grownup mystery book *Perry Mason* by Earle Stanley Gardner. My school load was not very challenging. I learned that my tutor was a typing teacher so my time in English studies and arithmetic was basics only. He enjoyed history and social studies, which really only added reading to my day, but I lacked skills that would be apparent in the near future.

Then *it* happened—puberty. Even though we had purchased all the supplies months before and though Mom and Aunt Kaye had talked to me and had shown me how to put everything together, I was in trouble. The one thing we didn't plan was how to keep the sanitary belt up with the cast. Ultimately, we used cup hooks screwed into the plaster on either side of the cast, but it wasn't a very efficient solution, and we still had more than a year to go. I knew things would have to get easier for me soon. After all, I was a queen, wasn't I? Then why did I feel like a monster?

I wondered if my big brothers from the *Mispillion* ever thought about me. I looked at the cruise book so often and my picture album with my marine daddies. I loved to read my father's letters. I guess the kids at school didn't know I was once a queen, and it sure wasn't doing me any good now. In fact, the only reason I was looking forward to the impending surgery was returning to Camp Pendleton. Maybe I would see Larry again or even some of the people that wrote letters to me when I was so sick. I secretly wondered if Daddy was still alive somewhere but couldn't find us. I think I kept that secret hope because the military said they never received his body back from Korea. I dreamed that he would show up one day and fix everything for us. There was a grave in the Black Hills of South Dakota because my daddy loved that area so much. It had his name on the marker but the grave was empty, so maybe...someday...just maybe.

My three months were up, and it was time to get rid of the cast. I was thinking that Mom would scratch my back all night, and I couldn't wait to get in a bath and just lay there. Even swimming sounded good to me, so getting ready for this trip to the hospital was easy.

Larry wasn't on the base when we got there. I was disappointed, but there were some other guys I remembered and they remembered me. I could hardly sleep that night and was ready when the nurses made their rounds in the morning. I laid there listening to the men marching and singing in time, "Sound off, one—two, sound off, three—four, sound off, one—two—three—four." Taking the cast off was quick and very easy. In fact, I was surprised that no one made a big deal about it except me. Of course, they weren't the ones having to live in that turtle shell. The doctors were satisfied with the correction and eager to operate, so they scheduled my surgery, October 13, 1961, a Friday. Some of the corpsmen said they couldn't believe anyone was going to operate on me on Friday the thirteenth, but I knew everything was going to be fine and so did Mom.

I soaked in the tub, and I got my back rubbed and scratched. Now it was time to prepare for my most dramatic surgery yet. Nothing that had been discussed had the same importance. The very thought of no more crutches and of no more leg or body braces or a hunchback deformity was thrilling. The very idea that I would wear pointed-toed shoes was more than overwhelming. We were excited yet prepared for the long and difficult road ahead.

HIDE THIS NUGGET IN YOUR HEART

Boot camp: when the going gets tough, the tough get going; and they keep their eye on the prize.

EMERGENCE

Checking into the hospital the night before was good because it gave me a chance to say hello to my friends and get my mind off the surgery. After I was ready for bed, I went to the recreation room. I started to work on a puzzle when I noticed two of the duty nurses laughing and pointing at the door behind me. As I turned, I just knew it was Larry.

"Hey there, Marine, did you re-up or something? What are you doing back here?" Like he didn't know.

"I missed you when I came in to have my experimental cast removed, Larry. Where were you?"

"Well, I'm here now, and I have the privilege of escorting you to surgery in the morning. I tell you, you have a lineup of top docs, so you better hit your bunk because morning is coming quick. I'll walk you to your room. It's lights out. By the way, did I mention you look like you have lost a lot of weight?" I loved his laugh and the way he squeezed my shoulder when he made a joke.

Morning did come quickly, and before I knew it, the nurse was in my room to take blood—not fun.

Then Mom came in. "Good morning, honey. Are you ready for our big day?"

"I am, and guess what, Mom. Larry is taking me to surgery."

"I know; I saw him at the front desk. They're getting everything ready for you right now."

"How long do you think I will be in surgery, Mom?"

"Dr. Bingham said it would take about four hours; then you go to the recovery room, and I'll be waiting there for you."

"Okay, Marine, you're to report for duty pronto, so let's roll!" He meant that literally and roll we did. Again, the lights overhead seemed to connect one to the other as he pushed that gurney to the elevator.

"Larry, will you still be here when I get out of surgery today?"

"I will. I put in for special duty and got it. Besides your mom promised me one of her pies if I hung around."

"Pick cherry; it's my favorite. I know you'll like it." The elevator door opened at my head, and Larry pushed me through to the operating room.

"Here you are. I'll see you soon, Penny," he said as he pinched my cheek and winked.

There were voices all around, nurses, doctors and anesthesiologists with bright lights and plenty of action. The nurses moved me from the gurney to the operating table.

"Penny, are you ready to count for me?"

The doctor used one of the tubes in my arm to give me the shot instead of poking me, so I knew I was going to like him.

"Good, here we go; start counting," he said as he turned something and tiny drops went in the tube.

"One hundred, ninety-nine, ninety-eight...I'm floating... ninety-seven, ninety-six..."

Waiting upstairs, Mom started pacing after four hours had passed and she'd had no word from the surgeons. It had been five hours and still no word. She asked the nurse to check and see if there was a problem of some kind. Six hours, now she was certain something had gone wrong. "Oh God, have I gone too far? Have I pushed her too hard? Did I expect too much?"

"Mrs. Nelson," said a nurse, "they have just called from O.R. to tell us that everything is fine and they are going to finish soon, and Dr. Bingham will explain the delay, but there is no problem."

I opened my eyes and was stunned that I couldn't move anything. I had a tube in my mouth, and I couldn't open it. I was on my stomach, and it was obvious to me that I was still in the operating room because I could see lots of feet with slippers over them and drops of blood and could hear them talking. I didn't know what to do. I tried to make noises so they would know that I was awake.

"What's that noise all about?" someone said. "Looks like our patient woke up a little early." Not for long, seconds later I was back to sleep.

As I woke up in the recovery room, I saw my mother across the room talking to the doctors.

One of the nurses said, "Hi, Penny. My name is Sue, and I'll be taking care of you for the next couple of hours. Your mom will be here in a minute."

I closed my eyes to wait for Mom. I was sleepy. I wasn't able to move much.

"Wake up, sleepy head," Mother said, giving me a big kiss. "You were such a good patient that Dr. Bingham just told me they were able to fuse all sixteen vertebrae today so you will never have to go through this again."

I knew that was good news, and if I could have jumped up and down, I would have.

"You are my number one trooper," she said, as we both got tears in our eyes. "Larry came by to see you, but you were still asleep. He asked me to tell you he would check in on you later."

It had been a long time getting here, but I could see that it would not be long now and my life would be like other girls.

"I'm tired, Mom."

"Go to sleep, honey. Go to sleep, and dream big dreams."

The waiting was over. I had come through the surgery fine, and everything was looking good. I needed a new cast, but no stretching was needed!

The big day came. Friends came by throughout the day to sign my new cast and wish me well. It would be months before I needed to return for a checkup. Many of the guys would be going home, having finished their "hitch." It was a happy and sad day for me, but I knew I was a very lucky girl.

With the major work complete at Camp Pendleton, Mother decided it was time to move back to the desert. She explained that the dry desert air was healthier for me, so even though we were moving again, I knew that at least I shouldn't get pneumonia.

Tom was home again. He'd had an encounter with God. He brought us some books and a Tennessee Williams album, and he wasn't drinking. We were glad to see him again mainly because Mother seemed happy. I would never look at Tom with the same innocence or feeling of security again. I would never again hear him come in my room without getting tense, and I would for all time suspect evil in every touch.

With Tom home, Aunt Kaye moved to an apartment nearby taking a job at a restaurant called Sambo's. I missed her living with us because I knew she was looking out for me when Mother was at work. I called her just to hear her voice. Making small talk, I would say, "What are you doing?"

She would answer, "It's my turn to wrestle the tiger for tiger butter today." Then she would laugh that big laugh. Just hearing that laugh helped to steady me. But now, there was a difference in Aunt Kaye. I knew she was mad at Mother for letting Tom move back in. She seemed tense. I realized in later years, she was always listening for me to say Tom was up to his old tricks. Things were never quite the same for us again. She took on the role of protector and was no longer just my playmate.

Mother got a job at the Riviera Hotel in Palm Springs and found a trailer park near her work. This move was a great one. I was able to go to work with Mother some days, and I became acquainted with the owner, Mr. Schulman. He became my dear friend. He was so gentle and kind. He dressed so beautifully every day and made sure that I had everything I needed. Some afternoons, when Mr. Schulman had time, he would order Jewish rye toast with marmalade and hot tea for two. It was like our own private tea party. Often during these times, a famous movie star would sit down with us. He included me in every conversation, introducing me to amazing people.

"Penny, let's go. Get in the car, honey. We have a long ride." Mom was putting my suitcase in the car.

"Why are we taking that suitcase, Mom?"

"Mr. Schulman sent a surprise for you in case your old clothes didn't fit when your cast comes off."

"Oh, I forgot about that. I guess I am too excited. He thinks of everything."

As we were driving, I was thinking about what a kind man Mr. Schulman was. I remembered how he reacted one night when the police called to have him press charges against a man who had tried to sell property he had stolen from the hotel. The man was an employee that worked in the kitchen at the Riviera. When he got the call from the police, Mr. Schulman said, "I'll be right there."

Later, I was talking to Mr. Schulman, when I noticed the man coming out of the kitchen. I asked, "Didn't you have to put him in jail for stealing?"

"No, I didn't, Penny. You see, honey, he has been working for me for a while now and has had problems at home. His wife is ill, and he has small children. Since he works for me, I believe it is my responsibility to know what is going on in his life."

Mr. Schulman explained that he needed to do something for this man because he felt hopeless. He wanted me to understand that hopelessness was why he stole. Mr. Schulman didn't press charges but gave him extra money to help at home and raised his pay. He told me he wouldn't do that for just anyone.

He said, "When you know in your heart that you are in a position to do good and don't, you must turn that situation around. You must make it right."

I had never heard anything like this before, but I knew the man he helped was grateful. Over the next several months, I saw what a great employee he was. I believed Mr. Schulman was a wise man.

We didn't have to spend the night in San Diego. In fact, it didn't take any time at all to get out of the cast, take new x-rays, and put on my new short set. I had been nearly sixteen months in body casts. At last, I was free.

"How do I look, Mom?" I asked, looking at myself in the mirror. I noticed that my body had really changed, and I was certainly flaky and white. I couldn't wait to get home and lay in a bath. Mother had a bottle of Estee Lauder Milk Bath that had been sitting in my bathroom just waiting for my unveiling.

About that time, Larry's friend knocked on the door. "You decent, Penny?"

"Hi, Paul," I said. "Have you heard from Larry since he got out?"

The smile that he had coming in the door disappeared at my question. "No one told you what happened?"

"Told me what?"

"Penny, you know Larry was getting married to his high school sweetheart when he got home, right?"

"Yes."

"Well, they got married and were in Chicago on their honeymoon. We were told he had left the hotel to get cigarettes and was hit by a car. Honey, Larry was killed a couple months ago."

I couldn't take it in. I sat down.

"Sorry to have to tell you that. I know you two were good friends. Anyway, I wanted to see how you were doing before you left today. I have to go. Hang in there, Penny."

"Thanks, Paul," I said, not able to look at him, thinking I knew what people meant when they said their heart was breaking. It felt like mine was. I was quiet on the way home and couldn't understand what I was feeling. I was happy to be out of the cast. I felt funny in my body after so many months with that shell. Nevertheless, I was so sad about Larry. I wondered about death and stuff like that. I wondered if I would see my daddy again or baby Pam. People said I would, but I wondered, and now Larry. I should have been more talkative on the way home, after all, I had been waiting a long time for this day, but I was quiet and so was Mom.

Once we did get home, Mother ran the tub for me. As I got ready to soak, I could smell the milk bath. I could hardly wait to get in.

"What do you want to wear after your bath, honey?" Mother asked, walking into my room.

"My bathing suit," I said.

"Your bathing suit?" She laughed.

"Yeah, I want to go swimming."

Mom and Tom drove me to the pool and pulled two chairs up to watch me while I swam. I started to the steps and without even thinking turned to the deep end and dove in.

"Penny," Mother screamed, jumping to her feet, "are you crazy?" I heard her say as I swam to the side.

145

"Oh, this feels so good," I said as I put my head under the water and started for the bottom. It was good to feel something besides itching. It was good to move through the water because in the water I was free and graceful. A few more laps, and I would be ready for bed.

In the bathroom, I finally looked in the mirror. I took a long, hard look at what had become of me. I had developed breasts. I was slender, and yes, the hunchback was nearly gone. My skin was a funny color and puckered from all the swimming and soaking in the tub, but I was becoming. I needed a haircut, but my hair was thick, and a pretty color blond. I could see just enough of my back to know that I didn't want to look any closer. There was a scar, but I would save that for another day.

"Penny," Mother said, watching as I turned to her, "it's time for bed, honey. Do you want me to put some lotion on you?"

"Yes, Mom." It was wonderful to feel her rub my back and my arms. It had been a long time since I felt the warmth of her touch or the refreshing feeling of lotion on my skin. "I'm a bit like a butterfly, aren't I, Mom? I went into the cast like an ugly worm and emerged out of my cocoon just like a butterfly."

"Well, fly to bed, little butterfly, before I clip your wings."

HIDE THIS NUGGET IN YOUR HEART

Weeping may endure for a night; your night may be very long, but joy comes in the morning if you endure.

FAIRY TALES REALLY DO COME TRUE

Birthdays mark time, and with each one since I got polio, I saw improvement. This year, however, was huge to me. Not only was I free of all the paraphernalia associated with my aide and recovery, but I was officially a teenager! My birthday celebration would be at the Riviera Hotel in Palm Springs, California, with a family dinner and dance. Mr. Schulman had his hand in the planning, but I didn't know that. I thought it was just dinner with the family at my favorite place.

Movie stars frequented the Riviera. During several of my visits, I enjoyed lunch with some that were well known. One day, John Wayne came into the restaurant and spoke with Mr. Schulman while I was at his table. I found out he loved his mother too. Another was Buddy Hackett, the funniest man I knew. However, the one I shared the most in common with was Johnny Weissmuller, the famous swimmer and star of the Tarzan movies. I liked Tarzan movies, and he liked to swim in the hotel pool. He told me he had to exercise in the pool as a little boy because he had been sick, too. He said he had worked hard and won gold medals in the Olympics and became a movie star. He said I should work hard and stick with it so one day I would be healthy and strong too. I thought he sounded a lot like Mom, and I knew it was true because I was getting stronger. When I looked back to where I started, I could see that good health would be in my future. What I couldn't see was being an Olympic swimmer and winning gold medals, but *maybe a movie star...no that's just silly.*

I had a new dress for the big occasion. Mother was right; I was going to need some clothes after all the changes my body had gone through. Nothing fit properly or was too "little girl" for a teenager. My birthday dinner was terrific, and I really couldn't believe my eyes when I saw Mr. Schulman. He came out of the kitchen followed by the whole crew carrying a beautiful cake with candles and sparklers headed my way. Can you believe it? Paul Peterson of the *Donna Reed Show* was in the dining room, and he sang "Happy Birthday" to me along with the rest! I'd not been one to want people to look at me, what with all the attachments I once had and the limp and scars; but sitting in the booth surrounded by friends and family, I was overwhelmed with the shared joy of overcoming a ten-year battle, intact.

After eating cake and getting kisses, Mr. Schulman whispered, "Mr. Weissmuller asked to have you and your mom come to his room so he can wish you happy birthday."

"Mom, can we go?"

"Sure, honey." She smiled as if she was keeping one of those secrets again.

Mr. Schulman got to his feet and led our excited party to room 216. He knocked on the door saying, "Johnny, I have Miss Penny with me as you requested." We waited; me dancing on the inside while trying to be grown up on the outside, but no one answered the door.

"You try knocking, Penny," Mr. Schulman said.

I knocked but nothing happened, and my heart sank. I thought maybe we had waited too long at the party and Mr. Weissmuller had left.

"I'm sure he would want us to go in and wait," Mr. Schulman said, taking a key out of his pocket. "Here, Penny, open the door."

I did, and then I froze in my tracks. Everywhere I looked, on the drapes, on the beds, on the dresser and on the floor were clothes and shoes and jewelry, delicate underwear, and things for my hair, but not one maternity top or saddle shoes.

I was speechless as the lights flashed before my eyes from strangers who were standing in the room.

"So, Penny, what do you think of your surprise?" asked one of the reporters for the local paper.

I turned to Mother. We were both crying.

Then I noticed so was Mr. Schulman as he said, "Penny, this key belongs to you now. This is your room, and it will be available to you whenever you wish. We have planned for you to spend the night here in your room with all your new clothes and other beautiful gifts. Happy birthday, dear girl. Oh, yes, and if you get hungry tonight, just call the kitchen. They will send you whatever you desire, okay?"

"Thank you, Mr. Schulman," I said as he handed me the key to tuck away in one of the purses on the bed.

"Goodnight," he said, slipping out of the room.

I had so many thoughts going through my mind. First, all the clothes; I wanted to touch everything and try everything on, the shoes with pointed toes and different colors and styles, the bath things and the pj's and robe. Everything was so beautiful. I was thinking of the room being mine. I always wondered what it was like to stay in a movie star room. This was a dream come true.

Then I had another thought, it was a favorite poem by Edna St. Vincent Millay called, "The Ballad of the Harp Weaver." The poem was about a mother's love for her son and the poverty that had come upon them after his daddy died. The final lines of the poem after he discovered his mother was dead were... "And piling up beside her and toppling to the skies were clothes meant for a king's son, just my size." I thought I knew how he felt as I looked again, blinking at the room, and piling up beside me were clothes meant for a queen, just my size.

"I feel like a queen," I said to the reporter. "I feel just like a queen."

HIDE THIS NUGGET IN YOUR HEART

When you wish upon a star, makes no difference *who* you are, anything your heart desires, will come to you…when you wish upon a star, as dreamers do.

HERE COMES THE POSSE

We had a pattern to our lives that included moving. Every time things "seemed" settled and right, I would start getting that funny feeling on the inside of me.

"Guess what, kids?" Mom laughed, reading a letter from her old friend at General Telephone Company. "They want me to come to Long Beach. I could have my job back now that you are finished with surgery. Isn't that exciting?"

I'm sure it was to her since she had been working as a waitress and cashier again. It was Mom's turn, and we were ready to go to Long Beach no matter how hard it was to leave Aunt Kaye, Mr. Schulman, and my very own hotel room.

"Mr. Schulman," I said, holding back tears, "I'm going to miss you so much, and I wanted to thank you for everything you have given me and done for me. I love you." He looked so handsome in his white wool slacks and shirt and had his big smile on when he leaned to hug me.

"You can always come for a visit and stay in your room. Just call me when you're ready, and I will be sure the room is prepared for you. Now, go tell your other friends good-bye while I talk to your mother."

I did, getting and giving hugs to so many people who had convinced me that Palm Springs was the best place in the world to live. I made a promise that one day this is where I would get married.

We moved into an apartment across the street from the yellow pages sales office in Long Beach, and Jon and I got ready to start school. I was going to be in a different school than my cousins, Durm and Hank who now lived in Buena Park. Uncle Bill and Aunt Donna had divorced so they had moved, too. Uncle Bill remarried a woman named Matilda. She had three children, George, Nancy, and Kelly. We called her Aunt Till. George was my age, and he would be going to the same school I was. He was a great cousin, and Durm and Hank had already prepared him for looking after me. George was dark like my dad and Mom, with brown eyes, dark hair, and deep olive skin. His last name was Felix, and we called him "Felix the cat" after a cartoon character. George was a fighter and had a reputation, but the flipside was all the girls loved him.

"Mom, do you really think I look okay in this outfit?"

"You're beautiful, Penny."

"How is my makeup, too much, not enough? What about my hair? I don't know what the style is here, Mom, and I want everything just right."

"You'll know the style today, I promise. You can do anything with your hair, so relax and check it out. Besides, honey, everyone is feeling just like you on the first day of school."

I thought to myself, *Well, maybe this year will be different because I don't have crutches, braces, or funny shoes. No, I am finally in style.*

"Come on, Mom, we're going to be late. Jon, we need to go," I said, holding the door open to leave. Jon came running out of his room ready to go, worried about nothing. Mother looked beautiful and was all smiles because she was doing what she loved at work. Tom was nowhere to be found, but I was sure we would hear from him again. It was just a matter of time.

"Here we are, Penny. Go to the office and check in. I've done all the paperwork. You just need to get your class schedule. I'll pick you up right here after school. Okay?"

"Okay, Mom," I said, getting out of the car.

I was so nervous and excited that I really didn't notice anything until I was in the administration office waiting with the other kids. The girls looked at me, then at my feet, then back at me, then at each other. *Oh no*, I thought, *not again*. It was just like the old days, but this time I decided to look at them, look at their feet, and back in their eyes, so I did. I was stunned beyond belief and surely gasped aloud. They were all wearing saddle shoes and bobby socks—I was the only one wearing pointed-toe shoes. I would have to think about this, but I knew I would never wear saddle shoes again.

"Penny Nelson," a woman behind the desk called my name.

"Right here," I said, moving to the desk. I turned to see some of the girls repeating my name, talking low, and watching my every move. I left the office losing the joy that I had started out with that morning when I nearly tripped over a big guy running down the hall.

He had a friend running behind him, calling his name. "Dale, wait up."

Dale looked at me, gave me a dismissed look, and replied, "Come on, Bear; the bell's gonna ring."

They brushed by me and once again picked up speed. I asked a girl for directions to my class, and she said, "I'll walk with you. My class is in the same area."

We didn't talk much, but I was glad to walk with someone. Right at that moment I knew if I could get to my class without another push or mean look or whisper, I was going to make it. My teachers were nice. The students were busy finding their friends and making plans for the weekend between classes. The lunch bell rang, and I heard a noise behind me.

"Hey, Cuz, come on. I want you to meet some of my friends on the way to the cafeteria." It was George, and I felt safe and loved without even seeing his face. When I turned, I was shocked to see Dale and the Bear standing next to him; they were a little shocked, too.

"This is your cousin?" Dale said.

"Yeah, she's my cousin, and you guys are gonna watch out for her, ya know what I mean?" he said in his best "I am so cool and in charge" voice. He was very cool and quite obviously in charge. George started something that day that he'd do with me for the rest of my school days. Whenever he saw me on the school grounds, in the hall, in the administration building, or parking lot, it didn't matter where, he'd pick me up, swing me around, and say, "I love you, Cuz." Oh, I just knew things were going to be different this year. Yes, I was ready for school, and the girls that wanted to "get to know Georgie" sure did treat me nice, in spite of my pointed-toe shoes and funny walk.

Several months passed quickly, we were settling in, and I was fitting in. Sometimes I thought I should just pinch myself, to make sure I wasn't dreaming.

One afternoon I came in from school and found Tom in the kitchen cooking up something wonderful for dinner.

"I sure have missed you guys," he said without stopping what he was doing. I went to change my clothes and knew that he was home again without anyone saying a word. Just when I thought things were going to settle down and hoped we would be staying in one place, Tom was back. That meant everything could change again in a moment's notice. Jon started calling those times that Tom was gone, a "tour." It sounded military, but it wasn't. He just needed to straighten out because Mom wouldn't put up with drinking. No matter what we called it or what we wanted, we just braced ourselves.

Tom had a serious problem with success. Anytime he achieved what he set out to do, he got drunk. The fear of losing what he gained started this cycle, and before we knew it, "here we go again." Of course, after a binge, Daddy would be sorry and beg for forgiveness, promising never to drink again, and we forgave him. Tom would tell funny stories about places he had been and things he had done while away. We didn't know how much was true, but he sure told interesting stories. One night he was telling Mom about a place he found in Arizona. A Victorian house had been turned into a restaurant. It had a funny name like The Big Mouth Frog. He said it had living quarters upstairs and was for sale. It wasn't often that Mom made a move in the middle of a school year, but somehow we knew that we'd be taking a trip to Prescott, Arizona, during the school holiday to look around. Just as I feared, we were moving again.

Prescott, Arizona, had served as the capital of Arizona twice and was full of historical places, even a town square. The Goldwater department store was on one street and "whiskey row" on another. The area had beautiful Victorian homes and just outside of historic Prescott was the restaurant that had caught Tom's eye. Taking a scenic drive down a winding road through beautiful mountains, you discovered just to the left, a dirt drive with a wooden bridge over a little creek leading to the parking area of the white two-story Victorian. We renamed it the Willow Creek Inn. My room had a peak ceiling with windows on three walls with pink and white striped café curtains.

There were three dining areas on the ground floor. The middle, very plush area was the main dining room. The next room to the right of the front door was a dark cozy room full of old pictures and relics from Calvary days. This dining room was called the Calvary Room, and it had a bar. The last was on the opposite side of the house. It had linoleum floors, plastic-covered chairs, a simple bar, and was perfect for the cowboys that came to eat. We called it the Rodeo Room.

The kitchen was small and organized but tight. Tom spent half his time yelling "Hot, hot," no matter what he had in his hands so that people would move quickly out of his way. He wore his whites with the tall hat and a diamond ring to knot the kerchief at his neck. He would serve flaming skewers of meat, flambé desserts, and tossed flaming entrees at the tables in the main dining room. It was my job to hit the lights as he swung open the shutter doors from the kitchen, making a grand entrance. The room would be silent and then…*ahhhh*. It was dramatic and well received in Prescott.

I got up early one morning feeling, as if I was coming out of my skin. We were going shopping for something very special, a horse. We saw many horses that day, but none seemed to be right for me until the very last stop. A man had advertised a Gelding, fifteen-hand quarter horse—Tennessee Walker, and to me, he was beautiful. He was red with a white blaze on his face and four white stockings. This was the one, and I was going to be just like National Velvet. The man explained that the horse was a bit jumpy to begin with, but once ridden for a while, he calmed down and was gentle and easy to ride. We took him home the next day. I named him Apache.

Jon was next, and he chose a Palomino filly just two years old, something like Jon, in fact, needing to be broke. He named her Venus. About the same time, one of our customers gave us two calves. One was black and white and one was brown and white. We named them Powder and Puff. It was all a dream come true.

Apache was so much fun for me. I rode him every day. My brother would run him up the mountain fast and then Apache would be ready for a nice slow ride with me. One afternoon Jon asked me to ride with him.

I said, "Jon, no funny stuff."

He promised he would be nice, so off we went. I didn't know enough about horses to know that Venus and Apache had shared a stable and were inseparable. We were doing fine. In fact, I had only my flats on that day, no boots, but Jon was keeping his word, no funny stuff. We halted our horses as a group of bikers came down the hill near us, revving their engines. It spooked Venus. She bolted, throwing Jon off, and galloped away. Before I could even think about what was happening, Apache took off determined to stay with the filly. He bucked and spun around and did everything he could to throw me off, but I was holding on for dear life. One last, fast stop nearly threw me over his head, and then a buck knocked me out of the saddle. There I was being drug by that stiff foot stuck in the stirrup. I was sure he was going to step on me and kill me, but finally my foot was free, and he galloped off after Venus.

I could hear Jon calling "DeeDee" as my body came in view. He fell down laughing, and then he held up his arm to show my other shoe in his hand. A neighbor who had been outdoors during our little escapade carried me to his house and called my mother. He then went after the horses and returned them to us that evening.

I knew I had to get back on Apache. It was hard for me to consider, but I knew if I didn't get back soon, I'd never ride again. The next day I rode him, did tricks with him, and rejoiced that I faced that fear and won.

One afternoon as I was going to the school office, I noticed classmates at the flagpole crying and praying. When I got to the front desk, I found everyone huddled around a radio crying. "What's wrong?" I asked a counselor.

"President Kennedy has been shot." I sat down on the bench and waited. It was obvious that school was out for the day.

The next few weeks were unbelievable. The television was on constantly. First, we waited for news, then his death, the funeral, the assassin, the overwhelming sadness of our country and the world. The magazines were full of pictures of the Kennedy's throughout their lives and even in the White House. I knew how little "John-John" felt holding his Mother's hand and trying to understand why his daddy wouldn't be coming home.

Everyday activities were a blur as though a cloud hung over us. The success we had enjoyed was weighing heavy on Tom and the grieving of our country gave him the excuse he needed to start drinking again. The "Southern comfort" he used to bring a beautiful flaming dish to tables was disappearing fast, and he was speaking slowly.

Since it was difficult for me to walk the stairs, Tom had a telephone with my own personal number installed in my room as a birthday present. Having my own phone was as liberating as my first car had been. One day while the restaurant was closed, I was in my room when I heard Mom and Dad arguing downstairs. Tom was getting very loud, which was unusual, and he was saying odd things that made no sense at all. I went to the edge of the balcony, leaned over the railing to see what was happening and to hear him more clearly. What I saw was Tom looking at himself in the mirror, holding my mother by the neck with a rifle in his other hand. He was threatening her.

I yelled, "Put the rifle down, Daddy!"

Tom looked up at me, held the rifle over his head, and pulled the trigger. I jumped back and then saw the bullet had stopped but only by the carpeting beneath my feet. I went to my room and called the sheriff, telling him to come quickly.

I watched out the window as a station wagon pulled over the bridge and up to our front door. Then the sheriff's cars arrived. The sheriff told Tom to put his weapon down and come out with his hands up. They held the man back that had come in the station wagon, and they were putting Tom handcuffed into the car.

I could hear Tom telling the sheriff, "I just bought her a phone for her birthday, and the first call she makes is to the sheriff on her daddy."

The officers were talking to the man in the station wagon. He told them he was delivering ammunition from the sporting goods store in town. This, of course, caused the police to question why Tom wanted all the ammunition. It was becoming obvious that he was having war flashbacks. I knew we had been very lucky that day, but I also knew we were moving again.

HIDE THIS NUGGET IN YOUR HEART

When life throws you a curve, get up. When evil penetrates your security, look up. When trouble escalates, take a stand; neither your position nor your age determines bravery or wisdom.

Are you seeing a pattern of a downward spiral? Don't hesitate, wondering what next; you are able to be empowered to take action before it is too late.

ONE DOWN,
THREE TO GO

We were getting used to moving, starting over and making new friends, but I knew that I wanted to stay put through my high school years. I asked Mother to promise that no matter what, we would stay in one place until I graduated from high school. She promised, so, *Long Beach*, "*California, here we come, right back where we started from*"...

Millikan High School opened in 1956, so it was a "new" school. The entrance was open and expansive. Just walking into the front area of the school, I felt grown up. There was no playground equipment and no cartoon characters on the bulletin board. I can still hear the sound of typewriters clicking away and see the steno books standing A-framed next to them. This school was nothing like Prescott. I could see I was going to have a new and wonderful experience.

"Hi, Cuz. What's your schedule look like? Do we have any classes together this year?"

"Hi, George. I don't know, are you taking typing or short-hand?" I said, laughing, knowing that wasn't on his schedule.

"No, but I'll catch up with you later, maybe at lunch," he said, kissing me on the cheek and waving at some of his friends who were telling him to hurry.

"I have to go, but you let me know if anyone messes with you, Penny."

My schedule was full. The time I had been out of school with a tutor was costing me now. I was struggling with English and math. My required math for high school graduation was "consumer math," which taught us daily life finances like buying groceries. Simple math, nothing complicated. Other subjects were exciting to me like homemaking where I would learn to sew and cooking, which would be a breeze. Public speaking, typing, and shorthand were right up my alley. Social studies and history were a bit dull until Mr. K's class. He had red hair, was tall and slender, and he loved the subject he taught. I wasn't a problem student. However, one day in history class, I was talking to a girl behind me and the bell had already rung. Our conversation wasn't finished, so I just kept on talking.

"Miss Nelson," Mr. K said in a voice that made me know I was in trouble. "Stand up," he said. "Miss Nelson, I'm sure you're aware that to continue talking in class after the bell rings is rude."

"Yes, sir," I said, humiliated because I did know better. "I'm sorry, Mr. K. It won't happen again."

"I'll take you at your word. Now take your seat," he said and returned to his lesson plan. I squirmed in my seat through the entire class, and when the bell rang, I waited around to tell him again that I was sorry.

I knew many of the Millikan High School kids from junior high and knew they'd help me make new friends. I met a boy in typing class named Ken. He was in a club called Thadeus. It was a club for tough guys—not bad boys, just all boy. My cousin George was a member, too. There were many clubs for girls, but the one I wanted to be a part of was ANU, a community service club.

The social life of high school students was a new experience. They did things as groups like go to drive-in movies and picnics where they played baseball or went on beach outings where they played my favorite sport, volleyball. I didn't have many young people as friends. During the elementary years, I wasn't able to keep up physically with the things they wanted to do so adults were my playmates. Yes, I was about to step across another line and develop socially.

Now established in a high school, Mother began looking for a home for us, but she limited herself to looking in my school district.

———————————————

"Guess who called me today?" Mom said, as she was putting dinner on the table.

"Who?" I said, helping her get everything ready so we could sit down together.

"Jon, let's eat," Mom yelled out the front door. "Put your bike up so no one trips on the sidewalk, son.

"So, who called, Mom?" By now, my radar was up, and I was sure I saw that look in her eyes again. Was it hope or longing? I didn't know but my stomach was in a knot.

"Tom. He's going to be in Long Beach this weekend and wanted to come by and visit a while. He has new recipes for cheesecake and thinks he will open a place like thirty-one flavors ice cream. You know thirty-one flavors of cheesecake." She laughed and added, "He said the chocolate cheesecake is going to be called the Charlie Brown." I was babysitting a few apartments away and had promised I would work Saturday night.

I thought, *Hmmm that would give me an excuse to leave the house if things were going too fast for me.*

"Mom, remember I'm babysitting for Kathy Saturday night but not until seven, if that's okay?" I asked, hoping she wouldn't want me to change my plans.

"I don't want you to miss babysitting, so we'll eat early enough for you to visit with Tom and get to work on time."

The atmosphere had suddenly changed. We were now talking about school and things that happened at work with Mom that day. Jon was talking about going surfing with Durm who loved to surf and drove a hearse as his surf mobile. Nevertheless, we all knew Tom was coming home.

I didn't want to move again, no matter what happened with the two of them, and for a moment, my heart sank. Then something came over me and somehow I knew Mother wouldn't break her word to me, not this promise. It was the central piece of my bigger dream and we both knew it. We'd been planning a long time for high school, prom dresses, and graduation. We'd worked too hard to turn back now.

"Okay, I'm glad he is coming. We have missed him. Do you think he'll cook dinner?"

"Finish your dinner, smarty." She laughed, taking her last bite. "Let's get the kitchen cleaned. We all have an early morning."

I was getting older now and thought I understood a little more about "relationships." I just couldn't understand how they were ever going to have a stable life like many of my friend's families. Their parents had stayed together for years. I was amazed that some of them had lived in the same house since they were born. I thought it was funny when my friends said their lives were boring. I thought their lives sounded great. That's when I realized most people think someone else's life is better than theirs.

Other things were starting to make sense too, like "time flies when you're having fun" because time was flying. In fact, before I knew it, Ken was my "steady boyfriend," summer was fast approaching, and we hadn't moved.

HIDE THIS NUGGET IN YOUR HEART

The grass is not greener on the other side. The grass is always greener where you tend it.

FACING MYSELF

The summer was a blur of activity. We did find a house. It was ugly but had lots of potential. My room was at the back of the house, and I had my own bathroom. Tom was back, and we were all busy opening up walls and making a dark house ready for a bright future. The kitchen was getting brick built-ins and fresh paint. The living room was my problem. I even had to scrape a mural off the wall.

Jon and Tom worked in the front with a sledgehammer knocking out the glass enclosure so you could see the front door and putting in brick planters. This was the first house with no pool. At last, my physical therapy was over. There was just enough grass to keep Jon busy on weekends, mowing and weeding the planters. He also had a paper route that started very early in the morning. I could see we were becoming that all-American family I had dreamed of all my life. Summer sped by, and I looked forward to starting my sophomore year.

Even though it was the second school year for my big romance with Ken, we were still too young to drive. Our parents took us to the movies and friends houses.

Ken's sister, Cheryl, was in ANU. She was older than we were, and she "asked me out," meaning she sponsored me to become a member. Once you were "asked" out, you "rushed," which included several weeks of doing things with the club members; silly things to prove you were willing to be a part of their group. The club members called us "pledges." The members would have a secret meeting and vote on the ones that were rushing the club. When they voted on the pledges, a white marble was dropped in the box if they agreed that the pledge should become a member and a black marble if they were not in favor. If *granted* membership, you were kidnapped, blindfolded, and taken to the "hell night" location. After a fun and scary time, your blindfold would come off and all your new "sisters" would hug you. This was all in secret. Of course, your parents knew you'd be kidnapped, so they could leave a door open. All the kids in school knew what weekend the clubs voted so every pledge lay in bed waiting to hear the door open and giggling girls approaching.

I'd been to the pledge tea where we met everyone rushing the club and the members. I'd done all the silly things during the rush and found myself lying on my bed waiting for the sound of victory. It did not come. The clock slowly ticked along, and I ultimately fell asleep knowing that my imperfections had kept me out. All the members were perfect, beautiful, every hair in place. Their clothes perfect, and they didn't limp. I was crushed and didn't know what to do. Everyone would know that I hadn't "made it" on Monday morning.

Mom was quiet as she watched me at breakfast and knew that I had something on my mind.

"Penny, what's the matter with you, today?" she asked, taking my breakfast dishes to the sink.

"I didn't make ANU, Mom," I said. "They didn't want me because I'm not perfect. I limp and have this stiff foot and skinny leg and all my wishing and dreaming about being an ANU girl is just that, dreaming."

"That's a pretty convenient excuse for not making your club, isn't it, honey?"

"What do you mean excuse? It's true, Mom. You've seen the girls, and you know they're all perfect."

"That may be true, but if you blame your limp or anything else like that as the reason you didn't make ANU, you'd be wrong.

Those are all things that you can't change. However, you need to look for things that you can change. Maybe your personality or the way you act is the problem. Do you understand? It really isn't the end of the world. You have plenty of time to think about what you can change, and do it before the next rush. Think about it, Penny," she said, as she went to her room to change clothes.

Think about it was all I did the rest of the weekend and even into the next week. Could it be me and not my limp? I thought about making excuses and blaming everything that was too hard on having polio. Sure, I'd been a trooper and hadn't complained, but the motive was so the doctors and nurses would like me. I didn't realize that when it came to relationships with my peers I might be full of self-pity or excuse making as Mother said. I thought of the times I'd felt hurt through the years, and how I was afraid to confront those who hurt me. I thought about the times that I didn't push to do things when Mother wasn't there to push me. Instead, I would slink out of the picture never wanting to say, "I can't or I need help." Therefore, I just didn't participate in things that would've helped people get to know me. *Maybe there are some things I need to work on*, I thought, getting ready for bed. One thing I knew, it was easier to think about things others needed to change than it was to think about changing myself.

Mother was right. It was not the end of the world. There was to be another rush, if I was "asked out" or even had the courage to try again. My friends who made the club were nice to me, and those who didn't go out for ANU but made other clubs said I should rush one of theirs. Ken didn't care one way or the other about me becoming an ANU girl, and his sister just said I should just try again. I held my head up, took a deep breath, and went on through the year looking forward to summer and my sixteenth birthday.

One day, Mom called and said Tom was picking me up, and we would meet her for a surprise. It was a great surprise, a teal-colored Chevrolet Corvair with push buttons instead of a stick shift. I was thrilled and couldn't wait to drive my new Corvair.

I studied the manual on the rules of road and was confident to pass the test on August 3rd, 1965, my sixteenth birthday. Mom took me to the Department of Motor Vehicles, and I got in line waiting my turn. Once through the first line, I stood in another, waiting to have my test checked…passed…"Yippee!" Now I was ready for my driving test. Parallel parking was the terror of everyone, and I was grateful to have my Corvair instead of Mom's Lincoln. I passed again; now for my picture. I had my hair piled high in the beehive fashion with a long curl casually thrown over my shoulder.

"Smile," said the woman behind the counter.

Smile, I thought, *I bet she can see my wisdom teeth my smile is so big*. I had a new car, a full tank of gas, and a list of people I wanted to visit. Off I went from house to house and friend to friend making plans at every stop. I found having a car was a great privilege and would open new doors for me.

"Telephone's for you, Penny," Mother said. I was surprised that she was giving me the phone since we were still eating dinner. What was Mom up to? Normally we'd have to call the person back.

"Hello, Penny. My name is Tina, and I hear you have a car. I like going to the drive-in movies on Friday nights, and I need a friend with a car."

"I do have a car, but how did you know my phone number?" I asked.

"My friend Mary DeRouchey gave it to me and said it would be okay if I called you."

"Sure, it is. Do you want to go with us sometime?"

"Yes, this Friday is good. I'll meet you in the front of the school in the morning. I'll be with Mary, and I'll tell you where I live. Okay?"

"Sure, see you tomorrow."

"Who was that, Penny?" Mother asked, helping me clear the dishes.

"A girl that knows Mary wants to go to the show with us Friday night." Little did I know that the phone call was the beginning of liberty for me throughout the rest of my high school days.

Tina was five foot ten and I was four foot ten. She was a straight-A student that understood trigonometry while I stumbled through consumer math. She could spell, punctuate, conjugate, and articulate anything. I couldn't. She could sew a suit for a man, and I was still ripping out zippers. She loved horror movies, and I loved mysteries and love stories. Yes, we were destined to be best friends.

Tina made ANU and so did Mary, but that didn't stop us from enjoying each other's company. In fact, every weekend I stayed at Tina's house or she stayed at mine. Tina shared a room with her older sister, Sue, and no one ever went in to *inspect* it. At my house, if our clothes weren't neatly folded in our drawers, Mother dumped the drawers out and we started over. They were one of those families that lived in the same house with the same husband, that I so admired. When I was at her house there were no chores, but there were plenty at home before I left. That was the rule, finish our work, get the weekend off. When Tina stayed with me, she had to wait until my chores were finished and inspected, so she always pitched in to help.

There was just one little thing that worried me. Tom had not visited my room in years, and none of us ever spoke about it.

However, recently, if I were lying on the couch watching television, he would sit down by my feet and try to put my foot on his lap in a way that made me uncomfortable. Sometimes when I needed help with a zipper, he'd move his hand too far around the front of me. Therefore, in either situation I would have to get up or even leave the room. One day in the car, I noticed Tom put his hand on Tina's knee and left it there for just too long. I was worried about my friend sleeping over or being alone with Tom. I knew I had to do something.

"Tina, listen. I want you to keep something in mind that may never happen, but I want you to know to watch out for yourself. My stepfather has hands he can't keep to himself. If he ever puts his hands on you at all, get up and leave the room and tell me, okay?"

"Has he touched you?" she asked, in a protective way, not frightened at all.

"Yes, but that was a long time ago. Now he just tries little things, but when I leave the room, it's over. I didn't ever want to tell anyone about this, but I don't want you to be hurt by him."

Later that night while finishing up in the kitchen, I told Tom what I had said to Tina. I told him if she ever told me he touched her, I would call her father and the police. Tom acted shocked as if I had shamed him in some way, but it was quite the opposite. I'd been shamed, but never again would he hurt me. I sure wouldn't allow him to hurt my friends. I was changing and taking control of my future and the way I wanted to live it; no more secrets and no more fear.

HIDE THIS NUGGET IN YOUR HEART

Mirror, mirror, on the wall, who's the fairest of them all? Who? Not me?

Don't be afraid to examine yourself.

THE MUSTANG,
MIMI, AND ME

"Penny, leave the keys to your car on the counter. We're taking it in for a tune-up today," Mother said. " I'll drop you off at school this morning, and Tom or I will pick you up after class, so please be in front of the school right at three fifteen."

"Okay, the keys are on the counter, I'll be ready in five minutes."

I was "asked" out for ANU again and decided this time would be the last time, even if I didn't make it.

I heard a horn honking…long, short, short. Looking up I saw some of the ANU girls driving past the school.

"See you tomorrow, Penny!" they shouted. I waved back as I noticed Mom pulling up to the curb.

"Get in, honey. I have to get back to work."

"What time will my car be ready, Mom? How can we pick it up if you're going to work? I don't want to be without it an extra day."

Mom laughed but didn't answer. She had a funny look on her face as we drove to the house. Tom was in the driveway drying a car that he had just washed. It was green and sporty looking.

"Who's here?" I asked, getting out of the Lincoln.

172

"I didn't know anyone was going to be here," Mother said. "Let's go see."

"Tom, whose car is this?" she asked, looking inside the driver's window. "Penny, look there's a puppy in there." She pointed at a wiggly little thing in the front seat.

"Oh!" I squealed. "Can I pick it up?"

I opened the door and slid in the car, scooping up the puppy. It was a little poodle, and she started licking my face.

"Isn't this the cutest dog?" I asked, looking up at Mom who was holding an envelope toward me.

"This has your name on it, so I guess you better open it," Mom said, handing the envelope to me.

It was hard to open the envelope with a fidgety dog, but I was giving it my all when a key fell into my lap. I opened the card that read, *Happy belated birthday, honey. May these be the best years of your life. Love, Mom.*

My Corvair certainly did have a tune-up. In fact, they had traded it in for a new Ford Mustang. A new car and a new puppy! I named my puppy Mimette, calling her Mimi for short; and we were inseparable, the Mustang, Mimi, and me. Mother was good for her word, and I was living my dream for high school, even more than I could have thought possible just a few years before.

McDonald's had started serving strawberry shortcake that year, so when I would go for my french fries and Tina for her fish sandwich, we would all share the shortcake, Tina, Mimi, and me. I would laugh as I looked at Mimi with whipped cream on her nose sitting on the console between us. We were quite a sight, the three of us, in that fancy car.

"Penny, I'm not telling you again to get yourself to bed," Mother said in a stern voice.

I had been a "night owl" as she called me all my life. As a little girl, I would sneak out of bed and watch television, like *The Town Hall Party*, so I thought she was acting strange.

"Do something with your hair, and what is that on your face?" she asked, looking into the bathroom. I was trying something the girls were doing with rags to make a long curl in my hair, and I had a facial masque on, so I guess I was a sight.

"I'm getting ready for bed," I said, trying not to move my mouth much since I didn't want to crack the mud.

"Well, hurry up and go to sleep." I saw her try not to laugh, but it was obvious that she was laughing all the way back to her room.

Tom said goodnight, and I thought, *What a nut*. He had a pink sponge roller in his hair, right in front, which was odd looking since the back was bald.

I shook my head thinking, *This has to be the strangest family*, as I went to my room.

I was in a deep sleep when I felt someone on my bed, and then there was something wrapped around my eyes blindfolding me. I knew it was Jon. He was always pulling pranks in the night, so I yelled "Jon!"

Then I heard girls giggling as I was being gently shoved out of bed and down the hall. I felt Mom put a kiss on my cheek. I was an ANU girl at last, as hard as it was to believe. I still had my limp, so Mom was right again. Hell night was just that but only for a little while. The seniors were the most intimidating, but they were having their kicks before moving on to college and the big sorority scene where they would be the pledges again. Once that was over, the blindfolds were removed, and we saw who had made the club. It was great. The old members hugged us, laughing because we were a sight. One by one, we dropped off to sleep at the official ANU slumber party. It was good to belong, and I now had forty-two sisters; I would be honking, long, short, short.

It was the custom to put your club name on the back window of your car, and most of the girls used small letters. However, not me, I went for large: ANU. The club colors were green and white. Most of the ANU girls wore white zippered sweatshirts with green lettering on the back or green pull over sweatshirts with white lettering on the front. I had to have it all, the green sweatshirts, the white sweatshirts, and the ANU lovalier to hang on my neck. I wasn't going to miss a thing.

Club meetings were on Tuesday nights. I don't think I ever missed one. I thought these were wonderful days, but Mom wouldn't have agreed with me completely. She was so happy for me about ANU and supportive in everything I did with the club, but Ken was a huge issue.

Tina became my legs. When ANU would be in a baseball game with a sister club, I'd hit the ball and Tina would run. Then she would come up to bat, hit, and run. Then it was my turn and again and again she would run. If we were playing volleyball, she always had me on her team. I served, she played the net and any other place I should have been. One afternoon, we had finished a baseball game and I was wound up, ready to go and have more fun. Tina was slouched in the passenger seat with her eyes closed and one arm hanging out the window.

"Tina, I swear. You need to ask your mom to put you on some vitamins or something. You're just way too tired for a girl your age."

I was being serious, but when I saw the look in her eyes, I realized why; and at that moment, I loved her even more, and we both laughed. Poor Tina was so tired from being both my legs and hers, too.

Tina made every club event possible for me to attend and participate in. When we went to the drive in on Friday nights,

Tina would say, "All right, I'll go get the pizza, and when the boys follow me back to the car, you do the talking."

We figured since I was sitting in the car, no one would notice my limp, and I could make up for her being too shy to talk to boys by carrying the conversation.

It worked. In fact, it worked so well that I had dated a football player for several weeks when one night he asked what I had done to my foot.

He said, "How much longer before your foot is better?"

I looked down at my feet, "What do you mean? My feet are fine." Then it dawned on me. "If you're waiting for my limp to go away, you have a very long wait." I explained in detail.

"No, no, that isn't the reason," he said, but that was the last time we went out. I didn't mind though as I was secretly engaged to Ken. Nevertheless, Mother had put her foot down and insisted that if I didn't date other boys, I couldn't date Ken.

She said, "You are too young to just stick to one boy and be talking about marriage." She was right; of course, I was too young. But I was sure I was going to marry Ken.

One afternoon, Ken and I went to the park to feed the ducks. As I was getting into his Volkswagen bug, he handed me a brown bag full of bread and said, "See if I dropped anything in there." I dug around in the bag for a minute, and sure enough, there was a box in the bottom of the bag. It was the engagement ring that Ken finally got out of layaway. I was thrilled and hated that I had to take the ring off before going home, but I didn't dare let Mother see it.

I had another reason to sneak around my mother, and that was smoking. I had my first cigarette while in the hospital in San Diego. I was trying to be grown up while hanging out with my navy friends, and over time developed the habit.

By now McDonald's had become a popular hangout for teen-agers. They had the best French fries. The burgers were fifteen cents, and the guys that worked there were nice. I met one boy working there who had already graduated. His nickname was Skip. Every time I ordered fries, he'd fill a bag that normally held the whole meal. When I got to my car, he would come outside to clean the parking lot and flirt with me. I told him I was going to marry Ken. I explained that my mother insisted I date others or I couldn't date Ken.

"That's rough on you two, I bet," he said, smiling at me really big. "You know I might be able to help you with that. Would you like to go to a movie or something? I'm off Friday."

"I never date on Fridays. That's girls' night, but I can go on Saturday."

"Great, give me your phone number. I'll call you."

I was thinking driving home that he probably wouldn't call me. He was older, and what guy his age would want to have a date with me knowing I had plans to marry someone already?

"Telephone, Penny," Mother called down the hall.

"Who is it, Mom?"

"A boy named Skip. Do you know him?"

"Yes, I'm coming." Walking down the hall, I realized I was excited he'd called.

Mom smiled at me and said in a whisper, "I'll need to meet him before I give you permission to go out."

"I know," I said, taking the phone. "Hello."

"Hi, Penny. It's Skip. How about Saturday night? Do you wanna go the movies or miniature golfing?"

I was just a little hesitant, "I think they both sound good, but you'll have to meet my mother before I can say for sure."

"That's fine. How about later tonight? I get off at seven."

I confirmed with Mom on the time but forgot to mention to Skip that he would need to take off his shoes before coming into our house.

Skip was good for his word and knocked on the door promptly at 7:30.

"Come in," Mother said, "but take your shoes off first."

The look on his face was worth a fortune. He slowly slipped his shoes off and turned his toes under. Skip had been on his own for a while; it was clear by the holes in his socks but even funnier was their pink tint.

He smiled, looking down at his feet and said, "I got a mechanic's rag in the white load, and all my underwear is pink."

Mom loved him instantly, and I was thinking he was terrific too.

Ken and I had been together since we were fourteen and were best friends. We were a part of a fun loving group, and it was common knowledge that he and I were *a couple*. It was rare to hear someone talk about us without hearing "Ken and Penny" as if it were a hyphenated name. Ken was so friendly and equally comfortable with girls and boys. He was always smiling and planning mischief. The only concern I had about our relationship was that he and his friends managed to get their hands on beer on the weekends. At first, I didn't mind, but I noticed it more and more. Being sensitive to alcoholism, I told him one night, "Kenny, you guys shouldn't drink so much. You could end up like Tom."

"Oh, Penny, everybody just drinks beer. It's no big deal. We're just having fun."

"I don't."

"I know, but you're a mother." In fact, that is what all his friends called me.

I didn't know if that was good or bad. I trusted Bear, my buddy from the first day of junior high, so I asked him. "Bear, is it bad to be called mother?"

"Depends on how they say it—mother or mutha." He laughed. That was something to ponder. Maybe Ken was right; it's no big deal.

Just a bunch of guys having fun together, I thought as I joined the rest of the group. The girls were going to the movies, and the guys to "cruise Bellflower Boulevard," which was how they spent their Friday nights, showing off their cars, sitting low in their seats, and acting cool.

One Saturday morning I was sneaking a cigarette in my bathroom, blowing the smoke out the window, when suddenly my mother's face was framed in my screen. She was working in the planter beds under my window when she smelled trouble. It was against the rules in ANU to smoke in public or carry a cigarette while walking. They said it made a girl look trashy so I learned to "hide" the habit, but that Saturday morning, I was caught!

Right on top of the smoking revelation, came the night I had told my mother I was going out with one boy, but he only took me to meet Ken. Ken and I had a wonderful time with our friends at the beach looking at the phosphorescent water and talking about our future. I had a ten-year plan for us. Year one was for Ken and I to get settled in our home, then babies. Three babies, one every third year, and like Mother, I thought two girls and a boy would be perfect. All of a sudden, we saw I was late for curfew. Driving as fast as we could, my friends dropped Ken off on the corner and took me home. As I entered through the back door into the kitchen, I didn't see Mother sitting in the dark. When I lifted a glass of water to my lips, I noticed a glimmer of light reflecting off my engagement ring. Just then, the kitchen light came on, and I knew Mother had seen the ring. You'd have thought it was a ten-karat rock; it looked huge on my finger at that moment. She took the ring, and the next day put it in her safety deposit box saying I couldn't date Ken and wouldn't get the ring back until I was eighteen. We were at odds for the first time. We weren't working together, we were at opposite ends of understanding, and I was digging my heels in.

I thought there was no way my mother could make a decision about who I would marry, just look at all the trouble she had with Tom. I never thought for a moment she had my best interest at heart or wanted me to have a good life. All I thought she wanted was to tell me what to do; never thinking of all the years she worked so hard to give me a future.

I had been buying household items with the money I earned babysitting and putting them in my cedar chest for my first home. Mother bought things to put in my hope chest, as well. I would be ready by the time I was eighteen to move into my own beautiful home. Mother was helping me toward my first home but not marriage. Even though she knew my ten-year plan, she just didn't want year one to begin right after my eighteenth birthday. Every penny I earned went toward having my own home except needed gas money. I was earning $.75 an hour babysitting and gas was $.35 a gallon. Mom had been putting money aside, too, as graduation was coming, and it wouldn't be long before we would go shopping for that prom dress.

One afternoon Mother asked me if I would do a special holiday program for the yellow page group she worked with. It was a large crowd with many company "big shots" attending.

"What do you want me to do?" I asked her, hoping it wasn't one of those routines with the splits because I still couldn't get up from the floor without help.

"That poem about the mother and son you memorized for public speaking class," she answered, and I was relieved.

"Sure, Mom."

We tried on clothes for weeks. The selection was broad, and the styles varied from that princess look, to springtime flowers and everything in between. We found a beautiful bell-shaped cream linen skirt with a pearl and crystal beaded bodice that had gold threads and gold mesh flowing throughout the beads; it was a dress fit for a queen. I thought it was the most beautiful dress I'd ever seen, and perfect for the program I was going to do for General Telephone Company, however, too grown up for the prom.

My high school years had breezed by each one more wonderful than the last. I didn't have any surgeries, and if I was very careful, I could disguise or compensate for scars, the limp, or a shoulder that stuck out; or so I thought.

Mother was sure she could help me find someone who would cause me to toss out the marriage at eighteen idea. One day at a supermarket, a checker named Joe made a comment about the pretty girl in the picture she had in her wallet. Oh, Mother went on and on, giving him my telephone number. When Joe called, he explained he had met Mother and would like to get to know me.

He asked, "Would you like to go the beach on Saturday?"

I knew I couldn't manipulate my way out of the date, so I agreed. I had a bathing suit I liked very much. It was a one-piece suit but the center was black webbing and top and bottom sections were black and white check.

Saturday arrived, and I got ready for the outing, wearing a terrycloth shift over my bathing suit. I had my sandals and big dark glasses. Joe was three years older than me and seemed nice. He thought we should stop at the local A&W and have a root beer float. That sounded fine to me. I noticed that Joe's money looked like new as if it had just been printed, so I commented on it.

He said, "I press my money." I was sure I'd never tell Mother since I was in charge of ironing, and we ironed everything now.

When we got to the beach, Joe grabbed the radio and beach towels to lie on, a small ice chest, and me by the hand. I knew that if I lay on my stomach I could put that stiff foot of mine in the sand, and he wouldn't notice it. We talked about silly things and his college plans.

Unexpectedly, he asked me, "Penny, have you ever thought of plastic surgery?"

I immediately laughed and thought he was talking about my big nose.

I said, "No, Mom had it, and I don't think I'll ever get over her black eyes after the surgery."

"No," he said, "I meant for that big scar on your back. You're such a pretty girl, and maybe they could fix that."

It is funny how you can forget about things when you don't see them. I guess that saying "out of sight, out of mind" fit the moment. I had forgotten about that scar and had moved my long hair to tan, while being careful to cover my foot.

"No, I've never thought of that."

I knew the date was over. I hadn't felt a stab of hurt like that for a long time. I wondered why my mom would put me in that position instead of letting me meet people and then letting them decide if they wanted to date. Of course, I knew that Mother thought I was gorgeous and wouldn't have given the scars or limp a second thought. At that moment, I forgot how she saw me and only knew how he saw me. I was ready to go home. Shortly afterwards, I mentioned I was getting hot and burned easy.

"Maybe we should go," I suggested.

Once in the house, I cried just as I did when I was younger. I felt ashamed of the tears because I was such a fortunate girl achieving all the things I had hoped for—my sorority, my boyfriend, and my soon coming prom and graduation.

Prom night I wore an ankle-length white lace sheath with a hot pink empire sash; it took forever to find the right shoes with pointed toes and a dainty heel about one inch high, but we managed and had them dyed to match the sash. Ken looked great all dressed up in a formal suit, but he let me know right then that he wouldn't be dressing up like that again. However, tonight he was the perfect prom date, and I would worry about tomorrow, tomorrow.

There was a flurry of activities at school as graduation approached. The actual ceremony was practiced repeatedly. Our caps and gowns were ordered, and the prom was planned. We had school picnics and the signing of our "annuals" was a big deal.

At last, the big night came, our large graduating class tried to stay in a perfect line beside the bleachers, but we were giggling and excited. Finally, we heard the loud speaker announce the beginning of the graduation ceremony. Each student walked across the football field to the platform, receiving their diploma from the principal who announced special awards and credits. Then each student took the microphone and announced their plans for the future. Parents were crying and clapping. The line was moving me closer to the steps of that platform, and I was hoping that my leaning on the student behind me wouldn't be noticeable as I climbed the steps.

I heard one classmate say, "I'm going to Long Beach City College in the fall and then to a university."

Another "I'm going to be a lawyer," or "I'm going to a beauty college," and then it was my turn. I walked to the principal and received my diploma, which was such a thrill to me. Then I took the microphone and announced that I was going to marry Ken Torgerson. I'm sure Mother wanted to kill me. If I had been paying attention, I no doubt could have heard her gasp! Nevertheless, the ceremony was too exciting to think about anyone in the bleachers. We were getting ready to throw our caps and scream. I'm sure Mother wanted to scream, too!

"Congratulations to the graduating class of 1967" was the last thing I heard as the crowd of graduates pressed toward the barrels that would receive our robes as we headed off for our futures.

HIDE THIS NUGGET IN YOUR HEART

Celebrate the victory. Blow that horn. Long, short, short. Shout, and be exceedingly glad.

MAKING OUR OWN WAY

Now that I had graduated, I wanted to put my skills as a secretary to the test. I had scored high on shorthand, taking dictation faster than most executives could dictate; and my typing was ninety wpm with few errors on the average. My first job was in the installment loan division of a Long Beach bank. I assisted nine men who handled delinquent accounts and car repossessions. I learned to skip trace from the guys when they needed a woman's voice to gather information.

I started looking for an apartment when I turned eighteen and found one in my budget and close to work. I went downtown to the furniture store my mother had shopped at for many years and asked Mr. Schultz, the owner, if I could buy furniture on credit.

"Absolutely," he said. "Have a look around, and we'll start the paperwork."

My heart was beating fast, and I realized that my dreams of a lovely home were happening. "Good choices," Mr. Schultz said. "Now all I need is for you to fill out the credit form and sign the contract."

Mother had raised me to be independent and self-sufficient. She said she didn't know if she would be around to take care of me, so she taught me to take care of myself. We laughed, later, as she would tell me I was too independent. I told her she had made me that way, and now she'd have to live with it. Mother was a little surprised that I had an apartment and was moving so quickly, but when she saw it, she was happy for me. She did make it clear that the Mustang would not be moving with me, so the ugly station wagon that replaced it was a hard pill to swallow. About a week later, I heard a honk in the alley behind my new home. It was Mother.

As I came to her car, she smiled and said, "I thought you might need a few things," handing me a box of house warming items. Bleach, cleanser, dish soap, toilet paper, and mirror cleaner; it would definitely smell like home before the day was over.

Ken and I decided on October 28, 1967, as the date for our wedding. I was so excited looking for my gown with Tina and planning the big event. Mother finally realized that we were going to get married and was busy helping me plan when Ken announced that he just couldn't be in a big formal wedding. In fact, the justice of the peace at the courthouse was enough for him. I was devastated and so was Mother. So Ken and I decided to meet in the middle and have a small intimate wedding in Palm Springs where I had always planned to marry and later have a reception with our family and friends.

I wore a ribbon-lace knee length dress with a three-quarter–length sleeved jacket. Ken did put on a suit again but swore it would be the last one he'd wear this side of the grave. Ken's mother prepared a multi-tiered wedding cake, and Tom prepared the food, which was served buffet style from meats and seafood to salads and sides. Mother, of course, prepared mouth-watering pies and made sure we were in our places for pictures.

I was surprised to see Mrs. Neff but so happy that she would be part of the memories of my wedding reception. Mr. K., my high school teacher was there supporting and congratulating us; I couldn't believe how many people attended the reception. So many people who had been cheering me on over the years were now clapping, laughing, and wishing us well. We danced *that dance* that I had seen in my imagination from the time I was a little girl. As I leaned into my husband's embrace, I felt my heart swell and thought, *This is where I belong; at last, I am loved and safe.* We opened presents and ate a huge meal. We fed each other cake, drank to a champagne toast, and received best wishes from our friends.

"Thank you, Mother," I said. "Everything was beautiful."

"You should have had the wedding of your dreams. Look at all the people who love you and didn't get to share that day," she said, crying.

"We have this day, Mother, and I will never forget it." I answered, kissing her good-bye.

Ken was working for McDonald-Douglas Aircraft Company. This was the same company Mother had worked for in the fifties. Douglas paid a good wage to a young man just starting out. They had great benefits. A plus for young couples planning their families, and I was working my plan. The doctors had told Mother and me years ago that I'd have difficulty getting pregnant. The doctors said even if I did conceive, the pregnancy and delivery would be too much for my back. I was sure they were wrong and started talking to Ken about stopping birth control so we could have a baby. He wasn't in favor of it, but after several months, we went off the pill.

We found a great two-bedroom apartment and even opened a revolving credit account with Sears to purchase a new Kenmore refrigerator. Yes, we were fast becoming an old married couple. We went sailing with my boss, picnicking with my cousins and brother, played cards at home on the weekends, and worked hard all week. We talked about doing something fun for our anniversary like going to Big Bear Mountain or Lake Elsinore but decided to return to the Ramada Inn in Palm Springs to celebrate our first year. This was an important anniversary to me according to my plan. Our first baby, conceived on schedule one year after our marriage.

Brian Thomas Torgerson was born July 31, 1969, in St. Mary's Hospital in Long Beach, California, by Cesarean section after twenty-three hours in labor. He was beautiful, weighing eight pounds thirteen ounces and eighteen inches long. I hadn't planned a little boy, and I had put a canopy on the crib. When the doctor said I could announce on the speaker to the waiting room that we had a boy, I said "Ken, take the canopy off the crib," and he knew he had a son.

I remember asking God to let my dad know that he was going to be a grandpa while I was in labor. I was amazed to see Brian right after he was born. I had hoped for what I called a chocolate baby; one with olive skin and dark eyes like my father and Mother, not one that was pale like me. There he was, as I hoped with dark hair and the blackest eyes, looking just like my dad. At last, they rolled me out of surgery where my husband stood waiting.

I said, "Kenny, did you see him, honey? He looks just like my dad, dark skin, dark hair, black eyes."

Ken laughed, saying, "Well, then they switched babies on us because the one they brought to me had silver hair, a red face, and I think his eyes will be blue."

That is impossible, I thought and then thought apparently God had comforted me and let me know that my father knew he was a grandpa after all.

───────────────

We moved into a little house and Ken bought a washer and dryer for me so that I could keep up with all those diapers and baby things. Brian was on a perfect schedule. He woke up at dawn and passed out by 8:00 p.m. He ate every three hours and easily went to bed. I could see at least a dozen babies; there was nothing to it.

During my pregnancy, my aunt Donna convinced me to take up china painting. At first, I laughed, saying, "Aunt Donna, china painting is for old ladies who paint roses."

"How about doing some clowns then for the baby's room?" she countered.

"Okay, but that's it," I said, thinking I would just hate it. I was wrong. I really enjoyed painting, and just as soon as I could pack Brian up, we were going to classes so I could master the art. I laughed to myself, thinking about all the years I had dreamed of being an artist and had nearly let my chance go by.

Hank had married Vivian, and we continued spending time together playing dominos and cards while our babies played together. Durm was doing the lighting for bands in clubs all over California. I remembered him telling me to save his autograph that he had signed on a napkin when I was just a little girl because one day he would be famous. Durm loved everything about performing, and he talked about the big band he wanted to produce. He was my wild cousin, by now involved with the arts which included rock and roll and of course, alcohol and drugs. Ken thought it would be great to take me to a club where Durm was handling the light show for my twenty-first birthday. I could see I had a gifted cousin and wondered…*where I had put that autograph.*

I also knew that being twenty-one meant a new and very serious responsibility in voting for a president. I had trouble understanding all the different items coming up for a vote and thought, *I wish I had listened more in school.* Suddenly I knew what to do. I called my high school and asked if Mr. K could call me back on break, and he did. When I told him my concerns, he set up an appointment with Ken and me, coming to our house to answer our questions and show us how to participate in elections. I'll never forget the time he took to follow up with a student, *one that had once interrupted his class,* and thought about how important and influential teachers are. I remembered the little schoolroom I had in my fancy bedroom as a child, teaching my dolls, never dreaming that I would be teaching art in just a few years.

Brian was the center of my world. We were together all day, every day, so I talked to him constantly. He spoke early and clearly, skipping the baby talk stage completely. When his dad was home, he was ready to go anywhere Daddy went. Ken said he wouldn't take him in the car until he was out of diapers, so Brian trained in no time and was ready to go bye-bye. I started thinking about getting pregnant again. Ken was far from agreeing with the idea, and he said the timing was bad as Douglas had to lay off workers and we needed more space. Ken wanted to buy a home before we had any more children. We found the perfect house in Lakewood, and with a little help on the down payment from Mother, we bought it.

Ken heard that Atlantic Richfield was hiring and put in his application. He was hired for rotating shifts. Each week the hours changed from days to swing, then graveyards with increases in pay according to the shift.

Brian was getting so big and so easy to handle that once again I started with the, "Honey, if we don't get pregnant now, I may never want to have another baby. Brian is getting independent, and I won't want to be tied down again."

I persistently prodded him until finally he said okay.

However, within two weeks, he said he came to himself. "What were we thinking? What if something happens to you this time? Who will raise Brian or help you? No way, Penny, no more babies."

Ronald Craig Torgerson was born on his brother's third birthday, according to "the plan." He was six pounds six ounces, twenty-one inches long. My doctor had told Ken that this child would be born at Long Beach Community Hospital, as he intended to tie my tubes preventing any more babies. Since St. Mary's is a Catholic hospital, they wouldn't allow any type of birth control. So there I was, once again, in the hospital next door to the Tichenor Clinic where I had spent many nights. I was completely surprised that I didn't have a girl this time.

"Maybe I should have found a pickle jar." I laughed, dozing off to sleep.

I felt someone take my hand and thought it was Ken ready to tell me all about our new son, but it wasn't Ken. It was our pediatrician.

"Penny," he said, "do you trust me?"

"Yes, Doctor. What's the matter?"

"Your baby needs to go with me to Children's Hospital where I can take care of him. He has Hyland Membrane Disease and is having seizures. We think he may be mentally retarded, and he will need close attention around the clock for the next seventy-two hours. This is the critical time. Can I take him?"

"Yes, but can I see him first?" It was at that very moment that an incubator was wheeled into my room, and all I could remember seeing was Ronnie's eyes as they turned the incubator around and left the room as quickly as they had come in. The doctor followed the incubator out the door to the ambulance that was waiting. A nurse brought me something to help me sleep. I heard the siren before I drifted off.

That evening Ken came to visit. He'd been at the children's hospital with Ronnie all day. He looked drained and was having

191

trouble trying to convince me that all would be well. He just sat there holding my hand while we both cried. Finally, I told him to go home and try to get some rest, and reluctantly he did.

Ken's parents rallied their church and a prayer group would be praying nonstop for the next seventy-two hours for Ronnie's healing. I'd never heard of anything like that, but I was very glad that someone was praying.

The next morning before I was completely awake, I heard nurses talking in the hall near my door. "Do you know who she is?" one said.

"Yes, I was here when she had foot surgery as a little girl. She sure has had a rough time, and now this."

"They say the doctor doesn't know if the baby will live. Should we wake her for breakfast, or just let her rest?"

"Let her sleep. I'll bring her something later."

I didn't speak. I lay there perfectly still. In fact, I could hardly breathe.

Mother had moved to Texas. She had gone to work for a woman's figure salon a few months after I found out I was pregnant with Brian. She was going to open new locations in the Houston area. She immediately flew in to take care of Brian and our house. The next seven days would find Ken running between the two hospitals visiting me and then rushing to be with our son.

I finally got out of the hospital, and Ken took me to our son. I'll never forget looking through the window at his little body. It seemed as if it had melted like wax. He had wires in something that looked like putty stuck to his head and body. There were tubes everywhere, but he didn't move. My heart broke. The nurses saw Ken and signaled us to come in. We had to wear white jackets, masks, and gloves to put our hands through the sides of the incubator to touch him. We still couldn't hold him. The doctor said the critical time had passed and that Ronnie would live but that he had suffered brain damage and was epileptic. They weren't sure of the amount of damage, but they would test him periodically.

Going home without my baby was very hard. I thought of the years that Mother spent leaving me, and I noticed in the look she gave me that she understood completely. Nine days had passed since Ronnie's birth. I was wondering what was going to happen to him.

We were sitting down to dinner that evening, when the telephone rang.

"Hello," I said, expecting to hear a friend asking about the baby.

"Mrs. Torgerson, will you hold a minute? The doctor wants to talk to you." My heart stopped as I realized it was very late for a call from the doctor.

"Penny, are you guys just going to leave this baby here forever, thinking I am going to take care of him, or are you going to pick him up?"

"Ken," I screamed, "we can pick Ronnie up. When, Doctor, now?"

"No, I'll tuck him in tonight, but you get here first thing in the morning."

"We'll be there. Thank you."

Everyone was so excited that it was hard to eat. Brian kept saying, "Are you bringing me my baby?" He had asked for a baby for his third birthday so when Ronnie was born on that day, he assumed the baby was his.

"You bet we are, Brian. Are you ready to take care of Ronnie?" I answered.

The hospital looked more colorful that day than it had, and the nurses were smiling as we approached the neonatal section. I wanted to grab Ronnie up and head out the door as fast as we could, but that wasn't going to happen. We first were told about the medication for seizures, then how to change the circumcision bandages and things to watch for and things that should not concern us. My head was spinning, but we were going home. The doctors had watched over Ronnie for ten days. All his brain wave tests came back "damaged," and it would be months before we knew the extent of that damage.

Brian was at the front door when we arrived. As the door opened, he reached his arms out to take his baby.

"You have to sit down first, honey, and then you can hold your baby."

Brian quickly scurried to the sofa, wiggled all the way back, and put his arms out again. "Ready," he said. It was good to be home.

HIDE THIS NUGGET IN YOUR HEART

"Be still, sad heart, and cease repining; behind the clouds the sun is still shining;

Thy fate is the common fate of all, Into each life some rain must fall."

—Henry Wadsworth Longfellow

"Anyone who says sunshine brings happiness has never danced in the rain."

—Author Unknown

DREAMS TO NIGHTMARES

The next several months were busy with doctor's appointments and managing our household. In addition, I opened an art studio, Penny's China Shoppe. Oh yeah, my little adventure with painting clowns turned into a passion. I taught the art and sold materials for china painting. My studio had a big room in back where the children could play, following my mother's example as a "family-operated business." I remember telling Mother that for all the things we did together, there was a serious generation gap; however, that wouldn't happen with my children and me. We may have similar ideas on working together, but men had walked on the moon the month Brian was born, so we were very modern and would be able to identify with each other.

Tom and Mother were divorced by now. Mother was on a new path, a path that was not to include the chaos of years past. Tom had been gone for some time when he called to ask if he could visit and meet the kids. I talked to Ken about it, and he agreed that Tom could come, but he didn't want him deeply involved in our lives. So Tom came to town.

It was hard seeing him; he had changed so much physically. It was obvious that alcohol had taken a toll on his body and that the way he was living was far below the standard we had maintained through the years. He enjoyed the boys and called them "two Charlie's" in reference to his chocolate cheesecake days. We talked for a few hours and showed him the china studio. He cried remembering all the years that we worked in back rooms and restaurants, building businesses until his addictions brought changes that destroyed us as a family. The day ended with Tom asking me to forgive him. I found I was able to easily forgive and let him go, as he was more broken than I could have imagined and I refused to carry the hurt of the past into my future. This would be the last time I saw Tom alive. He called a few times, but he seemed resolved to continuing in his way of living and knew that we wouldn't participate in that lifestyle.

―――――――――――

Mother called frequently checking on her grandsons and encouraging us in so many ways. Brian was in school, and she loved hearing about his exploits and the way he was looking at his enlarging world. His kindergarten teacher was pregnant, and he announced to the class that he knew all about how babies were born.

His teacher tried to stop the next sentence, but he quickly added, "You just cut open the tummy and take that baby out."

―――――――――――

As Christmas approached, Brian asked what he could do for a school art project, which was "Christmas around the world."

"How about making clothes pins into children from different countries as ornaments?" I suggested.

"What's a clothes pin?" he asked.

"Brian, honey, don't be silly. You know, what we hang clothes on the line with!" He still just looked at me, and then I realized he had never seen a clothesline, all he knew was a dryer.

I laughed and said, "I have to call Grandma. She'd get a kick out of this *generation gap*." I really missed Brian while he was at school and was amazed as he took everything his teacher said as gospel. To him, she was the smartest person in the world, and I felt it, especially when he would tell me, "My teacher said… My teacher said…" One afternoon I wrote Brian a poem.

"A PROMISE"

I've tried, my son, to show you just what this world would be
I've tried, my son, to tell you just how much you mean to me
I've tried to show you life is just a mea-
sure, our loss against our gain
For would we really know happiness unless we'd felt some pain.

When you were just an infant and I held you in my arms
I used to marvel at your being and all your baby charms
Part of you has left me and gone its way to school
You've learned about your numbers
And you've heard the Golden Rule

Now you stand beside me just a fraction of my size
And yet I see a different world through your tiny little eyes
You turn a flower in your hand and the wonder does appear
You tell me stories of other lands and now I shed a tear

The world is ready for you, it waits with open arms
And now it's not just Mother who will be seeing all your charms
So go through life slow my son, never let it make you run
Savor each and every day
It's only once you'll pass this way

And when you hold your first child
Look deep within its eyes
You'll see these things, I promise you,
It's your turn to cry.

He'll turn a flower in his hands and the wonder will appear…

Shortly after that, my brother, Jon, came for a visit, and I shared the poem with him. He picked up his guitar and made a ballad of the poem for Brian; he knew just the right chords and really brought the poem to life for me.

I painted on small porcelain disks and mounted them on rings. I sent one to Mother, and she liked it. She said she wanted several pieces to sell for me. Boy, did she sell them! She had so many orders that I spent most of Ken's graveyard shifts painting. I had a great desire to paint like some of the famous painters of my day and from years gone by. Teaching classes at my studio and painting and selling jewelry was bringing me closer to my goal. I wanted to paint a masterpiece.

One artist I admired was Jayne Houston, a popular portrait artist. She had a line of specialty paints and a book that I had been saving my teaching money to buy. The very day I was able to purchase those items, my mother happened to call.

"Penny," she said, "I have a lady in my office who just loves the ring you painted for me, and she's a china painter too. I told her about my *famous* daughter who painted it, and she would *just love* to talk to you. Her name's Jayne Houston."

I almost fainted.

When she said "Hello," I blabbered, "Oh, Mrs. Houston, I just bought your book and paints today; you know my mother is well, my mother."

"I am looking forward to meeting you one day, Penny," she said and complimented me on the ring.

I was completely embarrassed as I knew that ring was far from great and yet Mrs. Houston was as generous and kind as she was talented.

Another day a friend of mine brought a woman to my shop to show her how lovely the studio was. My cousin Hank had built display cabinets to show the blank porcelain pieces. I had an antique cash register and shag carpeting throughout the teaching and sales areas. This was not normal for painting studios.

"Hi, Annette," I said, as my friend walked through the door.

"Hi, Penny. I have a friend with me today that I want you to meet. Penny, this is Jean Sadler. Jean, this is Penny."

"Jean Sadler," I said, "you may not know this but one of *the* most famous china painters was named Jean Sadler, but she died a long time ago. Her designs are a favorite of mine; hers, and Catherine Kline."

I heard Annette clear her throat and say, "Penny, this *is* Jean Sadler.

I almost fainted and quickly excused myself for a minute, going to the back of the shop so I could get control of my emotions. I was star struck and embarrassed.

I can't believe she is still alive, I thought to myself. Now she's in my shop! When I returned, Jean was looking around and complimented me on the way I displayed the blank porcelain and painted pieces. We talked for a long time about the art and artists and then they were gone. I was completely undone by the meeting, after all, she was like a movie star to me, and yet she was so genuine and full of fun.

Two days later, I got a note from her saying she was going to open a studio and teach seminars in the near future. She said I had inspired her so she was sending a surprise for my shop and she signed her name through a heart. UPS arrived with Jean's full line of designs and lessons! She told me I could send her a check as I sold her designs. In addition, when her studio opened, we would paint together, and we did. That is when I learned that a personal hurt had caused her to become reclusive. Over the next two years, Jean mentored me in many ways including china painting.

I was demonstrating for a retailer at a large International China Painters Show and found myself surrounded by other china painters watching and asking questions about the art, the paints, and the brushes I used when suddenly it was as if someone had sucked everyone out of the room. I turned and noticed at the far end of the building a crowd jammed together trying to see something.

I asked one of the floor attendants, "What's happening over there?"

"Jean Sadler is demonstrating," she said.

I returned to my booth knowing that I was able to take a break because she was truly the star of the show and I couldn't imagine anyone missing her demonstration. When she was finished and out of the room, some of crowd returned to my booth. Now women were asking me about lessons, when I taught, was there room in my classes, and so on.

Wow, I thought, *what brought this on?* When a woman told me, "You know Jean Sadler said you were a wonderful teacher and that she recommended you. She said you'd never create the masterpiece, but that you would create masters."

Initially, I was undone.

What, I thought to myself, *I* wanted *to paint a masterpiece.*

However, later, much later, I understood that it was greater indeed to be a part of the training of masters. This realization follows me today in every area of my life.

Jean allowed me to take her original paintings to shows out of state when she would introduce new designs. This was like the "holy grail" to porcelain artists. She honored, inspired, and encouraged me to continue with all my heart and made a way for me in a community of very famous artists.

Ken and I enjoyed traveling on weekends, and when they could, friends went with us. One weekend as we were driving home, we passed by a bank where our friend Josie had started working.

She said, pointing out the car window, "Well, that's where I work, if anyone ever wants to take me to lunch."

Oddly, something on the inside of me stopped me from answering, but I knew something was different that day. It wasn't long after that, I came home from the painting studio and found Ken lying on the couch.

"What's up?" I asked, coming in the door. He never would lay around unless sleeping between his shifts.

He rolled on his side, looking toward me, and said, "I want a divorce."

I laughed and said, "What have I done now?"

But then I realized he wasn't kidding.

"I'm in love with someone else," he stated.

I knew at that moment who that someone was and when it started.

"Josie," I said.

He nodded yes and asked me, "How'd you know?"

"Well, that's that, then." I walked into the kitchen, thinking my heart would break, not wanting Ken to see the pain in my eyes. This was my "safe" choice, the one who wouldn't hurt me, cheat on me, or leave me. Ken's drinking was an issue throughout the seven years we had been married, but I believed that he would mature and stop. However, I was unprepared for another woman or for divorce.

Jean called one afternoon, and she knew I was crying. She gave me great counsel and strength.

"First," she said, "what scares you most about this? We will solve that problem, and everything else will fall in place."

"I'm afraid I can't support my children alone," I said.

"So let's think of the ways you can earn money."

She was more than a mentor; she was a friend. What I didn't tell her was that I was afraid I would be living my mother's life and that I had failed to provide that secure home for my children that I always dreamed I would.

When I spoke to Mother, she asked, "What do you need—me or money?"

"I need both," I said.

"Okay, I'm sending a check, and will make arrangements to come."

The check arrived, and Mother came to help me. In only a few weeks, Ken decided to come back home. Mother went back to Texas, sure we would survive this storm. I don't know what changed for him or if he ever really got over Josie. I knew everything had changed for me. I became critical of my body, my weight, the scars, and I still had that pesky limp. Therefore, I didn't know if I ever could get over the hurt, Josie, or the sadness

I felt as I compared myself to her and every other woman I knew. I couldn't carry "her" into our future and have one. We tried to put it behind us. However, there was a guard on my heart, as it seemed my bigger dream had become a nightmare. Tom had violated my trust. Now Ken had violated my trust. I wondered if I would ever trust my heart to another again.

One day Mother called saying she had news that wasn't good. She was diagnosed with cancer, in the late stages according to her doctors. She asked if I would come to Texas to help in her office for a couple of weeks. Ken and I agreed that it was the right thing to do. I packed up the boys and took the next flight available to grandmother's house in Houston.

Mom had never used a typewriter, and though she was wonderful in business, her office skills were zero. This was not a problem as I had trained for office work and was happy to help organize the things that were concerning her. I sat in her big pink chair in the bedroom with a lapboard and went through everything in order to see what we needed to do. We talked about the business she was in—selling franchises in the weight-loss industry throughout the United States and how it was helping many women achieve their weight-loss goals. I remember wiggling in my chair as she had tried to get me involved while she was still in California. I hadn't gotten my figure back after having the boys. I knew I was heavier than was good for me, physically and emotionally.

Mother had decided to buy a new Lincoln Continental and said she would sell her old one to us. Ken took a week of vacation and came to Texas to get us and the new car, as my work there was done. I was excited to be returning home. We had recently added on to our house in Lakewood. We had a new master bedroom and bath, laundry room, and den with cathedral ceilings. We updated our kitchen, lowering the cabinets to make it easier for "short" me. Durm, Hank, and Ken had done most of the work designing around my art including hand-painted bathroom sinks and tiles. We were certainly feeling settled in and established, or so I thought.

We were about five minutes out of downtown Houston, when Ken said, "I'm moving to Texas, Penny. What do you want to do?"

I was more than shocked, but considering everything, Mother's illness, and the "temptations" in California, I agreed. We placed our home on the market as soon as we returned. Within a few months, our house sold, and we were packing for a big move to Texas.

HIDE THIS NUGGET IN YOUR HEART

Let go of the hurts of your past so you can move into your glorious future.

MY THOUGHTS ARE
NOT YOUR THOUGHTS

I taught a final china painting class, promising to return for seminars the next year. I packed my car, my best friend Tina, and a painting friend Sophie, and we all headed for Texas. Ken, Brian, and Ronnie had an all-boy-adventure following the moving truck in the camper.

Driving straight through from California and arriving in the middle of the night on May 1, 1977, tired and uncertain as to the directions, I spotted a Safeway truck exiting the freeway just in front of me.

"This is great," I said to Tina and Sophie. "Mother said her street was just past the Safeway Market so we can follow that truck."

Soon the truck slowed down and turned into a residential area. We turned with him. The next thing we knew, the truck stopped in a cul-de-sac, and Houston Police surrounded us with their guns drawn. They told us to get out of the car.

Sophie, way past sixty-five years old and afraid of nothing, jumped out of the car, and told them to "put those guns away."

As Tina and I got out, an officer told us that a group who drove black Continentals hijacked several Safeway trucks. When the driver saw us on his tail, he radioed the police who told him to lead us down a dead-end street. The officers checked our identifications and called my mother to verify our story. Once they were certain we weren't part of the notorious Safeway hijacking gang, we followed them out to the main street. There stood Mother, in her bathrobe with her hair in rollers, standing on the grassy median waving to let us know we were on the right track.

Later that evening, Jon showed up with some buddies.

They all had their guns and rifles strapped to their bodies, saying, "Welcome to Texas, DeeDee." You talk about the wild West.

Now that we were living in Houston, I agreed to continue to help Mother with her business. I put an office together, which took no time at all. Mother then enrolled me in her company's training school so I would understand the health and fitness business at every level. Once I finished the course, Mother sent me to a salon she had just opened in Odessa, Texas. This was the first time I had been away from my children, and I wasn't thrilled about it. Mother sent pictures every few days of Brian and Ronnie water skiing and playing in the pool, so I knew they were making memories while I was learning the business.

Within the first year and a half in Texas, I had regained my figure and developed in the business from investing to operations to teaching the program to franchise owners and their managers. Ken was working in the family business too. He was traveling, mostly by air, and enjoying all the drinks served. He was also around "high rollers" who socialized and took him to dinners and business functions. Again, with a lot of alcohol, and that scratchy feeling I had as a teenager in love was stronger than ever.

It had been seven years since Ken had the affair with Josie, but there were others, and I knew something had to give. One night I was soaking in a bubble bath when Ken came home. He was sitting on the bedroom floor with his back against the love seat telling me about his day. His birthday was coming up, and I was famous for over-the-top birthday gifts from chrome rims for his '32 Ford to gold nugget jewelry. Nevertheless, after fourteen years of marriage, I told Ken I was ready to give him the gift he had been asking for, for years.

He smiled, saying, "What?"

"A divorce," I answered, and the room went silent. Ken moved to Oklahoma near my cousin Hank while the children and I stayed in Houston.

I was so troubled about my children not having their father in the home. I knew firsthand what a loss that was, but the boys were strong in support of me and remained close to their daddy. Ken and I never said ugly things about each other so that our children could grow up in peace, not torn between us.

I wondered if everyone needed to be "loaded" to live with me; I was sure that the alcohol that had surrounded my life and the violation of trust with men was my problem. I just didn't measure up. I was damaged goods.

I had a lot to keep me busy—the business, the boys, and traveling. I was working with people from all over the United States. I convinced myself I was fine, but there was so much pain on the inside of me. Sandy, a friend in our business, was worried about me and told her sister that I was probably depressed. Her sister, Janice, said she would talk to me if she thought it would help. Sandy said, "Well, she's having a party at her house tonight and you could come by, but whatever you do, don't talk about Jesus because she is already so depressed."

I'd been rushing around getting ready for the party. Sandy was right. I wasn't happy and couldn't figure out what to do about it. I knew whining wasn't the answer and getting drunk didn't help, so I just put on a smile and tried to convince the world I was fine. I heard the doorbell ring; and when I opened the door, there stood a stranger with an appearance I can't explain. She had a twinkle in her eyes and a smile that captured me.

"Hi, I'm Sandy's sister, Janice. Are you Penny?"

I turned around and saw Sandy sitting on the back of the sofa. I turned back to the door and said, "Whatever you have, I want it."

With that, Janice, much taller than me, put her arm in a half nelson around my neck and said, "Awe, all you see in me is Jesus from the top of my head to my toes."

Sandy slapped her forehead and fell over the couch, but that was just what I needed, and that is just what I got. A double dose of the Savior at home with a bold young woman who was not ashamed of the gospel of Jesus Christ.

HIDE THIS NUGGET IN YOUR HEART

"...forgetting those things, which are behind, and reaching forward to things which are ahead, I press toward the goal... Press on." —Philippians 3:13, paraphrased

WHERE HAVE YOU
BEEN ALL MY LIFE

My businesses were open twelve hours a day, and I'd been pulling some very long shifts. Driving home each night was relaxing and a chance for me to unwind. One evening, I was listening to a Christian radio station and singing along.

I was overwhelmed with a sense of closeness to the Lord and said aloud, "Lord, where have you been all my life?"

That wasn't a question of doubt but a question relating the love I felt for Him, and instantly there was complete silence. It seemed as if all sound in the universe was turned off. I saw an ambulance with lights flashing, driving through the intersection in front of me, but heard no siren. I had not touched the radio dial, but silence filled the car. Then, very quickly across my mind were flashes of "picture" like scenes—the davenport in that trailer when I first got sick, saying good-bye to my dad as he left for Korea, the hospital room in the dark of night, the clown that did magic while I was in hot packs, the "stretching table" before my spinal fusion. I saw the birth of my children, worried nights when Ken was out late and had been drinking, the night he left home to live with another woman. I saw Tom with a rifle in his hand and a knife at my mother's throat and him telling me, "This is how daddies show their little girls they love them." I saw myself exercising in the pool alone and playing jacks on the playground at school. I saw the hotel room of my thirteenth birthday party, trips to the *Mispillion* and all *my boyfriends* on that ship, driving in the car laughing with Tina, going to the drive-in movies or cruising Hollywood, making ANU and installation as an officer, dancing at my prom. I realized tears were running down my cheeks as I felt His presence fill my car, fill my heart, and ease my mind from every worry and cleansing me from all the pain of the past, physical and emotional. Odd, I thought, that the times I questioned my future He was there. The times I was afraid, He was there. Times I was laughing and times I was crying, He was there but amazingly, He never showed me the times I was doing wrong, thinking wrong, or being angry.

I knew I would never be the same after that night, and I would never take His promises lightly, that He blots out my sin and remembers it no more. (Isaiah 43:25 and Hebrews 8:12.)

A song came to mind, *My Father's Eyes,* which says:

Eyes that find the good in things, When good is not around;

Eyes that find the source of help, When help just can't be found

From this verse, I was inspired and gained insight into the love of my Heavenly Father. I desired to see in others what he saw in me; and to be a source of help, when help can't be found.

I prayed that I would have His eyes as I heard Amy Grant sing and that He would give me a year of the pure Word because I so desired to know Him and serve Him.

I couldn't imagine what God would want with me or even from me. While talking with Janice, I told her I wanted to know Him more, so she offered to take me to her church. It seemed like we drove forever to get to a part of Houston I'd never been to before. She pointed to the huge flags and a sign that said Lakewood Church. John and Dodie Osteen were the pastors, and I became part of their sheepfold.

I'll never forget John saying, "Give me one year of your life, and you will never be the same."

I was sure this was the answer to my prayer in the car that night and thanked God daily for the truth of His Word. My first few services brought home the message of healing as Dodie, diagnosed with cancer, stood on the promises of God, and I would be privileged to watch and learn how to stand for healing, which would fashion my life and ministry.

One afternoon Mother called to tell me that Tom was in a hospital in a coma. She was leaving for Mississippi to see him and his family. Someone found him alone in the back of his van unconscious and bloated. Mother learned the bloating was from severe liver disease from the years of alcohol abuse. He never recovered. In his van were his valued treasures, mother's love letters with words he had underlined in red that he would never hear her say again and his expensive knives stored in a plastic five-gallon bucket. Everything else had been pawned as he stayed on his course of self-destruction. Tom was gone from our lives, and this time he wouldn't be back.

Tom didn't want to be buried in Richton, Mississippi, but that's where he would be buried, in an old country cemetery. Most of the headstones were limestone except for a few modest ones made of granite. Mother chose a large black marble slab and headstone. It looked like Elvis was the one buried there. The funeral was the typical small Southern town affair where a family member stayed at the funeral home all day and all night until the internment. Family and friends streamed in to comfort the grieving.

Mother approached the casket. She was cold even though she was wearing a full-length mink cape. The next thing we knew she was crawling into the casket with Tom. My aunt embraced her and led her away to a chair, trying to comfort her and help her regain control. Only then did I realize how much Mother loved Tom and understood why she took him back time after time.

Tom's mother, Grandma Holland, was nearly blind so she didn't realize what was going on even though she noticed that something unusual was happening.

I went to Grandma, and she touched my face asking, "Are you the girl or the boy?"

Grandma Holland was good to both Jon and I, but she really loved Jon. I'm sure she was hoping I was the boy. Jon had taken the Greyhound bus one year to stay with Grandma. That summer he came to love her and her southern ways. Grandma was so happy to see Jon again, and him just being there was a great comfort to her.

There was a commotion at the front of the funeral home. Someone had made a comment that Tom thought he was a big shot, but he had been a drunken liar and died flipping burgers at some greasy spoon.

Jon grabbed the man and pushed him to the wall, saying, "My dad was a big shot. He wore a diamond ring on his scarf to cook. He drove Lincolns and Cadillac's, had boats and homes…" Then he dropped the guy and left the room.

It was true; he was a *big shot* to us. I could see Tom laughing in his Bermuda shorts at the Salton Sea with a big cigar hanging out his mouth and a brown bag made into a hat to keep his baldhead from burning. I saw him coming through the swinging doors of the Willow Creek Inn with flaming dishes and his tall chef hat. I could see him on the back of a quarter midget racer teaching Jon to drive. He could have had so much more, but he slipped away—forgiven but alone.

Jon wrote Tom's epitaph: *Here lies a son, a brother, a husband, a father and friend—laugh now because we never cried, we had big fun until I died.* After the funeral Mother called to ask if I had heard the George Jones song, just released, "He Stopped Loving Her Today." I hadn't heard it, but when I did, she was right; it sounded as if it were written for them.

HIDE THIS NUGGET IN YOUR HEART

Key to a good relationship: follow God's example; love gives without thought of self, then *chooses* to forgive and forget.

FEELING THE HEAT
AND RISING ABOVE IT

I had a dream one night in June that a huge hurricane hit the coast of Texas and wiped out my businesses. The dream was so real that I couldn't shake it after waking. I called my insurance man and asked if there was protection for hurricanes as my businesses were on the coast. He told me about a new type of coverage called "interruption of business" and that he'd check it out for me. He did, and I signed up. The only problem was the agent found out the extra coverage couldn't be bound to my existing policy. He decided to start the new coverage when my policy renewed, which would happen in a couple of months; however, he didn't explain that to me.

My phone was ringing very late one November night. I couldn't imagine why, but the voice on the other end said that my business was on fire. The antique shop below my salon had been robbed, and the thief started a fire to cover his tracks. When the fire got into the electrical wires, it quickly enveloped a large section of the shopping center. I had fire, smoke, and water damage. I was thanking God for warning me in the dream and for the insurance policy. The next day I called my agent.

"No problem," he said. "I'll get back to you, and we'll start the ball rolling."

That was great news as my business was on a cash basis—no contracts—so being closed down meant zero income. However, my expenses would continue.

When the insurance agent called, he told me there was no protection because he was unable to bind this new type of coverage to my existing policy. Within ninety days, I was down more than two hundred thousand dollars.

I had always made my tax deposits timely, so when I was unable to make this one, I called the IRS to see what to do. They were gracious and asked for my tax ID number, which I gave them. It wasn't long before one of my managers called saying their paychecks bounced, stamped "tax levy" in red. It was Christmastime, and my employees felt they had no choice but to find other jobs. Next, my bank called my loans even though they automatically withdrew my monthly payment and I wasn't behind. I learned the meaning of the small print on a loan document that reads due *on or before* the ending date of the loan. They cashed in my CDs, deducting the interest as an early withdrawal penalty. Later, a judge made them return the interest saying it was legal but what they had done was immoral.

I was a divorced woman with too many businesses to operate, two little boys to raise, and trouble with the IRS. It was a trying time.

The storm was really blowing. In fact, one friend said she had always heard that when someone was *born again,* things like this happened. I thought about that awhile, but it didn't seem right to me. I called her later and told her that I was sure God saw this trouble in my future and knew I would need Him to get through. He was most surely there. With all that had happened, I still knew God was on my side.

Our swimming pool had turned green because I couldn't afford the needed chemicals. Then the pool vacuum stopped working and weeds overtook my planters. I was broke. I needed answers. I tried to read my Bible at night but always fell asleep with my face in it. I knew I wasn't really getting it. I was constantly calling Janice and asking her to explain things to me.

One night she told me, "Grow up, my little sister. It's time that you keep reading and ask Him these questions. You must learn to talk to God yourself. This may surprise you, but He is a better teacher for you than I am."

This sounded vaguely familiar. I was remembering my mother telling me I was a big girl and I didn't need her help.

"Okay, Janice, but can I still call you if I get stuck?"

"You can call me anytime, but I know it will be to tell me all the good things God is showing you. He wants you looking to Him, not me for the answers."

After several months, a woman from out of town was staying at my house while learning about the health and fitness business. She was petite like me, but she wore country lace western. I wore tailored clothes to work, and the only Western look I had was jeans, boots, and a cowgirl hat for playtime.

On her last day with me, she came into my bedroom while I was getting ready for work and said, "Ms. Penny, the Lord told me to give you this skirt. It's brand new, never worn."

I turned and noticed it was a Western full skirt with an unusual lace trim.

"Thank you," I said, taking the skirt from her hand, wondering why God would tell her to give it to me. I didn't have anything to wear with it. Just then, I heard a horn honking in my driveway and knew it was Mother. When I got to the car, she opened the window handing me a beautiful white blouse.

"I found this, and it reminded me of you," she said, as she was backing out. It had the exact same lace that was on the skirt.

I went back in the house and put on my new outfit. I thought to myself, *How weird is this? How could a skirt from Las Cruces match a blouse Mother bought in Houston when they weren't even made by the same manufacturer?*

Sitting down to finish my makeup, the phone rang. It was my neighbor asking if I wanted her to buy some wood chips for my front planter as she was going to the garden shop. I knew she was hinting at the mess my yard had become, but I made excuses for not using wood chips right then.

Shortly, the phone rang again. This time it was my friend, Bruce. He said, "Hey, I am picking you up for lunch." Bruce was also a friend of Janice, and a group of us met for Bible studies and had lunch together about once a month, each paying our own way.

"Oh, Bruce," I said, "I can't go today. I have appointments," not mentioning that I didn't have a dime.

"Not during lunch, you don't. I called and told the girls not to book you, so I'll pick you up at 11:30, no excuses!"

He was good to his word, arriving at my business right on time. As he opened the car door for me, I felt him pushing something in my pocket. It was cash. We had a great lunch, and I was refreshed and glad that he had insisted.

Driving home from work that night, I remembered the conversation with my neighbor and thought, "I really must do something about the lawn, but it's too dark tonight."

The car headlights showed bright on my front yard planter as I turned into my driveway. The planter was perfect with no weeds, and now it had fresh cedar chips. I opened the front gate and beheld my sparkling blue pool with its light on. As I went into the house, the kids exclaimed, "Mom, Bruce came by today and fixed the pool vacuum, and he taught us how to clean it. He brought us chemicals, and we shocked it. Doesn't it look great?"

I hugged them and told them what a great job they had done, but inside I was feeling ashamed.

I thought to myself, *My neighbors were fed up with the mess, and my friends had to bail me out of trouble.*

I took my bath and crawled in bed exhausted, then remembered I hadn't read the Bible yet. I opened it to Matthew, and my eyes fell on:

> Therefore, do not worry and be anxious, saying, what are we going to have to eat? Or, what are we going to have to drink? Or, what are we going to have to wear? For the Gentiles (heathen) wish for and crave and diligently seek all these things, and your heavenly Father knows well that you need them all. But seek (aim at and strive after) first of all His kingdom and His righteousness (His way of doing and being right), and then all these things taken together will be given you besides...
>
> Matthew 6:31-34 (Amplified Version)

Wow, that sure was what had happened to me today, I thought as I fell asleep. Janice was right. I was learning a lot. I was trying to get understanding about God, and He was showing Himself to me. I was watching Bible teaching on television and listening to great-inspired songs on the car radio. The words of the Bible seemed to be coming true. I had even started praying for some of my customers who confided in me about health problems, and they were telling me they no longer had the problem. I saw cancer healed, a goiter disappear, and a client who had five miscarriages finally carry a beautiful baby girl to term. People started calling me to pray, as there was a great witness of God's goodness with my business clients.

One day a client asked if I knew what to do about a boil. She had one in her ear.

"I don't know, but I have a friend who knows all that kind of stuff. I'll call her. I think the membrane from a raw egg..." In a little while my client called me to her exercise unit and asked, "Did you find anything out yet?"

"No, but I'll keep checking. Her line was busy." I went about my duties and forgot all about Mrs. Babin's ear, until she stepped into my office before leaving.

"I'm sorry to bother you, but could you pray for my ear?"

Ooh, I was ashamed, saying, "Of course, I can pray," wondering why I hadn't thought of it. I laid my hand on her ear and asked for healing.

"I'll call you if my girlfriend has any information about boils. Maybe it was a raw potato..."

The next day while I was driving to work, I was thanking God for healing a client's husband from the effects of a heart attack. "I healed Mrs. Babin's ear" popped into my head.

That's cool, I thought.

Again, I heard, "I healed Mrs. Babin's ear." I pulled off the road to think. What was I hearing?

Then with every fiber of my being, I heard, "Cancer is no more than a pimple to Me; it is you that makes it big."

Then I remembered John Osteen saying, "Instead of telling God about your big mountain, tell your mountain about your big God."

When I got to the office, there was Mrs. Babin waiting for me. "You will never guess..." she started to say.

"I think I know what you are going to say, Mrs. Babin."

"That the boil is gone," she said.

"Yes," I answered, "I knew it!" We both laughed as she gave me a big hug. *Wow*, I thought, *not only did the boil go away, I really did hear from God.*

219

Over the next several months, I was feeling more and more fatigued. I just didn't feel right but kept thinking I would feel better soon. John Osteen said one of his favorite scriptures was "and it came to pass." He said, "You see, it did not come to stay— it came to pass!" I took that word from my pastor and continued my hectic schedule knowing I'd feel better soon.

I liked to talk to God while putting on my makeup in the mornings, but some mornings the telephone would interrupt my God time.

"Hello," I said, feeling a bit put out.

"Hi, Penny, this is Mrs. Jones." (I had bought three businesses from her and still owed her $64,000 dollars on the note.) "We're getting ready to leave for Disney World with the children, and I felt impressed to call you."

I bet she did, I thought, but I knew I didn't have the money to make a payment. I was thinking it had been awhile since I had an afternoon with my boys and she was going on a dream vacation.

"Anyway, Penny, I want you to hear something… Did you hear that?"

"No, Mrs. Jones, I didn't. Will you repeat it, please?"

"I can't repeat it. It was your note to me for the businesses. I tore it up. I was reading my Bible last night, and the Lord reminded me that I had called you and begged you to buy my businesses. You know, I was getting a divorce, losing my home, and going bankrupt—but we're still married. We're happy. We were able to keep our home, and we have a good life. You owe us nothing, and I just wanted you to know before we left. Be blessed and good-bye."

I sat there stunned. I asked God to forgive me for my attitude as bitterness had tried to enter my heart. God's goodness arrested me and reminded me of the story in Matthew 18:23-35, King James Version, that tells of a man who owed a huge debt and asked for mercy and received it. Then that same man went out and found a man who owed him a pittance and held him by the throat demanding payment.

"Help me to never forget to give mercy, Lord, as you give mercy." Thank you, Mrs. Jones for showing me mercy!

Time seemed to pass so slowly, but one-by-one I would sell a business or make an agreement with the IRS or close a location until finally I wasn't so driven but able to see a light at the end of a very long tunnel.

I traveled for the business, supervising in other cities and states as well as becoming the company trainer, holding a school for management and owners each month. I opened a new location in Marlborough, Massachusetts, for a family that had just lost a child and needed help. I decided I would go there for a year to get them established as this was a brand new state for our company and the first location.

The boys and I flew to Marlborough to make a memory together.

Ronnie looked out the airplane window as we approached Boston's Logan Airport and said, "Mom, look, we are on the very edge of the United States of America."

In his mind, he saw the US map from his school geography book, and there was a new reality to his life. The boys' world expanded that day in more ways than one. We were soon to meet someone who would be part of our lives forever.

We met a brown-haired, brown-eyed, nineteen-year-old girl and immediately knew she was the reason I was in Massachusetts, and I knew instantly that I was going to love her. Noreen was like my own child, I adored her, and so did my children. Ronnie, fourteen at the time, asked her to marry him. She spent so much time with us; it was like having another child. The boys and I volunteered at a nursing home, and she went with us to play bingo and read. We polished nails, wrote letters, gave facials, and cooked Texas-style food for the residents. I taught Noreen and her sister about the weight-loss program, and they helped me write a training manual for the business while living in Massachusetts.

Sometimes we would crawl up on my bed and I would read the Bible to Noreen and tell her about Jesus. Other times we sang with Carmen, Amy Grant, Mike Adkins, and Kenneth Copeland with the stereo turned very loud while we cleaned house together. We talked about the words of the songs, which taught us about God's goodness and His love for us. I prayed with her to receive Jesus as Savior, and I was there when she received the baptism in the Holy Spirit.

Janice called to check on us. I shared with her regarding Noreen's salvation, and we talked about finding a church to attend in the area. She offered to contact Lakewood Church for suggestions. The church responded with a large box of materials including Bibles, books from several well-known authors, VHS teaching tapes, and pamphlets.

We were inseparable, but it was time for me to go on the road again. While unpacking, I found a letter she had tucked in my suitcase. She wrote, "If you ever really miss me a lot and you are far away or just can't get a hold of me, you can read this letter and know I think the world of you and I need you now and always will. I love you so much."

When I got home, I saw that being out of town was hard on Noreen, and I had missed her, too. I was thinking of my upcoming trip to Fort Worth. There was an annual convention I attended and wondered if I should take her with me. I asked her if she wanted to go, and her immediate answer was yes.

We stayed at a friend's house in Arlington, Texas, and had such a wonderful time. Noreen said she had never seen such a big house.

I laughed, saying, "This is *Texas*, honey." I learned she had never stayed in a big luxury hotel. That did it. I decided I would really impress her. On our last night, I booked a beautiful room in a ritzy hotel. Noreen and I made many memories like eating strawberries served in crystal bowls and breakfast in bed; it was hard to imagine ever being separated.

I was still very tired and in more pain than usual. Thinking it was all the traveling, I asked the Lord to help me find someone with a heart for our business to replace me on the road.

I had to leave town on the boys' birthday, in order to get to my next job assignment, meaning I was traveling on my birthday too. I was feeling a bit low. When I landed in West Texas, the owner of the business wasn't there to meet my flight. She'd sent someone else to take me to the hotel. Checking into the hotel, I learned the air conditioner was down and it was Texas hot. Things just weren't going well. I was in Odessa at the salon I had originally opened. A third owner was now re-opening, advertising under new ownership. They were increasing the price per session, had only one employee, and she was untrained. I would need to hire and train the rest of the team. "Lord," I prayed, "help!"

As I opened the door to the salon, the receptionist welcomed me, saying it was her second day and she didn't know a thing. I laughed and gave her a script that explained the exercise equipment and how it helped people. It was in her job description to act as a technician for all new sales. Educating the applicants on the equipment would be good practice for her. There were many appointments for interviews, but by late afternoon, I still hadn't found anyone right for the manager's position. I noticed a beautiful young blonde woman sitting in the reception room, perfectly groomed, her hair and nails, makeup and shoes; every detail was perfect. *Great*, I thought. This one would never do. I just couldn't see her getting her hands dirty scrubbing a toilet or polishing the furniture. I told the receptionist to just give her fifteen minutes on the equipment instead of the normal thirty and then bring her to my office. I was ready to visit with her a few minutes and send her on her way, knowing she was not looking for *this* job.

"Hello, Ms. Perkins," I said as she seated herself across the desk from me. "My name is Ms. Charles. I'll be happy to tell you about our program and the job opening." I noticed she placed her hands primly in her lap and shifted in her seat to one side. I asked her about the time she had on the equipment and what she thought about it. She answered professionally and then shifted again in her chair. I finally cut to the chase and asked her, "So what brought you to us today?"

She looked me straight in the eye then shifted again saying, "God."

I almost fell out of my chair. "You're kidding," I said. "I just prayed for you last night!" She was hired, and I was inspired. It seems that she had been on a modeling job earlier that day, and the woman she met there had been my unexpected ride from the airport the day before. She told Daina about the job opening, and me, suggesting she apply. Daina Perkins was perfect for the job. Not only was she a beautiful Christian woman, but she was a diligent worker not above cleaning toilets or any other tasks needed for excellence on the job. She was quick to learn the business and eager to advance in the company. I promised if she found someone and trained them to be better at her job than she was, we would promote her to supervisor.

That was all it took. The hunt was on for her replacement so she could replace me. I could hardly wait to work with her as supervisor.

It didn't take Daina long to bring a burgundy redhead into the company named Myrna. Myrna was a spitfire. Her background was nursing, and her family boasted seven generations of Pentecostal preachers. She was a gifted singer and pianist. It was certain that we would become a three-strand cord, and the friendship that developed would carry us through some difficult days while multiplying our laughter and joy.

We enjoyed good food, good music, and time in the Word. We worked, played, and prayed together as we built a strong company. Myrna was not to be left behind as sales manager. She was taught by Daina the rule for advancement; push the one in front of you and pull the one behind. She, too, was bound for the supervisor position that was rapidly becoming available.

HIDE THIS NUGGET IN YOUR HEART

A grateful heart is a position we must choose to establish, and practice on purpose, until it is spontaneous and habitual.

CELEBRATING LIFE

Weekends were times of refreshing and on Saturdays, I enjoyed pulling weeds in my yard and floating on a raft in the pool. Sometimes my kids would enjoy the day with me, but they were older now and had a network of friends of their own.

One afternoon, while walking to the pool, my legs lost all feeling, and I dropped to the ground, landing on a large clay pot and breaking three ribs. Later, the feeling returned in my legs and then amplified as a new kind of pain. It seemed my bones were in pain, not just the muscle. These incidents increased without warning. While I was bathing, suddenly I couldn't move my legs and didn't have the strength in my arms to get out of the tub by myself. At night, I would wake up with what felt like a circuit shorting out, causing a spasm in my body like a twitch in your eye. The next day I would see a "bite"-like spot where the muscle "shorted" out. I told the boys it looked like Pac Man had attacked me. My neck had been bothering me for months, but I didn't connect the two issues until I was having trouble holding my head up. My arms got increasingly weaker to the point I couldn't put my hair up or effectively apply makeup. I would get tongue-tied, and I'd slur my words. Then the symptoms would stop, but the pain and fatigue persisted.

A doctor in Arlington, Texas, held a franchise to one of our salons, and I was there helping. He was aware of my symptoms and agreed to see me. I made an appointment for a thorough check up. After he reviewed the test results, he diagnosed "post polio syndrome." I hardly knew what to think. I'd done so well for so long. In spite of a limp and surgical scars, this body had served me well. Now I was in unusual pain. The pain came and went all over my body, hips one minute, knees the next, then terrible headaches and neck aches. I was sleeping badly and suffered serious bouts of fatigue. I was getting colds and had loss of feeling in my limbs that ultimately resulted in no use of my legs. My doctor said I was using trick posture to walk. He said the spinal fusion coupled with a locking effect of my left leg allowed me to walk but medically speaking, he saw no reason I was able.

He asked, "Penny, why do you walk?"

I answered, "Because I want to."

Both of us had tears in our eyes and the doctor responded, "You must want to very badly."

The doctor explained what my future would be. He described the kind of wheelchair I would need, recommending a low flotation waterbed. He listed the medications we could try and said that I should pick the steps I wanted to take as I had very few left.

The doctor did try to encourage me, saying, "I won't rest until I find some answers for you."

I'll never forget the shock I felt when he said, "Penny, you have only a few steps left, so use them wisely. If you want to dance, then dance, but you should use a wheelchair to get from your bed to the kitchen."

I only half heard him. There were other voices, the familiar ones from my past that were ringing in my ears. "Think this muscle, Penny. ...If you'll do this, honey, you won't have to be in a wheelchair... This brace will help, and one day you may be able to take it off for good... This surgery will... Don't cry, honey, we know it hurts but one day we'll dance at your wedding... Be a good girl..." I wondered if I had been bad. Didn't I do all they told me to do?

"What do you mean a wheelchair, Doctor?" I asked in my head. What I translated was: "You have lived the best years of

your life and the rest is all downhill"—in a power chair to boot…
I was thirty-seven years old, and I cried.

I had been bold about being a Christian. I'd talked about
Jesus and His goodness to everyone, including this doctor. Now
I couldn't hold back the tears and was obviously distraught. He
cleared his throat and said, "Oh, I see, Penny. Your God gets off
the throne if you go into a wheelchair. Is that it?"

I knew, for certain, that wasn't the case. I answered, "No,
God's still on the throne in my life." I realized it was much easier
to talk about His goodness when I was walking. I needed to get a
grip on myself. He handed me the prescriptions and a follow-up
appointment.

I couldn't eat. I had "pity parties" every little bit. I vomited
constantly, a reaction to all the medications I was trying, and I
wanted to die. I begged God to take me, and when I woke up
alive, I thought of ways to take my own life. I knew I had to live,
but how God? All those years of therapy and now the doctor tells
me that I am going to be in a wheelchair. Wait. I did know how.
I knew I must take one day at a time and look to Him, not my
circumstances.

My next appointment confirmed additional physical loss.
The doctor updated me on what he discovered about post polio
syndrome. It wasn't good news, and moved by compassion, he
hugged me. The doctor's wife drove me back to the salon. We
talked about how to get healing. I told her, "I have the healer
right here with me now. I have His Word, and I trust Him." It
was so good to have people of faith all around me especially on
the days my mind would try to reason with me. In fact, I had
walked this faith walk out with Dodie Osteen when she was ill,
and now she was every bit whole. I remembered one of the scrip-

tures that Dodie stood on for her recovery: "The Lord is good, a strong hold in the day of trouble and he knows them that trust in Him. What do you imagine against the Lord? He will make an utter end: affliction shall not rise up the second time" (Nahum 1:7, 9, KJV).

Daina and Myrna were my champion prayer partners, and they massaged my hurting body, prayed, and pushed me to faith daily. I didn't want to be seen in a wheelchair, but they insisted we go shopping.

"You're going," they would say; and we went. They did everything they could to my keep my spirits up and keep my life as normal as possible.

Our company represented a facial machine that worked with probes. When the probes were placed in a tub of water with bath salts, it worked on muscles. Daina hooked me up, and I soaked, while Myrna sang "Blood Bought Church" over and over and over. "Sing it again, Myrna!" I would shout from the tub, and bless her, she would. One verse said, "Every stronghold of bondage must fall beneath my feet, every prisoner held captive must go free." I wanted to be free.

I sat in bed one night reading my Bible and came to a verse in Acts 17:28 (KJV): "in Him we live, move and have our being." I said, "Lord, I do live in you and have my being in you but I'm not moving and I want to."

The power wheelchair was special fitted, and I began using it. Mother had gotten me a Rascal three-wheeler for Christmas so that I could periscope up to reach shelves at the market or work in the kitchen. I wanted to walk and hated that she bought something that didn't match my faith. Besides, it wasn't beautiful, and I needed something beautiful just now.

When she saw the look on my face that Christmas day, she said, "Tomorrow—we go shopping." She bought me the most beautiful strand of pearls, a treasure.

Many people called or visited me and wondered what sin was in my life that would open the door for such a thing as this to happen. My thoughts about you right now would be enough to send me to hell, I mused, but I knew I had to get over people and not take offense. Gloria Copeland taught me that God doesn't make us ill to punish us for sin.

She says, "God don't rent a devil to teach His children a lesson."

One day I got a collect call from a friend in prison. A mutual friend had told him what happened to me.

He said, "Penny, I asked God why you were in a wheelchair."

"What did He tell you?" I said, with a less than lovely attitude.

I was thinking surely I didn't take a collect call to hear more religious junk when I heard Tim say, "He said if you had legs the size of toothpicks, you'd walk."

We talked for a while longer and then hung up. I had so much to think about, so much to remember about my good God. All the healings I had seen Him perform reminded me that what He did for others He would do for me. I thought about how He had never left me before, and I knew this word from Tim was a word of hope for me. I would use it as an anchor for my mind, will, and emotions.

Daina was in training to be my replacement, as I was deteriorating quickly and the prognosis for my condition was terrible. I was her training model on how to measure for loss of inches. When I started my personal weight-loss program, my thighs were twenty-seven and a half inches in circumference, and now at my structure weight, they were eighteen and a half inches. Month after month, I would lift my body up off the seat of the wheelchair for Daina to measure my thigh and say, "They are now eighteen and half inches," but this time she just looked up at me and said nothing.

"Hurry, Daina, I can't hold myself up any longer," I whispered.

"They are now sixteen inches," she said, looking me in the eye. I had lost two and a half inches of muscle in thirty days, and I was stunned. Obviously, the muscles in my legs had atrophied due to the post polio syndrome. I fell onto my seat and dismissed the class, turning the chair full throttle and hitting the double doors with the foot attachment to leave the room. Daina followed and leaned against the wall next to me as I sat there crying.

Suddenly Tim's words came back to me, and I looked up to Daina saying, "Sixteen inches sounds like toothpicks to me. What about you?"

"Yup, me too," she said with tears in her eyes.

"Daina, I'm coming out of this chair!"

We were scheduled for a management-training seminar in New Orleans that year. I was trying to believe it would be fun. Looking for the bright side, but knowing that I would miss the nightlife in New Orleans was troubling me. I knew I couldn't negotiate Bourbon Street in a power wheelchair, but I soothed myself by indulging in a pair of black high heel boots. Since I couldn't walk in high heels, I thought I could at least sit and look pretty in them. I had a beautiful black suit with a black fox fur collar. The boots had silver studs on them. Yeah, I was feeling better.

Mother opened the meeting, speaking to the three hundred-plus attendees and getting them motivated. Then it was my turn. My microphone was pinned to my jacket with the wire and battery pack attached to the back of my wheelchair. I felt good and managed to stand with my weight on my right foot while holding on to the podium. Mother took a seat in my wheelchair, and I believe intended to give me her undivided attention. She had heard me speak in training for years and she nearly wrote the book I trained on, so it didn't take long for her to get distracted.

First, she pulled out her fake fingernails and glue, replacing one she had lost earlier. Then she got her polish out and gave it a couple of coats. By now, the attendees in the front rows were trying to keep from laughing, and Daina pointed toward Mom. I smiled, thinking she would have killed me if I had done something like that. I continued speaking, when she reached in her purse and got her spritzer, giving her face a few squirts.

I couldn't resist and said, "Nelson, settle down, and pay attention."

She grinned and slapped my arm. Suddenly I saw Daina's eyes widen as Mother was studying the joystick that operated the chair (she didn't know it was on). She pulled it back, causing the chair to fly backwards at high speed, pulling the wire from the microphone and choking me. Startled she jumped out of the chair while the whole room broke out into hilarious laughter. It was definitely break time.

Because of the long hours we worked, we ate out a lot. There was a wonderful Italian restaurant near my office, which had the best fettuccini alfredo. There was a cocky French waiter named Henri that stole my heart and challenged me every time we went for lunch or dinner. He would click his tongue if we ordered something that he felt was wrong for us or if we rushed part of the meal instead of savoring each morsel. During the beginning of this trial with wheelchairs and medication, I was sick to my stomach all the time and the only food I was able to keep down was this fettuccini. Sometimes, someone from our office would order and bring it to me. Often, Henri would make a special delivery himself. Finally, he secured the recipe so I could eat fettuccini whenever I wanted. My weight had dropped to seventy-three pounds. Keeping food down was a big deal for me.

We were getting ready to expand our business into France. I asked Henri if he would mind looking over the brochure we were preparing for print.

"Madame, this is the worst translation I have ever read. You must have had a Canadian do it," he said, dropping it on the table in front of me.

He was right, but I hated to admit it.

"It has your mother's shoe size as an example of weight loss, and I'm sure that is not what you desire."

"Well," I said, "would you be interested in proofing it and making the needed corrections?"

"I can do that, but, do you think you should take your business to France when no one in your company speaks the language? Are you a fool, Madame?"

"What do you suggest then, Henri," I asked, trying not to laugh at his superior though completely correct question.

"I suggest you learn to speak French, Madame. We can start immediately."

I was terrible even at English and had no clue about verbs and such. In one lesson he said, "Today, we learn the verb 'to be.'"

As I had studied the lesson, I thought to myself, *What a horrible language this was... I be, he be, she be...etc.* I told him my thoughts. When he had finished laughing at me, he scheduled a time for the next lesson, abruptly dismissing the session.

I was embarrassed and asked the Lord that night to give me a love for the people of France, as I would never be able to learn this language without it. The next week Henri brought me a book on France, the culture, the architecture, and the people in the different areas. He brought all different kinds of pastries that his family would have on a typical Sunday morning. He brought wines and stories of the life in France. I was learning to love the French people. I hadn't mentioned the prayer to him, but I learned God could use a haughty Frenchman to change my life.

Henri was a champion in the area of celebrating life. He said I must learn one new thing every day; taste something new, hear something new, see something new, or smell something new. He taught me to have fresh flowers and a candle on my table when I ate even if I was alone. We shopped daily for food, not weekly, as was our custom. We prepared wonderful meals together with loud music in the background from every genre. We watched old movies, some with subtitles. Every class was a lesson in celebrating life, not just learning a language. Once he told me of a dream, he had. He dreamed he saw me on the top of the Pyrenees Mountains with snow skis and then I was at the bottom. He said he didn't see me ski in the dream but what other way would I have gotten to the bottom, in one piece that is. He introduced me to others from France, and a love for Europe was brewing in my heart.

Henri called me late one evening and knew I'd been crying. I was reading a book about a young Irish girl who had come to America on a ship at the turn of the century. She was ill and poor; the authorities quarantined her. The hair merchants cut off her beautiful red hair, telling her it was to prevent disease, but in fact, they stole it to sell.

"Why do you cry about that?" he asked me.

"It's awful to have someone lie to you and take away your dignity," I answered, wondering why he didn't see the tragedy in it.

"Madame, your tears do no good. It ruins your eyes and gives you a headache. Either decide to do something about a situation or forget it completely. "Now, go eat a bon-bon and dry your eyes."

He was right. Pity is never the answer, but compassion always does something. Love is a verb, an action word resulting in a deed. Here was something new to ponder from my French teacher.

When Tim told me I would walk even if my legs were the size of toothpicks, it brought me new hope. I was celebrating life as Henri had taught me, and this took my focus off my health. When you take your eyes off your problem, the problem gets smaller. I was purposing to enjoy my life, and I started noticing I was feeling stronger. Transferring from the wheelchair to a sofa, chair, or bed takes a lot of strength and energy. I noticed it was getting easier, so I started trying to do other things. I had a galley style kitchen and was able to walk from one side to the other, doing a little more each time. I then understood that healing was on the way. I had a new mindset. Instead of hoping, I knew I would get out of the wheelchair.

Before very long, I told Brian to put my wheelchair away in the garage, and I meant "the out of sight" kind of away. My mother saw me at work without the chair and called Brian. She insisted he bring the wheelchair back before I did harm to myself.

Brian answered, "Grandma, I tried, but Mom said she would drive that chair up my butt if I brought it out of the garage again."

Henri had become interested in our equipment and decided to open an office in France to represent us. During the time I was in the wheelchair, my doctor and our manufacturer designed a new exercise unit. We called it the Thera-Plex. It was especially for physically challenged individuals. This was a new market share for us, and Myrna used her medical background to oversee this division of our company.

Six weeks after I retired my wheelchair, I went to work in Germany. The next five weeks I *walked* through five countries including

France. Henri showed me the Pyrenees Mountains, but I didn't ski. I ate squid in its own ink in Spain. I saw the most wonderful tulips in Belgium. I toured Germany, dined in great restaurants, and saw the mountains of Switzerland. Being of German and French descent, my eyes were constantly searching the scenery, wanting to take in everything. I noticed while we were driving from Pau, in the distance below us, colors dancing as if in a stream.

"Henri, what's that?" I asked, pointing.

"It is a pilgrimage," he answered.

"A what?" I asked.

"You'll see." I did see, as he took me to the scene of Bernadette's visitation in Lourdes. I cried as I saw the multitudes of people waiting to go through the grotto, knowing so many needed healing in their bodies. They were the streams of color I had seen from the mountains, and they were carrying flowers. They were on gurneys, stretchers, wheelchairs and crutches and they were coming for a touch from the Master.

I remembered the scripture, in Deuteronomy 30:14, "The word is near you, even in your mouth, and in your heart that you may do it."

I was so grateful for that Word. As I walked through the grotto, I saw centuries old paraphernalia—hand made crutches and artificial limbs—things that had been left there as people received their healing. A point of contact for our faith was what I saw. Then I realized for some clients and friends, that I had been their point of contact, to stimulate their faith. For others, it's famous and anointed healing ministries and for others still, it was oil representing the Holy Spirit applied, or water from Lourdes, but the Healer is Almighty God. I knew I already had my healing. The post polio symptoms were gone. The doctor was surprised, but I was celebrating.

Henri wanted to be sure that my healing would last so he sprinkled water on me and told me "Drink deep, bébé," as we passed the spigots lined down the wall as we departed. Later that night I danced, danced, and danced some more.

HIDE THIS NUGGET IN
YOUR HEART

Search for the sweet fragrances, the rich flavors, the joyful sounds, the beauty and splendor, and the comfort of a touch in your life. *"Joie de Vivre"*

UNDERSTANDING
THE CALL

It was wonderful to be on my feet and traveling again. I once again was working as an independent supervisor. My time was my own as I could accept or decline an assignment as I wished. I had a deep desire to have more quiet time with God and to show him my gratitude for being able to walk again.

I had just returned from working in France and Germany and needed my hair trimmed. I had made an appointment at a new shop with a stylist named Robert. I was so tired I had almost decided not to go when my phone rang. It was Robert confirming my appointment. My answer was yes, I would be there. The conversation in the shop was less than desirable and Robert was right in the middle of it, the heathen. However, as soon as I was in the shampoo chair, I knew there was healing in his hands. I asked the Lord to save him so that he could minister to people while he washed their hair.

Out of the clear blue sky, he said, "My mother said I'm spiritually dead. Do you think so?"

I wondered if he read minds but answered him by saying, "Well, you are a spirit so you will live forever either in heaven or hell. It's your choice."

I thought, *Lord, this might be too subtle because he was full of questions that were bothering him.*

I went to the car to get my Bible. While retrieving it, I was reminding God that I was so tired I almost cancelled my appointment. God must have been laughing at me because I think He had set me up. Returning from my car, we talked about the Lord for the next few hours and Robert received Jesus and became my number one prayer partner.

Robert mentioned that he knew of a homeless shelter in another county that was in trouble. The pastor needed help, and the shelter needed everything. We prayed, and I started sending clothes and household goods with him whenever he went there. One day Robert called and asked if I would go with him to meet the pastor and see the shelter. We agreed to meet on a Friday night. Arriving at the shelter on time, we found it locked. The pastor had forgotten our appointment.

The next evening Robert called again. "Do you want to go the shelter Sunday morning for their church service?"

"Okay, let's give it another try," I answered.

The church was in a building next door to the shelter. It was the first time I had seen it in the daylight, and the building was such a mess I could only imagine what the hotel that served as the shelter looked like. We listened to the sermon and then visited a while with the pastor, but I couldn't get out of there fast enough. On the way home, Robert asked me what I thought. I really had no thoughts, except to send more stuff and never go back.

Myrna came to Houston for the weekend. I was really looking forward to having time with her. Robert was also Myrna and Daina's hairdresser, so we were all good friends.

Robert called, asking, "Penny, do you want to go to the shelter with me tomorrow? They're having an open house."

"Oh, Robert, Myrna is in town so I can't go," I said, relieved that I had a good excuse.

"Ask Myrna," he said. "She'll want to go."

I took the phone away from my ear and shook my head no, as I said, "Myrna, do you want to go to that homeless shelter's open house tomorrow?"

Myrna smiled real big and said, "I'd love to!"

I could have kicked her. I could hear Robert laughing. The plans were made to meet him there. Myrna's burgundy hair was beautiful that day, and she was dressed to the nines. I wore a soft pink lace suit, and we were both wearing sparkling jewelry. I had prayed that just the right people would show up and give the shelter the things it needed. However, when we arrived, we found only a handful of people in attendance. Myrna started playing the piano, and the kids gathered around. We sang, ate, and enjoyed the company of those that were there, but I was discouraged for the pastor. As we were getting ready to leave, *and I couldn't wait to go,* a little boy walked over to me.

As I bent to hear him, he took my cheeks in his hands, looked me in the eyes, and asked, "Are you an angel?"

I felt a stab in my heart and tears in my eyes, answering him I said, "No, honey, I'm no angel."

As we drove home that day, I complained to the Lord about the response to the invitations, but just as quickly as I formed my complaint, He let me know all those He called to the party were there. I couldn't figure that one out, well not right then anyway.

One night after Myrna had left town, I woke up with bile in my throat from a dream that was so real. In this dream, I was in an unfamiliar room and my children were small again. I was leaning over as I tucked them in bed and their eyes were sunken and sad. They were hungry, and I had nothing for them. In my dream, I slapped them on the face trying to erase that look in their eyes, which is what woke me. The look on my children's faces was the look of total despair. Suddenly I understood why some people would use drugs or get drunk or steal—to hide from that despair because it is too much for a person to face. I went to my living room and sat on the floor with my head on the coffee table crying. "Lord, I'll do anything you ask me to do for one year." The next day I called the pastor of the shelter and offered to help him raise money and get volunteers involved to improve the living environment at the shelter. He was skeptical but invited me out the next day.

I called Robert, and he thought it was a riot but encouraged me to go, saying, "You don't have the boys at home anymore; this is your time."

"It is my time all right, and you think spending it at a homeless shelter is what I was born to do?"

I met the pastor at the shelter office. It was even worse than I'd imagined. The full-length windows of the lobby had burglar bars on them, and there was filth everywhere. We talked about the shelter's needs and my qualifications. I was relying on my business knowledge which I was to discover later was a foolish thing to do. Before I finished for the day, I asked to use the restroom. I'd noticed a door off the office with a padlock on it.

The pastor said, "That restroom doesn't work."

Handing me a key, he pointed to room number five and said to lock it when I was finished. He warned me that no residents were to use it as he kept it ready in the event a traveling minister came through. I walked to the room and inserted the key. When the door opened, I knew this was neither my attempt to fix something nor just thanking God that I was walking. It was the room from my recent dream, and I once again knew that God had directed my path.

HIDE THIS NUGGET IN YOUR HEART

Sympathy. Empathy. Apathy. Three friends go walking, one falls in quick sand. The sympathetic friend, feeling sorry for her rushes in and they both start to sink. The empathetic friend, feels compassion and quickly finds a stick, and offers it to her friends to pull them out. The friends in the quicksand could not be apathetic and be saved, they had to grab onto the help offered. Get it?

THERE WERE GIANTS IN THE LAND

The very first day I volunteered at the shelter, a woman came in with her son, Eddie.

The mother, Effie, said to me, "He was in a gun fight last night. He'll be dead or in jail before nightfall if we don't get him off the streets."

He was a grumpy, skinny, black man with a scarf on his head, and he didn't have much to say. I gave him a hug to welcome him, telling him to sit down, so I could explain the rules. He agreed by signing the form, and I pointed to his room.

I said, "The door next to yours on the left is the kitchen. Take a shower, and meet me in there. Dinner will be ready in about thirty minutes." His mom watched as I handed him a welcome bag with soap, toilet paper, shaving gear and cologne.

Eddie strolled out of the office heading toward his room when his Mom said, "Do you expect him to bathe?"

I looked at her, shocked by the question. "Yes, I do."

Effie shook her head laughing and walked out saying, "You got a lot to learn, honey."

As I was preparing dinner, I wondered, *What if he doesn't shower?*

He was a mess, and the kids in the dining room would notice. I couldn't have rebellion the first day on the job, so I prayed he'd be cooperative. I heard the kitchen door open, and there stood Eddie, clean and taking a seat at the table.

"Okay," I said, "this is Eddie, and he's going to be staying with us." I started to put green beans on his plate, thanking God under my breath.

"I don't eat no green beans," he said, looking up at me with a fixed gaze.

I smiled that (oh, yeah) mother's smile and looked him in the eyes, saying, "You do now!" And he did. He ate every green bean on his plate.

The next morning Robert gave me a ride to the shelter. He was going to help clean the kitchen and cook while I tried to raise funds and get volunteers to do much-needed repairs.

When we arrived, I saw Eddie sitting on the grass out front. "Hi, Eddie," I said. "What's the matter?"

"My momma told the law where I was because there's a bench warrant out for me," he said.

"Well, she knows you'd be safer in jail than on the street. Looks to me like you have three choices," I said. "You can run like you want to do right now, or you can come in and wait to see if anyone shows up, or you can turn yourself in."

Turning, I called to Robert and asked him to pray with Eddie, never dreaming neither one of them thought that was a great idea.

When he had finished praying, I asked Eddie, "Do you want to talk?"

"No," he barked and gave me a look that was chilling.

That was enough for me. I turned and started toward the office. On the inside of me, I heard "Is that love?" I turned and went back to Eddie whose head was hanging down.

Taking his face in my hands and turning it upwards, I said, "Could you use a little love, Eddie?"

He looked up at me answering, "I reckon everybody could use a little love, Ms. Penny."

That was a defining moment for me, and my response was, "I give you my word this day, Eddie Miller, I'm going to love you."

Something happened on the inside of me. I felt my heart grow as one of my girl friends said, "Big enough to fit anyone in it." I had stepped into my destiny.

I went to the office, and soon Eddie joined me. He went into the kitchen and got to work cleaning and helping Robert prepare food. The property was on the edge of town, and the shelter kept pigs. Eddie slopped the pigs, rounded up the kids, and started putting things in order. Occasionally he would peek around the corner and flash me that smile I enjoyed so much.

When the pastor got in that evening, he told me I shouldn't have taken Eddie. He said that he was not interested in more residents as he had all he could handle. It wasn't long, just a few weeks, and I experienced a first when as a volunteer—I was fired. Shortly after that, he evicted Eddie.

I had heard that Eddie was on the streets again. I prayed that the Lord would send angels to pester him until he came off the streets, knowing they'd protect his life. I put the message out that if anyone saw Eddie to tell him Miss Penny wants him to come to her house. One Sunday, I heard from a man who had seen Eddie. I told him, "Please tell Eddie I have sent my angels after him and to remember love never fails."

I strung balloons criss-crossing my ceiling. On a bright pink poster board, friends and family wrote favorite scriptures and signed their names creating a special gift for Eddie for his return. I started calling him *Steady Eddie* as in "calling those things that are not as if they were" (Romans 4:17 KJV) because I knew that he would be back. Weeks passed when Brian came to my house to visit one day and asked me if I wanted him to take the balloons down. He said, "With all the air out, it looks like you have raisins stuck to the ceiling."

"No, Brian, they're not coming down until Eddie comes home or Jesus returns." So on the ceiling they stayed.

Eddie finally showed up at my house. The same man found him and brought him to me with a trash bag of dirty clothes. Eddie slept on my living room floor for three days. Every time he opened his eyes, I gave him ice cream and finally he came to himself.

"Eddie, are you sick or did you get bad dope. What do you thinks wrong?" I asked.

"Just tired. The dope wasn't bad. I just never rested. I stayed on the pipe. It was terrible. You wouldn't believe it, Ms. Penny."

I laughed and told him about sending the angels, and from that day on, he would tell others, "If she sends the angels for you, man, you might as well just give up." He did give up, and together we decided to find our own place to offer hope to the hopeless and help to the helpless.

Eddie and a friend he'd met at the shelter were looking for property for us. Eddie was telling him about our plans. It was lunchtime, and Eddie suggested they go to his mother's house to eat, as Effie always liked cooking for her son. Effie told the boys she would go to Church's (for chicken), but the guys thought she said she was going to church.

Effie left and Eddie said, "Well, let's go to my brother's. When they got there, he wasn't home. "So now where?" Eddie asked himself. "I know. Let's get barbeque at that place next door to the shelter."

While eating, they overheard a woman asking the whereabouts of the man who rented the shelter for his ministry. It was her family's property. She was saying there were plans to close the building because it was condemned and they were considering demolition. Eddie told her there was a woman from Houston she needed to meet before they made their final decision and she agreed. We met that evening. Two weeks later, September 18, 1991, the shelter I was fired from and Eddie was kicked out of, was now our responsibility. The other ministry moved to a new location, and we were ready to go. Later, we laughed as Eddie learned Effie enjoyed a big chicken dinner without him, but we knew Eddie was right where he was supposed to be, eating barbeque, which put him in the right place at the right time.

One afternoon, while bathing, I asked the Lord to give me a name for the shelter. I wanted a name that would be easy for people to remember and, of course, not give Him a bad reputation, like calling it "the Jesus place" and treating people like the devil. I laid back to relax and soon I was humming the song *In the Garden*. The words, "I come to the garden alone" were playing in my head.

Quickly I got out of the tub, hurried to dress, and then found Eddie, "We'll call it the Garden—they may come alone, but God will walk with them and talk with them, and He will tell them they are His very own."

I had $1,000 in cash when we started the shelter; we were full of hope and strong in faith. The next week the electric company came to change the service over to us; the deposit was $1,000. We stepped out with thirteen adult residents, a bottle of shampoo, half a bottle of conditioner, and one bar of soap. It seemed once we took the chains off the front gate and the burglar bars off the lobby windows, people just followed us in. I had told God I'd do whatever he asked for one year. It looked as though it was going to be a very interesting year.

Friends bought supplies, so I put together welcome bags. The women got makeup and earrings, perfume, and nail polish. We gave cologne and shaving cream to the men, with soap and toilet paper for both. It didn't matter that the water from the well was red, nor that the septic tanks were full or that my garden bathtub was really a tub in the garden. The tile was missing around it, and the wall was open to the backyard. I was in God's will, and He was making Himself big to all of us.

Out of the clear blue, Noreen and I got back in contact, and though it was more than six years since we'd seen each other, it seemed as if it were only days. She made another trip to Texas. This time she wasn't staying in a luxury hotel, oh no; nor was she eating strawberries in a crystal bowl. She stayed with me at the shelter, but I was sure we would again enjoy luxury together. I hated for the visit to end. I just knew on the inside of me that it wouldn't be six years before I saw her again.

Raising awareness about homeless people versus street people was quite a task, but I was determined to get my message across. To me the difference was that homelessness was a temporary situation brought about by divorce, loss of employment, medical emergency, or possibly some type of addiction or abuse. The people were embarrassed about their situation and tried everything they knew to do to get back on their feet. Street people on the other hand intentionally chose the subculture of avoiding responsibility, rebelling against authority, and refusing help, which carried with it accountability on their part. Mental health issues complicated many of the street people's lifestyles.

The financial support coming to us was minor, but I never doubted that God would supply our needs as there were so many promises in the Bible and commandments regarding the poor, the strangers, the hungry, the widows, and the orphans.

One afternoon I received a phone call from my pastor, John Osteen. "Hi, Penny. Are you mad at us?"

"Mad, why? What have you done?" I asked, shocked that he'd even called.

"It's what we haven't done. We haven't sent any money to you."

It took me a minute to collect my thoughts, and I replied, "I didn't expect you to since we're a Fort Bend Shelter, and you're a Houston church. I know you contribute to the care of the homeless there. Fort Bend churches should support us, but I figured you guys were praying for me."

"That is why I'm calling," he said. "The Lord told us you had passed the test. What test was it, Penny?"

Talk about feeling the pressure. I had been tested in several areas and wasn't sure I had passed any of them yet. This was John Osteen, my pastor, and I needed to answer. I said, "To never trust anyone, to only trust Him."

"That's the big one," he said. "You know, Penny, everyone wants a ministry like Lakewood Church, but they weren't there when Dodie was looking for change under the seats and floor mats in the car for lunches for the kids. Keep your eyes on Him. We're sending you a check for five thousand dollars, and we will send you five hundred dollars a month for one year."

We said our good-byes, and I wept for the joy of it, hearing that they were praying for me. It encouraged me, hearing that the Lord was talking to others about the work He called me to do. Knowing that money was going to be coming in monthly took some immediate pressure off. Of course, I knew every day had trouble of its own, but reading the center verse of the Bible, Psalm 118:8 (KJV): *it is better to trust in the Lord than to put confidence in man,* reminded me that God wants our trust in Him and Him alone. We all take this test every day.

There was a man in our area who told me it was time to start a church for our community at the shelter instead of having visiting ministers hold Sunday services for the homeless. He wanted to be the pastor. I told him as soon as I heard that from the Lord, I'd be glad to open a church.

I went to the Lord about it, and the only answer I got was "This is the church, twenty-four hours a day, seven days a week." There were many wonderful places to worship all around us, but this was God manifesting Himself to the "least of them, in men's opinion" (Matthew 25:40 LBV). We did have services every Sunday with visiting clergy from all around our city. I believed that when our residents moved out of the shelter they would need a home church in their new community and what better way to build relationships than by inviting others into our world. Sadly, the man who wanted to be the pastor was offended, and he told some of our residents he would have me closed down in two weeks.

There was a nasty newspaper article written about us, full of lies and half-truths meant to shut us down, and reading it, I was certain it would work. A local pastor read the article and came to me immediately sharing the Word and praying for me. The next thing I knew that article brought our needs to the attention of the community and caused more than a hundred churches, businesses, and civic groups to walk on our property and work to improve it. Every denomination working side-by-side, full of joy in the work and realizing as one minister said, "We have more that we agree on than what we don't."

We were so successful at improving that condemned property, the owners sold it out from under us. A court order was served, telling us we had only ten days to move. We had over seventy residents. One resident was diagnosed with terminal cancer two days earlier, another was about to deliver an "at risk" baby any minute, and there were no other shelters in our community to receive these people.

Churches offered rental programs and paid for apartments for some of the families. Others helped them rent mobile homes, and one man offered his commercial building to us to use for offices until we could relocate. To some, "out of sight was out of mind," but we never missed a day's services to our community or even missed a phone call.

I had no idea how to continue or where to start again, but a woman from Houston had dropped by to meet me on her way to her ranch one afternoon.

Before our visit was over, she called her accountant and said, "Send a check to the Garden for five thousand dollars to start a transition fund." Her name was Joanne King Herring. That fund gave me direction and confirmation to go forward. Then others started coming to join their faith with us. We were able to purchase an old hotel in downtown Rosenberg. This hotel was much smaller and didn't include additional land, so we bought a building in the old downtown business district as well, opening a resale shop. We called the store, the Garden Emporium. Donated items raised money, which allowed us to help many people in the community and helped offset the expenses for those living at the Garden.

Eddie moved into the new location with the other men from the shelter, and they started the necessary improvements with the help of a chief volunteer, some church groups and youngsters from the local schools. Another group of volunteers went to work on the store.

I made an office and a small bedroom midway through the building, and I had a medical unit there for continued exercises on the Thera-Plex.

Cajun Jim, an Alcoholics Anonymous member, brought a donation from the association my first day at the Garden and became a huge part of our lives, and precious to me from then on. He built a raised platform so the water would drain properly and I could bathe in an antique-footed tub. He built a New Orleans-style back porch where we could eat crawfish and listen to good music when we closed the store at the end of the day.

The Garden needed everything, but the biggest problem was the plumbing, and every penny of the donated money to relocate was wrapped up in other renovations. We dried out the Garden Emporium, which had sitting water in it. It was thoroughly cleaned, painted, and decorated. When we finished, we celebrated by having a street party with a Cajun band. All the stress and physical work to move our shelter, remodel the two new locations, and keep the financial support it had taken two years to build coming in, I found myself back in a power chair. I was determined it was not going to slow me down. I was soon to learn more help was on the way. Noreen decided to move to Texas and make a fresh start for her and her little girl. She volunteered at the Emporium, making her home with Kaye, my medical assistant.

I had been invited to speak to a group of children at a Christian school before the holidays about homelessness and what we as

Christians should do about it. At the end of the speech, I met a lovely woman from England who asked questions about our work and took information on how to contact us. A few weeks later, she brought her daughter to meet me. They brought two turkeys for our dinner table, shared some ideas on raising money at the Emporium, and left—mentioning what great faith I had.

I might have been full of faith, but it didn't look as though we would have the renovation completed in time for Christmas. A church put together a wonderful Christmas party at a community building, and we were soon ready for the New Year to usher in our newly remodeled hotel.

By spring, the work on the hotel property had advanced quickly, and we were ready for the major plumbing renovation—a big outlay of money; in fact, every penny we had left. May was always a difficult month for us because funds were short and volunteers were traveling or adjusting to the summer schedules with their children. I was busy at my desk when one of the volunteer coordinators came in and informed me that the plumber had come back on site during the night and stolen all the supplies and left town.

This was not my finest hour. I dropped my head on the desk and thought, *It's over.* I was sure I couldn't go on. The money was gone; I was tired in my body and mentally exhausted from trying to keep everything going. I had precious times with the Lord, but at this moment, I was sure that I had missed Him completely, and I had overstayed my call. Maybe I should have ended it on that year anniversary. Surely, someone smarter, richer, and stronger would never have found themselves in this situation. I cried all my makeup off and was lower than a Texas snake's belly. I turned in my chair, looking at the front of the Emporium through a two-way mirror and noticed my friend from England talking to the manager.

"Kaye," I said, "please go out there and greet her, but don't bring her in the office. I'm a mess, and I wouldn't want this to hurt her faith. She thinks I'm so strong." Before Kaye could get out the door of my office, my friend had left.

Coming back, Kaye said, "She asked us to give you this card, Penny. She didn't ask to see you."

Taking the card and opening it, I read, "Dear Penny, this has been in the works for months but just came through after a big delay. Please don't send us a thank you note as God asked us to do this, but we'll need a tax receipt for my husband. We pray that God multiplies this like the fishes and loaves to make a way for many." Her handwriting was so small that I had trouble reading with my swollen eyes, and then I turned the check over and gasped.

"Does this say eighteen hundred dollars or eighteen thousand?"

Everyone looked and agreed it was $18,000. Just the amount I needed to complete this phase of renovation. The part of her note that kept ringing in my ear was "This has been in the works for months." God still had a plan for me.

HIDE THIS NUGGET IN YOUR HEART

Purpose to love. Love is a decision that bears great reward. Love never fails.

DREAMS REDEEMED

Cajun Jim was faithful to help me with the shelter. One day he received a phone call from a friend who told him that his best buddy, Wayne, had been shot in the throat and was now a quadriplegic. The bullet had severed his spinal cord. He had been working in North Carolina when he was shot and was just now being released from the hospital to go back home to Louisiana. Jim had been telling me stories about his "wicked" life with his friends since we met, as only a Cajun can tell a story. But now (showing his good heart) he was so concerned about Wayne that he was determined to find him and even go visit him, if possible. At last, he got Wayne on the telephone. Wayne being back in touch with his rowdy friends didn't please his father.

John L. Robichaux was a retired chief of police and had enough of ole Jim years before. Nevertheless, he loved his son and could deny him nothing in his condition. Jim and Wayne talked on the phone daily, and though Wayne's voice was very soft, he tried hard to communicate. Wayne would say something about God and Jim would tell him about me, and that I could talk to him about God. He, also, told Wayne that I had a machine that exercised crippled people and that the machine had helped get me out of the wheelchair. I talked to Wayne and enjoyed hearing his story, how he had been born again the night he was shot. Wayne said he walked into the house and saw his girlfriend sitting there waiting for him. Because she was a jealous woman, she was suspicious and mad. They had been working on a twelve-pack after not drinking for fourteen months.

Wayne explained, "I knew she was upset but I didn't know she had my gun. She raised the gun and pulled the trigger. I fell over on the couch facing in, lying there bleeding but still conscious. I'm a real calm guy, so I started talking to her, and I convinced her to call for help."

"What did you say to get her to do that?" I asked, amazed.

"Well, I knew she had another bullet in my gun, but my face was turned into the couch so I couldn't see her. I said I would say it was an accident, and it worked. We didn't have a phone, so she went to a neighbor. While she was gone, I started talking to God and said if you are real, God, and can hear me, please help me. I promise I'll never do anything that I know would bring shame to you."

One night Jim asked if he could go and get Wayne and bring him to the Garden for a while to see if my medical unit, the Thera-Plex, would help him walk again. I said that would be fine, but I would need to know what Wayne's needs were so I could prepare for him.

On the drive back to Texas, Wayne said, "Jim, don't drop me in the grease, man. I can't even wipe my own butt."

They had been together for years, but not one of those years had been sober. Jim had been in recovery just over four years, and Wayne said he hadn't had a drink in fourteen months until the night he was shot.

"Tough way to quit," he said with a false laugh.

That twelve pack he shared with his girlfriend changed his life forever. Jim promised to get him to Rosenberg safely and knew that Kaye, the medical assistant, Big Eddie, and I would be able to help his friend; in fact, he depended on it.

I was finishing up in the office and had the overhead lights on. All the other lights were out in the store and it was a black night. Jim maneuvered Wayne out of the car and loaded him into the wheelchair, pushing him to the back of the Emporium to my office. We had set up a hospital bed in the Emporium and hinged three doors together, covering them with fabric to make a room divider for privacy. The shelter did not yet have a ramp or doors wide enough for a wheelchair to pass through. It was built in Bonnie and Clyde's heyday. Local folklore had it that this hotel was their favorite hangout in town.

I heard Jim's voice as he neared my office. As I looked up, Kaye opened the door.

Jim rolled Wayne in, and I waved at him, saying, "Hi, I'm Penny, and I am in charge of Bible study and rehabilitation."

Immediately, Wayne asked Jim to pull him outside into the hall again. I thought that perhaps the lights were too bright for him. I asked Kaye to turn the ceiling lights off, leaving just the lamp on my desk lit. They came back into my office, and we visited until bedtime.

I had never been involved in the care of a quad, but Wayne had the greatest sense of humor, a huge hunger for the things of God, and he was great at putting others at ease regarding his condition. To get him ready in the morning, it took a team. He had to be shampooed, shaved, dressed, and fed, then taken to work. Everyone had to work at the Garden. Wayne sat next to the cash register and visited with the shoppers who came by. He helped with ideas on how to fix things, and he encouraged the residents who worked in the store. He oversaw the disbursement of the donated items. He told stories, giving his own testimony. When people complained about having to do something hard, he would say, "Okay, let me do it. You sit in this chair awhile."

They would say, "Oh, Mr. Wayne," and then would stop complaining.

He thanked all the volunteers, and those who donated items for resale, telling them when the items sold that the proceeds went to the mortgage, food, and utilities. He was great at this job, but Wayne was not satisfied; no, he wanted more, much more. I could see that in his eyes.

For Wayne's first Sunday with us, I thought we'd better go to a small church in town where I had friends to help get him out of the car and into the church. Lakewood Church was more than an hour away and huge. It would be better to start slow and get some practice.

Wayne called me Saturday night on the intercom and said, "Are we going to church tomorrow?"

"You bet," I answered.

"Do you know of a man named John Osteen?" he asked.

"I do. He's my pastor."

"Well, I saw him on television when I was in the hospital. I thought if I ever got to Houston, I wanted to go to that church. Is that where we're going?"

I laughed. "It is now."

Lakewood church, often called the "Oasis of Love," is a drink of water to a thirsty soul. At the end of the service, Wayne wanted Dodie Osteen to lay hands on him and pray so I pushed him to the front of the church, just barely out of the wheelchair myself. Dodie embraced me and asked about my mother, and then she met Wayne. I told her Wayne asked for prayer. She sat on the arm of his chair and took him to herself, embracing him and praying for him. The gift of compassion is obvious in her, and she is gifted with a memory for people by name and their particular situations.

She sent handwritten thank you notes by the thousands, which made her my thank you note hero and an example of excellence to everyone. Wayne knew he'd found his church.

From the beginning, we put Wayne on the medical exercise unit twice a day. He couldn't wait to walk and would have taken a session five times a day if it would have helped. I was in charge of manicures, pedicures, massage, facials, and feeding dinner to him after a long day. Not to mention the nursing care involved in a bowel program required for anyone confined to a wheelchair. We became fast friends with such constant and personal contact.

Wayne could move his thumbs in and out like crab pinchers and had a good grip but still needed hand therapy and healing. I would ask, "Wayne, how do you want me to pray today? Something specific?" I would wait while he thought.

"Will you pray for my hands?

"Sure." Getting my bottle of anointing oil, I would apply it to the affected area and then pray, thanking the Lord Jesus for hearing and answering our prayers.

On July 17, 1994, Kaye was preparing Wayne for bed, and he had asked me to pray. He said to pray for anything I liked but to include that he wanted to "feel" God in his body and soul as he did during worship at church. I was praying that God would give me a Word especially for Wayne, to encourage him and speak directly to him, as he had hit a hard place emotionally.

Wayne's hospital bed was in the front section of the Emporium. He could see out the windows that spanned thirty feet. Many nights he waited to see the sunrise, unable to sleep. He told me he was walking in all of his dreams, so when he awoke to a new day, he was shocked that he couldn't move.

Some mornings residents would come early to open the store and forget to lock the door behind them. This left Wayne exposed to people staring at him and the urine bag hanging on the side of his bed. He would close his eyes and swallow the shame he felt. He told me that he was sorry he had taken so much for granted in his life, like the feel of water from a shower running down the length of his body or the cold floor on the bottom of his feet in the morning when he got out of bed.

In church, however, Wayne was free in the spirit. The hair on his arms would be standing up as he reached his hands up in worship. "Even my body responds to the Holy Spirit in praise," he would say with tears of joy in his eyes. I knew the Lord would help me, and He did—leading me to:

> O God, You are my God, *early will I seek You*; my soul thirsts for You, *my flesh longs for You* in a dry and thirsty land, where no water is; *To see Your power and Your Glory, as I have seen in the sanctuary.* Because your loving-kindness is better than life, my lips shall praise you. *I will bless you while I live; I will lift up my hands in Your Name.* My soul shall be satisfied as with marrow and fatness; and my mouth shall praise you with joyful lips; *when I remember you upon my bed, and meditate on you in the night watches.* Because you have been my help, therefore in the shadow of your wings I will rejoice.
>
> Psalms 63:1-7 (AMP)

"Wayne, the Lord showed me a scripture that was prayed by David and recorded in the book of Psalms asking the same things you have."

He was surprised as I read it to him. It fit so well. He was beginning to see himself in the Word of God.

The next day we continued our routine, and in the evening after bath time, we put Wayne on the exercise unit. I had a thin piece of foam rubber under him and a beach towel over the foam for safety. Wayne couldn't feel, so there was no way to know if the cushions pinched him. He hadn't seen the unit without the towel over it and didn't know how it worked. I was sitting on his wheelchair next to the unit reading to him from a book, *The Name of Jesus*. Every once in a while I would stop to check on him, perhaps move his leg into a better position and continue reading until the timer on the unit stopped. At the end of the treatment, he very calmly said, "Are there different moving parts under my back?"

"Yes," I answered, "how did you know?"

"I can feel it," he said.

"Feel it, for how long?" I shouted.

"Since the very beginning of this treatment," he smiled.

"What? Why didn't you say something? How could you be so calm?" I yelled, jumping up and calling everyone while he laughed at me.

It was a hot Texas night, and the Emporium didn't have air conditioning except in my office and bedroom so we had moved Wayne's bed into the office in front of my desk. After this treatment, we laid him on his stomach, and I rubbed powder on his back. I was overcome with joy for this answered prayer. I laid my face against his back, and had just gently moved my cheek while I silently thanked God for His faithfulness in answering our prayer.

"Is that your nose or your finger on my back?" he asked.

"My nose." I laughed and realized that he was able to feel even a gentle touch. We wrote the date next to Psalm 63:1-7 in his Bible. July 17, 1994, the day Wayne felt Him in his body.

It was time for the annual Southwest Believers Convention. I had always attended, but this year with Wayne, I couldn't take a week off, or so I thought. Wayne asked if I was going to Fort Worth, and I answered, "Not this year."

Wayne said, "I was kind of thinking I'd like to go. I think it would be great to have Gloria Copeland pray for me."

Then he said, "I have a check coming, and I would pay you to take me," as if I needed to be paid. I immediately checked to see if we could get a room near the convention center that would handle Wayne and be in our budget. I wasn't going to miss the convention after all. In just a few days, off we went on our first long-distance adventure.

Wayne had never been involved in anything remotely like this convention, but he was quick to receive. He laughed until he cried with Jesse DuPlantis, a Cajun preacher that spoke to his heart in a sermon called "Fits of Carnality. Have you had one today?" Jerry Savelle touched him with that "*never quit*" message that Wayne needed to hear. He was pressed to grow in the things of God when Ken Copeland preached on living a pure life. Then Saturday morning arrived. Ms. Gloria preached on healing, giving the day to the scriptures that Wayne so desired to hear. She prayed for him, and he quietly received strength. I know he wanted to jump out of the chair and walk. He had dreamt of that since he heard the Word on healing. Later, he cried at the hotel as we packed to leave, telling me that the anniversary of his injury was two weeks away and the doctors had told him that whatever he could do at the end of the first year would be all he could expect for recovery.

"Well, that's not what Doctor Jesus said," I answered, taking the suitcase to the car. The ride home was quiet, but a peace settled on him, and I knew that we were going to see changes. Little by little, we would take our mountain.

Mother called from San Antonio to talk to me about a noise in the Thera-Plex, and I said, "I have a guy here that is so sharp. He was a pipe fitter, welder guy. Let me ask if he knows what that is, and I'll call you back." I asked Eddie if he thought he could get Wayne under the unit to check something out. Eddie came up with a great idea. We put him on a sheet to make it easier to move him, put a little flashlight in his mouth, and pulled him under the unit.

A few minutes later we heard him grunt, indicating he'd seen enough so we pulled him back out taking the light out of his mouth.

"I could build that," he said.

Something on the inside of me was sure he could.

"Mother, this man said he can build the unit. If you're interested in hearing his ideas, we'll take a ride to San Antonio to talk to you about it."

The minute Mother met Wayne, she made a connection. She visited with him about the equipment and the problems she was having and listened to his ideas about improving it. As we were preparing to leave for home, Mother put her head in the window and kissed Wayne good-bye, sealing the deal. I laughed to myself watching that farewell kiss. Cajun Jim said in their younger days he called Wayne "Elvis" because they had to beat the women off with a stick. Obviously, he still had the knack.

At four o'clock, every afternoon Wayne would come in during my break and massage my neck and shoulders as his part in *giving back* since I massaged his hands and worked his fingers teaching him to *think this muscle*. Sometimes he'd pull up next to my office chair, and I'd lay flat across his lap so he could rub my back with the heel of his hand. He'd tell me about his day.. One day he mentioned that he told God he would gladly stay in his wheelchair if God would strengthen me and keep me out of mine forever. "Wayne, I have some very good news for you. Jesus took the stripes on His back and went to the cross so you and I could both come out of our wheelchairs. You don't have to sacrifice. He already bought our healing; He was the perfect sacrifice, so get yourself ready to walk."

Wayne was a real prankster and usually full of good cheer, but of course, there were days when he regretted the loss of mobility more than other days. I saw a look in his eyes one afternoon and asked if there was anything I could do to help him.

His answer was, "Yes, please don't let anyone see me naked again but you."

I didn't expect that answer; however, I understood completely. I had been studied, probed, poked, and handled by people all my life while regaining my health, so helping him maintain his dignity was not a problem for me. Wayne couldn't afford a caregiver and really didn't want anyone to help who reminded him he was "needy"; no, he wanted personal care from a fun and playful helper. He wanted to forget he was not physically whole, and he wanted a trusted friend. Actually, Wayne knew from the beginning that he wanted much more than that. He hoped to be whole again. He hoped for a full healthy relationship. I didn't understand what this commitment would mean, but I made a promise and I intended to keep it.

Wayne came to Texas wearing large, baggy pants to make it easier for someone to dress him. Wayne, not being able to help lift his body gave a new meaning to "dead weight." As soon as he had evoked that promise from me, he said he wanted to wear jeans, cowboy boots and more tailored shirts—Western was optional. We got him boot-cut jeans. I'd grab the leg bag and a diaper, for extra protection, socks and boots. There was grunting, pushing, pulling, and laughing as our Cajun cowboy suited up for his day. I was sure that God knew how handy that fusing my spine would be, allowing me to act like a crane to lift Wayne. I bent from my hips and said, "Grab around my neck, Wayne. Here we go," as I brought him into a sitting position. "One slide board comin' up," I would say as I placed it under his butt making a bridge between him and his wheelchair so I could slide him over. "Whew, that was work," I said as I started to pack his "man bag" for the day. Let's see, keys, sunglasses, water bottle, money, to-do notes, and...

"Don't forget some candy," he said before I finished zipping the bag.

"Okay, now what do you want for breakfast?"

The head of Wayne's bed bumped up to the front of my desk, making a solid workstation for me while dressing or undressing him. One night I was soaking in the tub thinking about how precious Wayne had become to all of us. What an inspiration he was to the residents in the Garden as he prepared to open a manufacturing shop. Just then, I remembered Kaye was sitting with Wayne, and I was sure she wanted to go home. It was time for his nightly reading, from E. W. Kenyon's book *The Name of Jesus.* I got out of the tub, wrapped my wet hair in a towel, and put on pajamas with a short, boxy top. Wayne was in bed so I turned the bright office lights off and adjusted my reading lamp so that I could sit on his bed and read. Kaye said she had to run an errand for Wayne and would see us later. That night's chapter was about the cripple who sat at the Gate Beautiful in Acts 3. I was bent forward under the small lamp reading, and my heart was touched as I read the part saying, "He sat at the gate in his own dirt," thinking of Wayne wearing diapers, when I felt a strange sensation rush through my body. At first I thought I was being touched by the Word as sometimes happens when you are receiving revelation, but this was not one of those times or feelings. No, Wayne had tried to walk his hand up my back to massage it while I was reading. When I realized what had happened (I hadn't felt like that since I was a teenager), I jumped off his bed, threw the side rail up, grabbed the fan that was hooked on the bedrail, pointed it toward my face, and started acting like I was drying my hair.

"What happened?" he said with shock and concern on his face.

"Don't ever touch me without telling me first," I said, thinking that my voice sounded harsh.

"I'm sorry, Penny. I just remembered I hadn't rubbed your back or neck and thought it would be all right. It never bothered you before," Wayne explained.

"Well, well, I, I…" I said.

What was happening to me? I wondered.

"I was ready before. I knew you were going to touch me."

I finished the reading and left for my room when I heard Kaye calling my name. She handed me a cassette tape that Wayne had asked her to buy for him to give to me. It was Dolly Parton's "I Wish You Love." I understood the words of the song that said, "I'm not what you need," and it troubled me because I didn't want Wayne to feel as if he were a burden since I had felt that way so many times in my life. I went to bed and listened to the whole cassette. Suddenly, I remembered that I hadn't cracked the door to my office, and Wayne would freeze unless some of the cold air could pass into the hallway. Temperature was a problem after his spinal cord was severed. His internal thermostat didn't work properly. Pain registered as cold to Wayne, so I was always making adjustments based on the air temperature. When it was too hot, his temperature would spike, and we would have to put ice on him; too cool and he'd be in terrible pain. Quietly, I pushed his door open a crack to slide in a doorstop.

"Is that a poodle I see?" He laughed as he saw my hair piled up and curly, sticking through the door near the floor.

"I forgot to put the door stop in," I said.

"Will you come in and talk to me a minute?" he asked. "Or am I still in trouble?"

"No, you aren't in trouble. Do you want me to read to you some more?"

"No, just talk to me."

"Thanks for the cassette. It was a beautiful gift, and I really enjoy listening to Dolly."

I noticed he seemed uncomfortable and thought maybe it was time for his every two hour turn to prevent bedsores.

"Do you need to move into a different position, Wayne?" I asked, getting ready to adjust him.

"I want up on my arm. Can you help me do that?"

"Let's give it a shot," I said, climbing up on the bed in order to be able to turn him. Wayne was now lying on his side, so I lay down on the edge of the bed so I could face him. He was propped up like a guy on the beach. We both wondered how long that would last, but he was looking completely whole and stable for the time being. A few minutes later, I thought he was falling over, but I was wrong. He was leaning over, and he kissed me—a long, slow, and wonderful kiss.

"Wow," I said, "you sure can kiss."

"I know." He smiled a wicked little smile. "That's what got me shot."

I'd heard the story of the shooting bit by bit during the time we talked on the phone when he was still in Louisiana.

He told me that the prognosis during recovery was bleak. A nurse even said to him that he'd never hold a woman in his arms again as she put pillows between his arms, saying you need to get used to this instead. Regardless of the medical report, I could see that Wayne had hope, hope that he would accomplish something worth-

267

while, and he was ready to begin. Of course, recovering from something as devastating as his injury took longer than he expected. After the hospitalization, he went through rehabilitation to help adjust to the limitations and special needs of a quadriplegic. It was months before he could return to his father's home in Louisiana. He knew very quickly that he wouldn't thrive there and was trying to figure out what life held for him. That was about the same time Jim called him to say he could come to Texas to try the medical unit.

Wayne said, "Pick me up June third. I'll be ready."

June third came quickly. John L concerned about his son's safety, followed Wayne outside while Jim was loading the car, and asked, "Wayne, why do you want to go to Texas?"

He answered saying, "To get a woman, Daddy."

John L shook his head and said, "Your womanizing days are over, boy."

I laughed just thinking about John L and thought this was the perfect time to say goodnight as it was now the wee hours of the morning.

I was having trouble sleeping after that. I was concerned that I had given Wayne the wrong idea and if so, he might get hurt. On the other hand, what if I had feelings for him that he wasn't prepared to deal with; I pondered and prayed about the situation, finally dozing off in peace.

The next morning Wayne gave me a picture he had of the two of us taken the first night at Lakewood Church and asked that I'd send it to his Dad with a note: "I got the boss, Daddy."

"You're a mess, Wayne Robichaux," I said as I addressed the envelope for him.

I wasn't looking to fall in love with anyone. I married Ken because he was safe, or so I thought. When he cheated on me, I felt unworthy, thinking the defects of my body were the problem. These feelings of rejection coupled with the violation by my stepfather taught me that any physical relationship was of no value. Then, too, my mother's voice rang in my ears, "Sex is a poor man's opera." I do not know what gave her that attitude, but at this stage of my life it seemed as right a theory as any other. Involvement in physical relationships seemed to hold little reward. I'd never really had a healthy relationship so I didn't understand the feelings I was having toward Wayne or the feelings he was stirring in me. Besides, I was full, or so I thought, with the Garden and the fulfillment that came from loving my residents and all the fabulous volunteers and friends that I'd made, but I was to find out over the next few months that God had a wonderful surprise for me.

Kaye had been sent on another late night errand for Wayne. This time the cassette was by Randy Travis, and the song titled "On the Other Hand." Wayne gave the cassette to me saying, "Listen to the words."

> "On one hand, I count the reasons I could stay with you and hold you close to me, all night long. So many lovers' games I'd love play with you and on that hand; I see no reason why it's wrong. In your arms I feel the passion, I thought had died—When I looked into your eyes I found myself, when I first kissed your lips I felt so alive, I've got to hand it to you girl, you're something else."
>
> Artist: Randy Travis Album: *Storms of Life,* written by Paul Overstreet

At the end of the song, he said, "I don't have a ring on my other hand, but I want to put one on your hand. Will you marry me?" So many thoughts went through my mind, but I knew in the very center of my being that God had brought us together. I remembered that soon after he came he told me he was useless, and I told him to see himself through my eyes until he could see his value.

My answer was yes. I saw that twinkle in his chocolate eyes that melted me. I knew we had connected on a level where together we could get through anything that came against us and together we could take on the world. We were whole in each other's eyes. We didn't see limitations in each other but on the contrary understood the possibilities.

"I always wanted me a blue-eyed blonde," he said. "In fact, I prayed for you once."

"Once? You need to pray for me every day, man," I answered, laughing at him and settling into his arms.

"I'm serious, baby," he said. "I was sitting in my father's backyard in Louisiana. It had taken him more than three hours just to get me dressed and ready to sit in the sun. I had a little New Testament Bible that I could hold, but I couldn't lift my arms enough to read the words. I could read my big Bible, but I couldn't hold it. I was able to move so little, a wild bird landed on my shoulder. I said, 'Lord, look at me, even this bird thinks I'm a statue. If you want me to know you, you're going to have to give me a good Christian woman who will teach me your Word.' I knew the very first night I arrived that you'd be my wife."

"Oh, sure you did, you honey dripper, you. I remember, you couldn't get out of the room fast enough that night."

"I know. I asked Jim to wheel me out so I could thank God for you. I wanted Him to know you didn't have to be beautiful, but I was sure glad you were."

"There you go again, Elvis, just like Jim said you would."

HIDE THIS NUGGET IN YOUR HEART

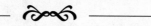

Leave room for God... "For he is able to do exceeding abundantly above all that we ask and think..." —Ephesians 3:20, paraphrased

DISCOVERING
OUR DESTINIES

We weren't going to rush into anything. We had both been married before, and we weren't successful at it. In fact, we studied the Word; we read Christian books on marriage and listened to good teachings on the subject. Wayne was also worried that I may have regrets, and he asked me about that one day.

"Are you sure you won't regret this? You know, I'm a lot of work, and you have so much to do now."

I thought about that and answered, "I only have one regret, Wayne, that we won't raise a child together. With the love we have for God and each other, what an environment that would be for a child to grow up in. The things I do for you are a joy, and God gives me strength. Just remember when you are walking, you can carry me. Deal?"

"I can't wait to do more than that, baby," he said, giving me that smile.

Wayne had once mentioned that he and his dad had never said they loved each other, not one time. Not long after Wayne moved to Texas, we made a weekend trip to Louisiana to his hometown so his father could see how well he was doing.

Wayne asked me to anoint his daddy with oil and pray for him before we left.

"Penny, you know my momma was Catholic, and Daddy was sure he would get to heaven because of her," Wayne said. "Maybe you could put a little cross on his forehead with the oil so it won't scare him. You know like the priests do on Ash Wednesday with the ashes?"

Wayne was already in the car, and I realized he was hoping I wouldn't include him in this prayer session, in case his father didn't like it. I asked John L to come with me to the car so we could pray. As we approached Wayne, I could see he was timid about this. I told John L his son had said he had admired his father all his life and had told me that his father was such an honorable man. I anointed John L as Wayne asked and told them to hold hands with me because I liked to touch when I prayed. John sat on the doorframe of the car as I prayed; holding my hand and facing his son, he took Wayne's hand.

After the prayer, he gathered his son in his arms and drew him to his chest, they both cried and said, "I love ya, boy," and "Yeah, me too, Daddy. I love you." I cried as I watched the healing God was bringing to this father and son. For months after that trip, they would talk long hours on the phone, and it was like two lovers, cooing and telling each other how much they loved each other. It was amazing.

Our kids were rallying to our side. Jade, Wayne's son and his wife Geraldine moved to Texas to be close to Wayne. When I first met Geraldine, I immediately loved her big time. She was a hard worker, eager to learn and had been the one that flew to North Carolina to learn how to care for Wayne when he got home from the hospital. She was an exceptional young woman. She helped me at the Emporium while Jade helped his dad build a shop. Together Brian and Jade remodeled a building to house the shop.

Since Noreen had moved to Texas she and Ronnie were discovering that Ron had been right at fourteen; they were falling in love, and he said, "You should have listened to me then, Noreen." It seemed like love was in the air.

Jade and Brian agreed to help Wayne open the shop to start production of the Thera-Plex units. Someone in Louisiana heard about the work Wayne was doing and sent him a three-wheeler to use until he got a power chair or he walked. Wayne wanted to have just the right name for this manufacturing division of the Garden and after much research on words and plenty of praying, he called it "Ability Unlimited." He'd soon be building the very unit he'd hoped would bring his recovery when he first came to Texas.

The property that Wayne negotiated and acquired for his shop was just down the street from the Emporium. Once our boys tore down some walls and built the manufacturing shop portion, we had enough room for a small apartment on the end. Wayne's father had been ill off and on for some time. Since Wayne was settled, we prepared the apartment so John L could live with us permanently. John visited with us for several weeks during the time we were putting the shop together. He enjoyed helping Wayne in his new business. I laughed as his dad answered the shop phone one day, "Ability Unlimited, you've got the big knocker."

I said, "Will you have the little knocker call me when he has a minute, John?" That evening while I was getting Wayne ready for bed, I mentioned, "I love your secretary."

Wayne said, "Awe, he's no good, baby. He didn't even tell me you called until almost an hour later." Shaking his head with that smile that said he was so glad to have his dad with us.

Everyone downtown knew John L. He was having a big time visiting the businesses, telling stories about WWII, police work, and the business his boy was building down the street.

One of the health problems he had was diabetes. After we gave John his medications in the morning, we would have to check his shirt pockets to make sure he took each tablet. I would come up close to him and peek in his pocket.

"You got a search warrant for that?" he would say, making me laugh. We enjoyed him so much but told all the merchants to watch him closely for us because he would sneak sweet treats. After that, the merchants would call us by the end of day to say they had given him a cookie, cake, or pie, which meant he couldn't con sweets from me at dinner.

During John's visits to Texas, we had our regular prayer nights. The prayer time Robert and I had started had grown to a large group, and one night Daddy joined us. Before the evening ended, we were preparing to take communion. I asked John L if he had ever asked Jesus to be his Savior.

"No, Bay, I never did."

"Would you like to now?" I asked.

"Yeah, I want Him," he said.

We all prayed with John and welcomed him into the family of God. We took communion together.

Wayne had promised his father that once he moved to Texas, he would take him home every month for a visit. It was hard to leave his house and daughter, grandchildren, and friends. He'd lived in Patterson, Louisiana most of his life. Wayne's mother had died before he was shot, and Daddy sure enough missed her loving, cooking, and care taking. John L had never even written a check or washed a load of clothes. Gertrude had taken excellent care of her man, so after she died he was totally lost. One night John and I were talking. He told me he didn't want to be sick or old or tired anymore. He said that he missed Gertrude with all his heart, but he was worried about Wayne. He had dreamt that Wayne had killed himself. He told me before Wayne came to Texas, he had asked his Dad to put him in the spare bedroom, the one where the firearms were kept.

He had said, "Daddy, I know what to do, just get me close enough to the cabinet."

John never got over that until he saw Wayne gaining strength, building a business, and planning a future with me. He felt he could return home without worry and get everything handled to make the move to Texas and live with us.

After John L had been home only a short time, Wayne's sister called saying Daddy had been admitted to the hospital. Wayne talked to his dad on the telephone, saying he was coming to get him as soon as the doctor released him. We got the call that Daddy was being released, and everything was packed for his move. Wayne said he would leave in the morning. However, the next morning, Wayne was depressed. It was the second anniversary of the shooting, and he was having his annual pity party. Wayne said he just couldn't go, telling his sister that he'd come the next day. Travis, John L's grandson, would spend the night with John in case he needed anything, so Wayne felt he would be fine.

Later that night, Wayne said he wanted one of our guys to drive him to Louisiana.

"I'll take you, honey," I said.

"No, Bill will drive me because I want to leave before day-light. We'll just load Dad in the car, turn around, and come home. I'm not even taking my chair. Just get me dressed in the morning. I'll be back before supper."

However, he wasn't. His father had gotten dressed in a suit and sat waiting for Wayne when he took his last breath, sitting on his bed. He looked so peaceful, just as if he had leaned back on his pillow for a moment. He wasn't old anymore nor sick. He was sliding down streets of gold with Gertrude. We would miss him, but we knew right where he was.

The funeral was difficult. Wayne felt he should have come the day before instead of feeling sorry for himself, but I reminded him Daddy never really wanted to leave his home and now he was happy.

We set the date of our wedding for December 2, 1995. We invited close friends and family to join us while we took our vows and made covenant with God, just a year and a half after we met. Wayne asked his grandson Joshua to be the best man. Josh was about seven at the time and asked, "What does a best man do, Papa?"

"Well, Grandson, if I change my mind or can't marry Ms. Penny, you would marry her."

Josh considered that for a minute and then said, "Maybe Justin (who was fifteen) should be best man. I like Ms. Penny, but he's closer to her age."

When the preacher asked Wayne, "Do you take this woman to be your lawfully wedded wife?"

Wayne paused for more than a pregnant moment. We watched the video of the wedding later. We were all seated like Wayne, and Josh was right behind him waiting for the answer… but it wasn't coming. At last, Wayne smiled and said, "I do."

The video shows Josh wiping his brow, breathing a deep sigh as he slid down in his seat.

The Garden was doing well, and we were at capacity. The Emporium was full and busy, meeting the needs of the community by providing furniture and clothing to the poor and elderly. We provided clothes and shoes for children for school through the help of churches in our area. We fed the hungry and made Thanksgiving and Christmas exciting for over 300 children every year. The apartment was getting finished and my footed tub was being installed. I was content, in love, and our first exercise units were getting ready to come off the line from Wayne's shop.

One morning my realtor called suggesting I look at a house that was recently listed. He thought I would want to buy it to enlarge the Garden.

"I'm not interested in looking at anything, Rocky," I said, "I just got married and…" I noticed Wayne saying something to me. "What, honey?"

"I want to see it," Wayne said.

"Okay. Rocky, pick me up, and if Wayne can get into the house, I'll arrange for someone to bring him over. He wants to look."

As soon as I saw the house, I knew Wayne would like it. However, getting up the steps in the back might be a problem, and there were steps at the front door, too. I called a friend who could lift Wayne in his lightweight Quickie chair and get him through the back door. He agreed, and they arrived ten minutes later.

The house was three blocks away from Ability Unlimited, one block from the Garden, and five blocks from the Emporium. Wayne made one pass around the house, stopped in one of the front rooms and waited until I came downstairs. I told him the upstairs was a duplicate of the downstairs as the house had been a four-plex at one time. It was now renovated to a one family home. He told the realtor what he would pay and suggested an interest rate and down payment, if the owner would finance.

Rocky answered, "Well, you guys think about this, and let me know if you'd like to make an offer."

Wayne looked at me, raising his eyebrows.

I said, "Rocky, that is an offer."

I could tell that Rocky didn't think the deal would fly, but that night he called and said he had a contract for us to sign if he could come by. The three of us sat on the bed and signed the deal to close in thirty days. I just couldn't understand why Wayne would want a home that size, much less a two-story house and him in a wheelchair.

It was 1996. During Lent every year, it was my habit to fast and pray. I had arranged for someone to cover my phones each morning and afternoon for one hour. Then, again, in the evening after Wayne was settled in bed, I would go to my prayer room and fellowship with the Lord. It was my determined purpose to hear what He wanted of me personally, professionally, and spiritually during this time. My desire each year was to rid myself of any areas of sloppy living, and check for a wicked heart of unbelief. I praised Him for all He brought me through and all He was taking me to, and oh yes, to come out a nonsmoker.

Noreen mentioned to me that she was having trouble entering into that prayer place where she could stay an hour and hear from God, so I invited her to join me the next morning during my prayer time. She did, and we had a glorious time together with the Lord. As Noreen was getting up to leave I heard in my spirit to be still.

I quickly said, "Noreen, the Lord's not finished with us yet."

Then I quoted a scripture from Revelation that I hadn't previously committed to memory. (I like the part that says "Come up thither" in chapter 4 verse 1.) The scripture that I quoted was Revelation 7: 3-4 speaking of the 144,000 sons of Israel. The word "marked" was magnified to me. Then I heard *in my spirit* that we were to pray for the immune system of the body of Christ all over the world, especially in the Middle East. I heard the word anthrax, which I wasn't familiar with, and then smallpox and bubonic plaque.

I asked Noreen, "What is anthrax?"

She looked at me, saying, "I don't know."

"It must be a disease of some kind because the other two are." I laughed and thought the Lord must have had to give me something familiar like smallpox to make His point. Then He showed me babies being left at the doorsteps of Christian homes and said clearly in my spirit, "Get ready."

I had no idea what any of this meant, but I did understand "get ready" so we made plans, getting baby things together to help those homes where children would be left. We established Jacob's House as a place of provision to meet the needs of these children based on the scripture in Luke 1:33 (Message), "And the Lord shall rule over Jacob's House forever."

Noreen called to see what time I was going to pray a few days later, asking if she could come over again. I was excited as I loved to pray and spending time in the Lord's presence was an even greater joy with her. I always expected to hear from the Lord, but this was a big day for both of us.

Noreen often commented, "You couldn't *give* me your life."

She thought I had no life, as it was poured into others. We started by turning on music, began to worship, and meditate on God's goodness. Then I reached for her hand with my left hand and lifted my right hand to the Father ready to begin praying. I couldn't believe the "current" that seemed to run from heaven through my body into Noreen's and would have asked her if she felt it, but I couldn't speak. I began to pray and then a prophecy came forward "like Elijah and Elisha, I will put a double portion anointing on you (meaning Noreen) that is on her (meaning me)." There was much more to this, and it was amazing. As the prophecy ended, I looked at Noreen, and she was crying.

She said, "I knew every word you were going to say before you said it. I tried to tell you, but I couldn't think or say any other thought until you finished. I could only think the next word." We both knew something huge was happening, but we had no idea how it would manifest.

By now, summer was upon us, and it was hot, hot, and hot in Texas. A woman named Michelle, her companion, and two little girls had moved into the Garden. She was big, pregnant, and due in August. She was going to put the baby up for adoption when it was born and needed a place to stay until her term was up. She became precious to me. Her children were full of life and personality. The oldest was ever ready to meet people, give tours of the Garden, and to be loved. It wasn't long before her companion got physical with her and we evicted him from the Garden, but she and the children remained. One night a friend was teaching a Bible study at the Garden and heard that the air conditioner in Michelle's room wasn't working. After class, he called me and said, "Listen, I have a window unit I'm not using. I will be glad to donate to her room if someone will install it for her tonight.

It was not a problem to find help, and within a short time, they installed the unit and everything was cooling off, or so we thought. No sooner had the room reached a comfortable temperature, when Michelle went into labor, and the Garden started jumping. We always kept a register at the front desk for residents to sign in and out. That night the book was signed with joy as the residents grabbed her, signed their names, and car-pooled to the hospital. One resident was even allowed in the delivery room with her. Later that night upon their return, they signed in, introducing the newest resident of the Garden, Jacob Paul, including his vital statistics.

The next week Michelle knew she needed to get a job as she had decided to end her relationship and raise her children in Texas. She had babysitters for the girls at the Garden but asked if we would watch the baby. Wayne and I became Jacob's first sitters, a new experience for us, and did we ever love the job and that little boy.

Several weeks later as is all too often the story, Michelle had spoken to her ex and he convinced her he had changed. He wanted her back saying he always wanted a boy, even though he wasn't the child's father. We tried to convince Michelle to leave all three children while she tried to reconcile; however, after being with us two and a half months, she got on a bus with all three children and left for Kansas. The house felt so empty with Jacob gone. I thought it strange because many children had come through our home, but we had never become so attached as we were to this little guy.

I was to address a large woman's group regarding the Garden and the work we did within our community. It was to be a very formal luncheon, so I invited Mother to attend with me. Mom was not sure about my career change and certainly concerned herself with my new living environment. I just knew this luncheon would thrill her. It was a perfect afternoon with good food and good friends surrounding us, making me very comfortable during my presentation. At one point in my talk, I mentioned that when I got to the Garden I found my purpose. In fact, the reason I was born. Mother made no comment about it that day, but several weeks later, she called.

"Penny, it troubled me during your speech when you said you found the reason you were born, your purpose, when you started the Garden. She said, I'd never thought about anything like that. I realized I didn't know my purpose or why I was born. *But I do now.* My purpose was to make sure you arrived at the Garden on time."

The holidays were approaching, and Wayne wanted his home decorated in Victorian style with garlands and wreaths and, of course, a big tree. I had collected ornaments for our family with all our children's names on them, adding a new one each year. As I was shopping for new ornaments that year, I found a little bear that reminded me of Jacob Paul, so I bought it.

While I was decorating the tree, I asked, Wayne, "Honey, do you think we'll see Michelle and the children for Christmas?"

He smiled that knowing smile, as I hung the little bear ornament on the tree. "No, but the boy is on his way home."

I called Barbara, my prayer partner and confidante, and asked her to pray for Jacob and his sisters as I missed them so much.

She said, "Penny, I have just put their pictures back in my Bible. I have been praying for them."

We visited a short while and then hung up, as there was much to do to get the Garden ready for Christmas.

Each year the Gypsy motorcycle club had a *toy run* for us. This provided donations, which allowed us to bless more than 300 children in our community on Christmas morning. Christmas Eve was so peaceful. We had helped grant wishes for every child on our list. The residents of the Garden prepared food to take for a surprise Christmas morning meal to a trailer park in our community. Wayne was asleep, and I was cleaning the stove thinking about Jacob Paul's little family and wondering how their Christmas was. It was after midnight when Michelle called from a pay phone to wish us a Merry Christmas. She and the girls had gone to midnight mass. We had a wonderful visit and everything seemed okay but I realized I wouldn't see the kids for the holidays.

Mother joined us for Christmas, and like all the years I can remember, great food, the world's best pies, and then we were cleaning out closets! Mother had a Christmas day tradition of her own. Clean out the closets…out with the old to make room for the new. Everyone else dreaded her Christmas day ritual, but she was in her element.

She found the baby stuff I had used for Jacob and said, "It's time to throw this stuff out. It's all opened, and you sure don't need it."

I was strangely affected, as I'd never been before. It was almost as if a sense of grief came over me. There was no way to explain it to her, and I wasn't sure I could put the feelings into words, anyway.

Later that day I heard the phone ring and someone said Richelle was on the phone. Richelle was Cajun Jim's daughter, and I thought she was calling to say Merry Christmas, but when I entered the room, Wayne was saying, "It's Michelle, Jacob's mom."

Quickly, I picked up the phone, "Hello."

Michelle was crying on the other end saying, "Can you come get the boy?"

I looked at Wayne sitting there wondering what was up and mouthed to him, "She wants to know if we'll take Jacob."

"Yes!" he yelled, loud enough for her to hear.

"Michelle, I don't know how we will get there just yet, but give me directions and, yes, we'll pick him up."

She then told me when she got home after going to church and calling me, she was beat up because of her late arrival.

"We're on our way." After I hung up the phone, I wondered how we could manage this. I'd spent all our money on the presents for the youngsters at the Garden. It was our purpose at Christmas that no child would go without their wish. Wayne remembered that Brian had gone deer hunting in Oklahoma, so we called him and asked if he would go get his baby brother.

It didn't take a second to get his response, "Give me the directions. I'm on my way."

Late that night, Brian called to tell me that he had safely picked up Jacob.

Brian said, "This baby needs a freckle or something. He's perfect and beautiful, except for a bruised place on his ear."

Brian had tried to convince Michelle to pack all three kids and come back to Texas with him, but she said just take Jacob. His heart broke as he left her, bruised and crying, waving at him as he drove away.

We had missed eight weeks of Jacob's life, but that would be it, I thought as I stared at him in the crib we'd purchased just minutes before he got home.

"Come to bed, Sarah," Wayne said, laughing, referring to Sarah and Abraham in the Bible. Kissing me goodnight, he reminded me that he had said, "The boy was on his way home." Now, I was a woman with no regrets. We were given the miracle of a child and a home full of love for God and each other.

Our days were full, and Jacob was growing quickly—taking all of us by storm. The word from the Lord regarding getting ready was getting clearer to us every day. Now Wayne and I knew why we were led to buy the two-story house that seemed too large for us. The children we were to *get ready* for were actually coming to our own house. Jacob's House was not just to be a place of provision but their home. Michelle had named her baby Jacob Paul. No one knew when we borrowed from scripture and set up Jacob's House that the first child to come under our roof would be named Jacob. Who knew but God. Jacob, more than twenty years younger than his brothers and sisters (our natural-born children) was like having an only child that is until we started moving so many others in. The next addition was a teenager in trouble, Jason. Then others followed, elementary-aged children filling our big house. It was clear we were to be more than a place of supply for infants. We were a place of safety for many.

One day I was on the telephone. As I put my hand up to quiet Jacob, I mouthed, "Wait a minute."

He looked behind him then side to side and looked back at me a little amazed, saying, "Why?"

I called his dad and told him, "We may have a problem here."

Up to this point, he had waited for nothing, and this was a disservice to him. Those only child days and ways were over, as Jacob now had to give up his room. With all the bedrooms full, he moved in with Mom and Dad.

Jacob normally slept between Wayne and me, but one night he had gotten on the outside edge of the bed. During the night, he fell off, hitting his head on the corner of a dresser. Wayne and I woke up to a loud scream and blood. I rushed to get a cold cloth and applied it to Jacob's head praying as I did that Jesus would heal him.

Wayne looked at the cut and said, "We need to get him stitches."

"Oh, I dread that," I said, "and I dread trying to get this blood out of his hair. He hates getting water in his face." We lay there comforting Jacob, and the next thing we knew we had all fallen asleep again.

I awoke having no idea how long we had slept and shouted, "Wayne, give me a strong arm," as I needed his arm flexed to pull myself up. I grabbed for Jacob, thinking we were the worst parents in the world.

Jacob said, "What's the matter, Mommy?"

I turned his head to check the wound, and it was gone. I mean, completely gone. The blood was still on his pajamas, in his ear, and on his pillow. The rag was there on the bed, still damp and stained with blood, but the wound was gone.

I said, "Wayne. Look." I was shocked.

Jacob squirmed and said, "What are you looking for, Mommy? Jesus fixed me up."

We would have thought it was just a bad dream had it not been for the blood on the cloth and a small line of missing hair where the cut was. Then I noticed there was no blood on his head, and his hair smelled like conditioner. It was clear to us that we were living in God's grace and abundance; in a circle of blessing almost like a bubble.

HIDE THIS NUGGET IN YOUR HEART

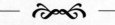

Jesus will set you up, fix you up, and carry you to the finish line.

UNCOMMON FAVOR

Joanne Herring visited us often when she drove from her home in Houston to her ranch in Fort Bend County. She was fast becoming Jacob's special friend. She tried to get others involved with my vision and invited me to parties and lovely dinners with her friends who included politicians, moviemakers, medical geniuses, and world-class businessmen. My friend was one of the affluent and renown, a television personality; she knew everyone who was known. Her fame increased after the movie *Charlie Wilson's War* was released. Charlie Wilson was a US representative who Joanne Herring, the honorary consul to Pakistan and Morocco, inspired to become involved with the resistance fighters against the Soviet Union. Quoting Desiree Lyon Howe, a close confidante of Ms. Herring, regarding Joanne's involvement in bringing down the Berlin wall, she said, "Russia's grand plan to overtake Afghanistan would have succeeded had they not had to reckon with a stalwart dynamo in haute couture."

Mrs. Howe was having a spectacular Christmas dinner, and Joanne invited Wayne and me to attend.

Wayne said, "Look, baby, if I back up wrong in this power chair I could destroy a museum quality antique. You go and tell me all about it when you come home."

I arranged a babysitter for Jacob and then tried to find something to wear that wouldn't embarrass Joanne, as my wardrobe had suffered during this phase of my life.

Arriving at the party, I immediately felt welcome as everyone I was introduced to received me graciously and brought me into their conversations as if I were one of their crowd. I was thinking back to another dinner she had invited me to in the home of one of her friends, an Italian baron. As the other guests spoke of their travels and discussed quaint restaurants they had discovered in Europe, I realized I had eaten in some of those same restaurants. We discussed menu specialties in European restaurants, bistros, and small cafes, laughing about our different unique experiences.

Now, I was again having dinner with the baron. Funny, I thought how God directs our paths and has purposes we may never dream of, even to the places we eat, using every experience in our past for good in our future.

Then I thought, *Of course, if He knows the number of hairs on our heads, nothing is too small for Him.*

Again, I was amazed at the wonder of God.

As much as I was enjoying the evening, I realized I needed to leave. I called my driver to pick me up as I had a covenant with that husband of mine that no one would see him naked, and it was well past bedtime.

As we pulled into my driveway, I said, "Park my pumpkin please. Tonight I ate dinner with a baron, but my prince is waiting."

Wayne *was* waiting. He was lying on the bed fully clothed. I had plenty to tell him while I prepared him for bed. He was soaking wet and freezing because he wouldn't let anyone else help him. Quickly, I began to make him comfortable, talking a mile a minute the whole time. He laughed as I told him about the party. I was talking so fast. I hadn't had an espresso for seven years, and boy, was I wired. That night, as I curled up in Wayne's arms, I realized I was the richest person at that party, and I was certainly the most content.

Early one morning, a stranger came to my door. She had another woman with her who smelled strong of alcohol and cigarettes.

She had a baby that was hot and screaming. I invited them in, and the stranger told me she remembered reading about us in the newspaper.

She said, "I saw this lady walking down the street in the heat with a baby. I circled around and stopped, asking what I could do to help her."

Of course, Lisa, the mother of the baby, was frightened that she would be in trouble with Child Protective Services but was assured by the stranger that she would take her somewhere safe. The baby was four months old and had a digestive problem requiring a special medication to keep his formula down. It was a special order with a very limited shelf life. I took Jeremiah in my arms and sat down praying for him to be healed and full of peace. Within minutes, he was asleep on my chest. Lisa asked if we would watch him while she got things together, and we agreed. Later in the afternoon, Eddie came to the office and laughed as he saw Jeremiah asleep on my chest. Shaking his head, he said, "You sure got a way with babies, Penny."

"I would've held you like this if you had been a little smaller, Eddie," I said with tears filling my eyes, remembering how we started.

"I know," he said, shaking his head.

Lisa called in a few hours and had changed her mind about leaving the baby with us. Back and forth, she went until I told her, "You can use me, Lisa, but you can't use me up." Finally, she asked us to pick Jeremiah up from the apartment she was staying in, giving me the address.

I had to pick Jason up from school first. He was finishing football practice, and I told him we were on our way to get Jeremiah.

He became angry and said, "Why? Don't we have enough kids at the house now?"

Jason was not pleased, but Jacob on the other hand, had thrown himself across my belly just the day before and prayed, "Jesus, please put a baby in Mommy's tummy just like Jeremiah."

Wayne said, "Hold up, boy." We all laughed, but it looked like Jesus was answering his prayer—but skipping the tummy part, thank God. Obviously, Jason was not in faith with Jacob, but when I pulled up to the apartment, Jason with his bad attitude got out of the van to get Jeremiah and whatever belongings he had.

The next thing I saw was Jason walking with the infant seat held up high talking to Jeremiah in baby talk. Getting into the back seat of the van, I watched in the rear view mirror as he leaned over and kissed Jeremiah, saying, "I make covenant with you, Jeremiah. I'll come and get you wherever you are, always. You will not live like I did, as long as I am alive." Then looking at me in the mirror, he said, "You should see the apartment. No furniture, a TV, the ashtrays all full, and beer cans everywhere. What a mess." Jason had remembered his years in that environment, and his attitude changed forever concerning the children coming to Jacob's House.

Jeremiah won his way into everyone's heart, including Wayne's. He thought it was fun having another baby in the house now that he was stronger and could help. I would lay Jeremiah on a pillow next to Wayne so he could hold the bottle to feed him. It was during one of those precious moments, Wayne nicknamed him with a Cajun name "Boudreaux" letting me know this little guy was destined to become a forever child in our home, just like Jacob.

Some of our teenagers couldn't read, and it wasn't because they were slow or had a learning disability. The families moved around so much that they were shifted from school to school, missing classes, and no one was there to pick up the slack. It was my practice to take them out of public school, pushing the pause button so to speak. Then we helped them catch up through home schooling to re-enter at the right grade level. Some were so far behind they had been placed in special education classes; others had been hanging around with gang members, getting pregnant, and using drugs.

It was September 11, 2001, and the phone interrupted the home school class. When I answered, it was Michelle, Jacob's birth mother. She was calling to tell me to turn on the television, and at the same time asking if she could come home.

I was stunned as I saw the second airliner crash into the World Trade Center. I answered, "Yes, honey, come home."

I had often wondered why God would have me teaching home school knowing my difficulties with English and math, but during this crisis, I found out at least part of the reason. I'll never forget the girls in my class thinking the song our senators and congressmen sang was written just because of this horrible situation.

"That is our national anthem," I said, realizing they had no clue. "Now I know why God has me teaching you. Before we're through, you will know God and love your country."

Within hours, I was to hear a word that I hadn't thought about in years—anthrax. Hearing from all my prayer partners, I was reminded of what I'd received of the Lord, and we continued to pray for immune systems with a heightened sense of urgency. Within a few days, I was to hear that there was a smallpox scare, and later that month a bulletin appeared on the bottom of my television screen "17 cases of bubonic plague, Jamaica." I understood it was time to be ready, not time to get ready, so I braced myself for the next instruction from the Lord.

Joanne had an historical church on her ranch property where we often conducted services. One Sunday I was giving the message in her church, and as I was closing, Joanne asked if one of my teenagers would be comfortable telling their story. Jason was quick to get up and tell about me trying to teach him to hang curtains and make a bed in his room. He had rarely slept on a bed and had never hung curtains, so in his frustration with my directions he threw the curtain rod on the floor and ran out of the room, down the stairs, and out the back door.

I couldn't run, but Wayne had built an elevator, which I quickly took to the first floor. When I got to him, I said, "Jason, don't you ever run from me; you run to me. I can't help what you missed in your life, but I have only two years to teach you what you'll need to know to make it in life. No one is going to cry for you, my son. If you go in the service, they won't care about your sad story. They'll expect tight corners on your bunk, so let's learn now."

Jason continued his story, telling them that he learned to make a bed you could bounce a quarter off, hang curtains, paint walls, and in fact, had helped paint and decorate another bedroom downstairs. He told them that he graduated high school, got a terrific job, and was the boss's favorite employee because whenever the boss needed something moved or changed, Jason was his man. He was the first in his family to graduate high school and was determined to break the cycle of lack. This particular Sunday, Dr. Michael DeBakey and his wife, Katrin, were visiting the church. They were dear friends of Ms. Joanne's. In fact, she affectionately called the world famous heart surgeon, her G.P. (family doctor).

When Jason was finished speaking, Katrin DeBakey said to him, "Jason, you are one in a million."

Jason smiled at her and said, "No, Ms. Katrin, I'm one *of* a million, and if Jacob's House had more money, there would be more stories like mine."

I didn't have time to paint china anymore as it required firing the pieces several times, but I had taken up needlepoint and water-colors for relaxation on the nights we had Wayne's bowel program. We called these "long nights" so that our children would not interrupt. I would watch them wink at us or the little ones giggle as they thought it was a romance night. I would smile thinking how wonderful it was that their thoughts of their daddy and I was always romance.

Wayne suggested that the thank you notes I'd painted in watercolor should be published. There was a special one that I had painted for my friend, Lady Bobbie. She was a gift to me from God when I needed a friend and prayer partner. She understood me from the moment we met and became that lifeline and heart connection kind of sister I pray every woman finds. I painted a card with pink roses on it for her, and when Wayne saw it, he made a decision. He had been investing in the stock market and decided he would rather invest in me. Taking his money out of the market, he had some of my artwork printed in hopes of providing an income flow for Jacob's House. We called the new division Treasured Possessions based on the scripture:

> Then those who feared the Lord talked often one to another, and the Lord listened and heard it, and a book of remembrance was written before Him of those who reverenced and worshipfully feared the Lord and who thought on His name. And they shall be mine, says the Lord of hosts, in that day when I publicly recognize and openly declare them to be My Jewels My special possession My peculiar treasure. And I will spare them as a man spares his own son who serves him.
>
> Malachi 3:16-17 (AMP)

This is how we desired to live and tried to teach to all those who crossed our path. To make a conscious effort to recognize God's presence in everything; to talk with Him about things as we went through our day, to turn to Him for help with problems and then be grateful for all the good things in our lives.

Michelle did come home with her eight-month-old Haley Renee, the little girl I had always wanted, always prayed for, and she stole our hearts, pronto. Michelle didn't stay long and decided to leave Haley with us, too. Wayne was mush in Haley's hands, and he delighted in her. He spent his days with the children, helping with Jacob's home schooling, and looking after Haley and Jeremiah while I worked at the store and office.

I told Wayne that I couldn't get Jacob to perform in school for me so I was going to send him back to the private school he had been attending on scholarship.

"You can't do that, Momma. He'll think he's being sent away since the other kids get to be home with you."

"Well, you will have to teach him then because I can't," I said, more than frustrated.

A few days later, Jacob came into my office and said, "Mommy, I want to read something to you."

I looked up but didn't see a book or a piece of paper in his hand, so I asked, "What do you want to read?"

Jacob picked up my Bible and read a scripture. I turned the page, and he read another. I was amazed and called his daddy on the phone, asking, "What did you do? He is reading my Bible!"

Wayne laughed and said, "Well, Momma, I won't pay a kid to clean his room or take out the trash because I pay for the house. However, I will pay a kid to read because in order to get a good job, you have to read. I simply told Jacob that if he ever wanted to see the inside of Eckerd's Drugstore again, he would have to learn to read, and he could earn money from me and spend it on candy."

That did it; in fact, the children had nicknamed Wayne "the candy man" since he had such a sweet tooth, and Eckerd's was his favorite afternoon stroll with the children.

Most children don't have the luxury of Daddy being so closely involved in raising them. Jacob had worked with Wayne even in the welding shop since he was less than a year old. They were inseparable, and Haley was moving in fast. At dinnertime, she would look at Daddy with her big eyes, and he would just melt, feeding her and laughing with the others. I remembered how we started out. I was feeding him, reading to him, and changing his diapers. I remembered how he had gained strength by lifting his infant son over his head. I remembered how he'd call me when I was stressed about something and say, "Come, lay on my chest, baby, breath like this," and peace would overtake me as I got in his rhythm.

I remembered once as I lay on the bed meditating on God's Word and His promises, when He asked me if Wayne wearing diapers brought Him glory. I paused thinking this was hard, wondering if this was a trick question. When I again heard in my spirit, "Does Wayne wearing diapers bring him glory?"

"No," I answered quickly. "He hates them."

"I hate them, too," the Lord said, and then He said, "Never buy a piece of a lie."

I realized that I should have known how God felt about Wayne's situation as quickly as I knew how Wayne felt, and I repented. I realized that total healing would bring God glory. My husband was wonderful to be around and brought many to the knowledge of Christ by his manner of living. However, I now knew Wayne walking would bring many more, so I knew to believe and never settle, until we had the full promise. We had come a long way, but we still had a mountain to take.

One afternoon I heard Wayne's voice in the backyard talking to the guys from the shop. Every one of them sounded excited, but when I opened the back door, they got strangely quiet.

"Okay, come clean, guys. What have you been up to?" I asked, just knowing I was going to have to pull it out of them. I took one of the guys aside and asked again, "What's up, Teddy?"

"Oh, Ms. Penny," he said, "today a customer came in to see if we could weld his gas tank, and Mr. Wayne said, sure—there is no job too big or too small. Then we found out it was still on his car. Mr. Wayne said, 'Come back in an hour, and it would be ready,' so the man left. Mr. Wayne said to lay him on the grass and drive the car over the top of him. He said he didn't trust any of us to do the job; he wanted to do it himself. So we did what he said."

I was shocked and started to say something when Teddy said, "But, Ms. Penny, we all leaned on the car so if it blew up, we'd go with him, cuz we told him you'd sure 'nuf kill us if something happened to him." He was right, but Wayne at last was feeling like a man with purpose and a man in charge. I smiled to myself thanking God for bringing so much healing to his spirit, his soul, and his body.

Wayne made sure that Jacob and I were in Fort Worth for convention every year, and our birthdays were at the same time. We also took our other children from Jacob's House. We stayed in the Worthington Hotel and lavished them with a lifestyle they otherwise wouldn't have experienced, letting them know that God had big plans for each of them, as they had the Word sown in their hearts. When times were tight, Joanne would pitch in and pay for our rooms, helping us to expose our youngsters to better things in their future so they would work to earn them for themselves.

Jacob was turning five. Wayne woke him up, saying, "Good morning, birthday boy."

Jacob asked him, "Daddy, am I really five years old?"

"Yes," he said.

"Daddy, is Brother Jesse preaching this morning?"

"Nope," his daddy answered.

"Okay, Daddy. Enough church, let's go shopping."

That's just what they did. They spent the day shopping, buying me a beautiful angel statue for my birthday surprise.

What a year it was. We were opening an antique store. Wayne said he wanted to be home more, so he sold the welding shop and moved his equipment into the building behind our house. We were blessed to have an office and school in the apartment above the garage and a house full of precious children.

A group of volunteers came to do a project for us in the apartment. It was a roll-in shower. This was something we never had access to except when we were celebrating at the Worthington each year. Once the information about what was needed in the bathroom was turned over to these wonderful volunteers, I wasn't allowed in the room. It was so hush, hush that I should have been more suspicious, but I had a full plate without being concerned about that.

One afternoon Wayne called and said, "Hey, Momma, take a break and come see me upstairs."

Usually that meant he needed me to be the heavy. He was so nice that when he wanted to get a resident to do something he would call me. Off I went thinking I would make quick work of this assignment and then start dinner. When I got to the apartment, one of the volunteers said, "Hi, Penny. I hear you like candles."

"I sure do," I said, passing him and looking for the wayward resident or my man.

Then I heard him say, "Could you come in here and tell me what you think about this?" He pointed at the bathroom.

"Oh boy, I finally get to see what you guys have been up to." I walked into the most beautiful bathroom. It had an ornate gold-leaf mirror hanging over the sink, with brass and crystal candle sconces on either side. Then he opened the shower curtain pointing to small shelves that were attached to the tiles with a candle on each.

"Can your short self reach these to light them?" he asked.

I had never missed a day caring for my husband and would have bathed him in bed from a bucket for the rest of my life, but there we were with a fully accessible shower. In a few hours, it would be dark enough to bathe my husband by candlelight and music.

"You bet I can. Thank you. Thank you. Thank you."

I was crying, but I didn't miss the tears in his eyes as he said, "Okay, I better get out of here and leave you two alone."

That night I remembered how Wayne had asked me to keep his home from looking like a hospital. To accomplish this, I moved the hospital bed out and put a double bed in its place. The first night in a regular bed, he had a muscle spasm so violent it caused him to fall off the edge of the bed. I was reading to him when he yelled, "I'm going down…"

I reached for his arm and tried to stop him, but gravity was against me, and all I could say was, "Yeah, but you are going down slow." We had a big laugh while I called the Garden for Eddie to help me get him back in bed. The first night in the shower was no different. His big power chair couldn't get near water so we had a special shower chair. As I tried to transfer him back, I nearly dropped him because he was "slick when wet."

"Don't lose me, baby," he said. "Can you imagine the picture if Eddie had to bale us both out of this shower naked?" Our life was full of laughter and peace.

That night we were watching a movie together in bed. We were enjoying the quiet time alone. Wayne grinned and asked, "Does that feel good, baby?"

"Does what feel good?" I asked, puzzled.

He looked down and moaned, "Ah, man, I've been rubbing my own leg for the last forty-five minutes." We laughed 'til we cried. I thought, *Who could ever ask for more than this?* It was our wedding anniversary and out of the abundance of my heart, I wrote:

> To my husband, my hero,
> My helper, my friend, my lover…
> The one I dream of and dream with…
> The one I look to for laughter when things just get too hard.
> In you I find my rhythm for breathing…

❧❦❧

> You are the strong arm that lifts me up…
> You are the last touch I feel before sleep overtakes me…
> And the voice that says, "It's time to get up"…

❧❦❧

> You are the joker…the counselor…the final word…
> You are always fair and just…
> You are slow to anger… You show mercy to all…
> You are Daddy—Provision—Protection
> Peace to our children…

Time with you brings me more Joy, and Passion
From a perfect fit, to a better fit…
From falling in love, to falling deeper in love…
It doesn't make sense, does it, honey?
But it is true…Obviously, God made me to Love You.

Penny Robichaux

HIDE THIS NUGGET IN YOUR HEART

"…your gift will make room for you and bring you before great men." Proverbs 18:16

When your desire is to do the will of God, your gift will fit right into the place God has already planned, taking you to levels you may never have expected to rise to—bringing you before great men and bringing great men into your life.

WITH LONG LIFE WILL
I SATISFY THEE

Wayne thought he would enjoy training German shepherds for protection and as assist dogs, so the search was on for the dog with the right bloodline, temperament, and size. He knew we needed property to train the dogs. Our house was on a main street, so he enjoyed taking us on long drives in the country, dreaming new dreams, making plans for our future, and looking for land. In fact, Wayne loved to wake up and say, "Let's go for a ride." His rides could be to Louisiana to see the kids or around the block. He loved to be free and spontaneous.

One afternoon Wayne called and asked me to close the store early. He had found the right bloodline and wanted to check out a litter of puppies. "Bring cash, Momma, and get a babysitter if possible. I don't want the kids begging for all of them, and it's a long drive. We'll need a driver. You can't drive and hold a puppy."

I arranged a driver, and Grandma Nelson was the sitter for our first evening out without the kids in years. We turned on old music and sang aloud with the radio, while we held hands. We picked our puppy, a beautiful female, and headed home. The children had been upset since we didn't take them on our date, but when we arrived with a puppy, they forgave us, and there were wet puppy kisses for everyone.

I was writing a grant that needed to be postmarked by midnight, May 31. I had been listening to a series with Wayne by Keith Moore entitled "The Honor of God." It was deadline on the grant, so Wayne told me to go to the office and he and the kids would watch a movie while I finished the paperwork. I finished the grant application, but there was one more tape in the series. I called Wayne to see if I had time to listen to the last one before he needed me. He laughed, saying, "Go ahead. I have five sweaty kids piled on top of me watching this movie. Have fun." I sat there taking notes from the teaching. I thought it was so profound.

I wrote on my notes, "I am changed." I turned off the lights, posted the grant, and went home. I was locked out, so I pounded on the door knowing that they were all upstairs with the television on loud. No one came to the door. I thought, *I'll call them*. I noticed my cell phone was not in my purse, so I headed back to the office to get it and to call for one of the kids to unlock the door. I didn't have the office key and had locked the door from the inside on my way out. I decided to go by the Garden and call, but that door was locked tight and I couldn't wake a soul. I thought, *This is ridiculous*. I was responsible for so many properties and couldn't get in even one of them. Laughing to myself, I stopped by the gas station next door to my house and used their phone, calling back several times, but the phone kept going to call notes.

"Finally," I said, as Wayne answered the phone. "I'm locked out, honey."

Wayne had fallen asleep and so had the kids. It took him awhile to get them off his arms so he could answer the phone, but I could tell he was laughing.

"I told Jacob to unlock the door so you could get in, but it must have been unlocked so he locked it. Let me get one of these kids up to help you, Momma."

When I squeezed my way into bed, I thought about how content I was and how grateful I was I could sleep in the next day.

"It's time to get up," I heard my man say.

"Oh, Wayne, this is my day off," I answered.

"Okay, baby, just get me dressed, and I'll feed the kids while you go back to sleep."

"Sure, famous last words," I answered while getting his toothbrush ready.

Once he was dressed he said, "I was serious, I'll feed the kids. You get some rest."

I didn't go back to sleep but was sitting in my favorite chair taking a breath when I heard Wayne shout up the steps, "Come on, Momma, we need a driver. I need to go look at that piece of land."

I was exhausted—wearing one of Wayne's old denim shirts, a pair of pink pedal pushers with no makeup, and my hair uncombed.

"Give me an hour, honey. I have to get ready," I said, dragging myself up.

"You don't need makeup. You're beautiful, and all we need is a driver. Come on now."

Then I heard the kids, "Come on, Mom, hurry."

"Okay, I'm coming," I answered as I was trying to find my shoes. Jeremiah was into shoes. That boy would put anyone's shoes on and leave the room. So there I was with one beige shoe and one blue shoe, but they matched in style if not color. We piled into the van and hit the road. It was June 1, 2003. The weather was beautiful but getting warm for this early in the morning. We sang songs and talked about what we would eat for dinner when we were finished at the property.

The land belonged to a friend of mine who was fixing it up with Wayne in mind. He was digging a pond for Wayne to take the kids fishing and putting in a trailer with a ramp and air conditioner so if Wayne got hot while training his dogs he could take a break. Our son, Brian, was digging the pond. The minute the kids were out of the van, they ran to greet him and started to explore. Brian had a canopy set up, so Wayne and I sought the shade under the canopy.

We were talking when he said, "Baby, see if I'm sitting on something under this leg," pointing at his left thigh. He pushed himself up, and I ran my hand under his leg.

"Nothing there," I said.

A few minutes later he said, "Check again. I think I'm sitting on one of the kid's toys or something," pushing himself up again.

I checked—nothing. Wayne had a strange look and said, "Get the kids. Something is wrong. We need to go."

I yelled for the kids to come back from the pond while Wayne headed to the van. I turned to check on him. He had backed his wheelchair halfway up the ramp and was slumped over the side of his chair bleeding from his nose, ear and mouth. He was unconscious, and I believed he was dead. I screamed as I pushed him upright. "Wayne Robichaux, don't you dare leave me. You get back here in the name of Jesus. I'm not raising these kids alone."

By now, Brian was driving the kids back in the truck. He heard me scream and saw Wayne bent over the chair. We got in the van as Wayne's eyes rolled forward, and though he was conscious, but he couldn't speak and was flailing his arms. I thought it was heat stroke and poured water on him and turned the air vents his way as we rushed to the hospital. Entering the emergency room, Brian said he'd take the children home and come back to be with me.

It wasn't long, and Wayne revived after they had poked him and probed him and given him injections. The emergency room is always cold, but that day, with his wet shirt he was freezing.

"Can I get a blanket or something?" he asked. "Or can we just go home?"

The nurse smiled and said, "I'll get you a blanket, but you need to see the doctor again before you can leave."

I leaned over and kissed him, saying, "Wow, you sure know how to liven things up, husband."

"Yeah, it was the strangest feeling. I can't explain it." Just then, the nurse returned with a toasty warm blanket.

"She really knows how to get to you, honey," I said as she placed the blanket over his chest and shoulders.

"Thanks, this feels great," he said. I moved around to the other side of the table when he said, "Did you bump my foot?"

"No, do you want me to?" I laughed.

"Is something on my foot?"

More serious now, I answered, "No."

"Here it comes again," he said. With that, he began to have a seizure and lost consciousness.

The doctor ordered a CAT scan and an MRI. We were to learn the next morning that he had a brain tumor, and we would not be going home. Because of the favor of God and the influence of Joanne and her friends, we left for MD Anderson, where we pressed on for our miracle.

Our neurosurgeon came through the door with Wayne's file in hand. He explained the location and description of the tumor saying, "My recommended treatment is surgery. "

"We believe in miracles, Doctor," I said.

"Good." He smiled. "Let's prove one together." He closed his file and again smiled at us.

I had prayed for peace, wisdom, and direction and felt as if I had received all of that in his short response.

The response was short, but the process was not. Every imaginable test was ordered, as they sought a primary tumor elsewhere, but with every test came the answer "clear," no sign of other tumors. I tended Wayne, in spite of the wonderful nursing staff, remembering our covenant while our family and friends tended to everything else at home, allowing me the opportunity to honor that covenant.

The nurses in both hospitals called us the lovebirds. I powdered his sheets, burned candles, and brought in a television so he could watch healing school with Ms. Gloria, laugh with Jesse, and sing with Len Mink. The nurses and other staff members would visit the room on break to enjoy the peace that flowed there and would ask, "What's the secret to your marriage?"

"It is not a secret, but a great mystery that is hidden in Christ."

"Okay, solve the mystery for us." They laughed.

We would tell them the scripture from Matthew 19:26, "With men it is impossible, but with God all things are possible."

Regardless of the trial, each day brought moments of joy. We did have one physician who came to discuss some test results. He said, "I have nothing definitive to report from the tests; however, I would say you have sixty days to live."

I watched Wayne's face and immediately asked the doctor to leave our room. Later, I requested he not speak to Wayne directly, but go through our primary physician. His words were etched in my mind, and I saw something in Wayne I hadn't seen before, a resolve, to the negative. The last tests were completed, and the doctor scheduled the surgery, ordering an MRI to be done the night before then we were released to go home.

We had some fair days, but it seemed every Monday, Wayne would go unresponsive and we ended up in our local hospital emergency room sometimes for a few hours and other times overnight. Then he would rally, we would go home, and then blue Monday came again. Just before the scheduled surgery, Wayne had an episode that landed us back in our local hospital with our family doctor. We were two days out from the surgery, and we were tired.

Ms. Dodie had asked Cisco from Lakewood Church to visit us in the hospital, but when he arrived, he found us in a cuddle taking a much-needed nap. He decided not to wake us, instead he would return the next day. Wayne went for the MRI with and without contrast as requested. While we waited in our room, Wayne was asking me what an electrolyte was.

"I don't know, honey, but they are very important." Just then, our family doctor danced into the room.

"Hey, Doc," Wayne said. "What's an electrolyte?"

I was watching the doctor and said, "Wayne, this guy is a Baptist. He doesn't dance. Forget the electrolytes." We were in a silly mood.

The biggest smile appeared on our doctor's face. "You got your miracle," he said. "The tumor is gone. There is a dent where the tumor was. What do you think that is?

"That is the fingerprint of God," I answered, and we rejoiced, laughing and crying tears of gratitude.

Wayne called our friend Barbara, and they were worshiping God together and thanking Him for the healing. All our children were rejoicing, when Cisco from Lakewood Church walked in. He talked to me and waited for Wayne to get off the phone, but Wayne and Barbara were in a wonderful place of praise and he wasn't going to be hanging up for a while. I smiled and sat with our visitor, telling him the good report, when he said, "I came by yesterday, but the two of you were so cute sleeping together, that I couldn't bring myself to wake you. I came today because the Lord gave me a scripture for your husband, and I want to read it to him. Psalm 63."

I smiled knowing how much Wayne would enjoy hearing that scripture read again. It was the same scripture that God had me read to him July 17, 1994, a real favorite. Now it was July 17, 2003. What a wonderful reminder of God's love. I knew that God had *set times*; this one we'd never forget.

People from all over the hospital came to celebrate with us. They laughed and teased us and asked, "What will you do now, Mr. Wayne, since you have your miracle?"

He thought only a moment and then said, "I'm going home to teach my children to honor God and honor their mother."

We had completed the series on honor a second time. It held us together through the challenges we faced, and he knew honoring God would take us through it all.

What a reunion we had when we arrived home after six weeks in and out of the hospital. The kids were over-the-top excited. Friends and prayer partners came by to celebrate with us. Cajun Jim came by to eat Jell-O with Wayne and talk about the "good old days and the days to come."

The next week it rained, causing all the windows in the house to fog over. Wayne was cold, even though I had wrapped him tight in a blanket and was getting ready to feed him a nice hot meal.

He looked me straight in the eyes, saying, "You know, baby, I'm tired."

"Okay," I said, with a catch in my heart. "Let's take a nap."

He looked at me long and hard. "You know what I mean, baby," he said; and I did.

All the steroids and seizure medications had cost him dearly. What had taken us nine years to build in muscle strength and function was gone, and I was again shaving him, feeding him, and keeping him bundled up, just as it was when we first began.

"Wayne, we are smarter now than we were. We know what to do to get everything back and more. I promise it won't be long."

That weekend many people dropped by to visit. By Sunday night, I knew something dreadful was in the wind. It was our "long night," but it was not going well. He was sleepy and didn't want to talk, or so I thought, but he was slipping away. Finally, I went to bed only to wake the next morning finding Wayne unconscious. I couldn't rouse him, nor was I able to find a vein to start the IV. I called the nurse who called the ambulance while I crawled back in bed and begged him, "Don't leave, Wayne. Talk to me, baby. Please come back to me." I put my hands on his cheeks. I kissed him and nibbled his lips, willing him to live— nothing. I wept.

The ambulance arrived, but this time I didn't go with him. I asked Eddie and one of the men from the Garden to go with him while I gathered up what I needed for another hospital stay. I called Noreen. "I don't think I'll be bringing Wayne home, honey. He said he is tired." With that, I broke down.

I knew Wayne wanted to go to heaven, but I couldn't let go. I had read that the Jewish sages taught how God had to woo those who loved the Torah, or the Word, and when that saint died, it was called "death by kiss." I believed Wayne had been so close to heaven he heard the angels singing. Still I couldn't let go. Then I realized it was July 31, my boys' birthdays, and I asked God, "Please have him wait, Lord. The boys would never get over Wayne leaving on their birthday."

The rest of our children came from Louisiana. I knew they needed to be there. The visit was good as they sat on his bed and remembered funny things and happier days, chatting and laughing, hoping to rouse him. By 3:00 a.m., they were ready to go to the house, eat, and bathe before returning to sit with their dad again.

They left our room, and I tidied up, nervously talking all the while, about how good the kids looked. Then as was my practice, I climbed in bed, laid my head on his chest, and began to pray. However, this time I heard myself say, "If I were you, little bird, I'd fly to the light, and when I saw Jesus, I'd run."

Wayne took one more breath and the next breath he took was with God. I heard the door open and the charge nurse come in. "Mrs. Robichaux," she said, "he's gone."

"I know," I answered her. "I was here when he left. It was death by kiss."

Because he has set his love upon Me, therefore will I deliver him, I will set him on high because he knows and understands My name (has a personal knowledge of My mercy, love and kindness—trusts and relies on Me,) knowing I will never forsake him, no, never. He shall call upon me, and I will answer him, I will be with him in trouble, I will deliver him and honor him with long life will I satisfy him and show him my salvation.

Psalms 91:15-16, AMP

In the past, Wayne had Hepatitis C and had used a lot of alcohol. Now with such strong medication, it was more than his liver could take and he had gone into liver failure. I realized it was August 1, 2003, exactly sixty days from the day he had the first seizure, just as the doctor spoke over him. Wayne took the doctor's sixty-day verdict as a release. It had taken nine years to gain a quality life. He just couldn't face that struggle again. I remembered that he said he was tired, and life in that wheelchair had been long enough for him. Wayne had faith to believe he could receive his healing from cancer, but he couldn't see himself out of the wheelchair.

It was after 5:00 a.m. when I got home, and I couldn't figure out how to go to bed. I just couldn't think what I needed to do. I walked around the house, through the kitchen, into my office, and there stood Jeremiah.

He smiled up at me. "Mommy, where is Daddy?" he asked as he reached for me to pick him up.

"Daddy moved to heaven this morning, honey," I answered and added, "Jeremiah, I have forgotten how to go to bed."

"Don't worry, Mommy. I'll put you to bed."

Jeremiah, just three years old took my hand and led me to my bed, helped me climb in, and covered me up, giving me a big kiss.

"Can we go visit Daddy in heaven?"

"Not right now, honey, but one day we'll go and live there with him."

Getting in bed was not the only thing I had forgotten how to do. It had been years since I got up and got ready for the day without preparing Wayne and the smallest in our brood. I didn't know where to find my clothes or what I wanted to eat. It reminded me of learning to walk again, starting over with baby steps. The difference was *I had wanted* to walk; I wasn't sure I wanted to live.

Noreen felt sure that Wayne had left for heaven in time for me to get to Fort Worth, but I told her it would be impossible for me to get a room on such short notice. We always booked long in advance. Without me knowing, Noreen called Joanne. I should have known that Joanne could move mountains, and she did. Noreen called back with my room reservations. I was soon on my way to Fort Worth with my children and two men from the Garden who drove and helped with the kids.

On the drive to Fort Worth, I had prayed that God would touch my children. I was empty and didn't know how to help them. When we arrived at the Worthington, we found that Joanne had secured a room for us on a different floor. As the elevator doors opened to our floor, there stood Kellie Copeland, a.k.a. "Commander Kellie."

I leaned into her shoulder and said, "Their daddy just moved to heaven."

Kelly threw her arms out wide and squatted down saying, "Are y'all gonna be in Super Kid Academy tomorrow?" as she gathered them to herself.

They all smiled and said, "Yes."

"Thank you, Lord," I whispered as we went to our room.

Through all the years we had been going to Fort Worth, we had developed a special relationship with the head valet, Ollie. He watched as Wayne would head for the convention with the children following behind his wheelchair like little ducks. He enjoyed our teens, encouraging them and, of course, remembering them year to year. The children and my friends from the Garden had left early for the convention center, to get in line for Super Kid Academy. I finished getting ready and went downstairs to get a cab. There stood my friend, Ollie. He gave me a big hug, saying, "I must have missed Mr. Wayne and the kids this morning."

Biting back tears I said, "Wayne is in heaven this morning, Ollie, and the kids have left for the convention, but they will be looking for you tomorrow."

Stunned, he asked what happened, and then he told me, "Wait here, I'll be right back."

A few minutes later, he came to the front of the hotel and, opening the door to a Cadillac, said, "I'll be taking you to the convention this morning. I know Mr. Wayne would want me to look after you." He did, making sure I had a ride for every service.

The convention ended too quickly. I wasn't ready to go home to an empty house, but I knew I must. Noreen called, wondering what my plans were.

"I want to go to Branson," I heard myself say, "but I'm on my way home." I had never had such a thought, nor did I know where that comment came from. Noreen told me later, she knew it was time to let go of me because I'd be leaving Texas.

HIDE THIS NUGGET IN YOUR HEART

What seems like the end is just a new beginning. "For I know the plans I have for you," declares the LORD, "plans to prosper you and not to harm you, plans to give you hope and a future." —Jeremiah 29:11

GRACE, GRACE, AND MORE GRACE

Grief is difficult and debilitating. I knew what the Bible said about death, and I believed it. I just hadn't gotten there yet.

"We would not have you ignorant, brethren, about those who fall asleep in death that you may not grieve for them, as the rest do who have no hope beyond the grave. For since, we believe that Jesus died and rose again; even so, God will also bring with Him those who have fallen asleep in death. For this, we declare to you by the Lord's own word, that we who are alive and remain until the coming of the Lord shall in no way proceed into His presence or have any advantage at all over those who have previously fallen asleep. For the Lord Himself will descend from heaven with a loud cry of summons, with the shout of an archangel, and with the blast of the trumpet of God. And those who have departed this life in Christ will rise first, then we, the living ones who remain on earth, shall simultaneously be caught up along with the resurrected dead in the clouds to meet the Lord in the air, and so always through the eternity of the eternities we shall be with the Lord. Therefore, comfort and encourage one another with these words."

1 Thessalonians 5:13-18, AMP

This scripture brought me comfort and peace, knowing that heaven was our home. As King David had said of his child, "He shall not return to me but I to him." It was living from day to day that was the battle for me.

One afternoon I went to buy gas. As I turned into the station off a busy street, I could no longer go forward. It wasn't a problem with the car. I just couldn't go anymore. The flood tide broke. I started crying and couldn't stop. I laid my head on the steering wheel and said, "Lord, I don't know how you can make anything right again." Then from deep inside me, I spoke the words, "I trust you." From then on, I knew I chose to trust him, in spite of my grief.

I have known people who go through life thinking that it is in their own strength they have accomplished things. Some credit their intelligence, or their finances, maybe even their bloodline; the famous self-made man, but I knew different. For the past twelve years, I'd overseen five entities; a homeless shelter that we called a living center full of "broken people," a children's home that included many troubled teens, a resale shop, a welding shop, and an antique shop. I had assisted in directing more than 8,000 individuals over those years, in the "way they should go." I had raised many little children and was the only caregiver to my husband. I had advocated in my community, managed speaking engagements, organized fundraisers, written grants, and ran the corporate office. I had precious personal times with the Lord, taught Bible studies, preached, and participated in prayer groups. I had wiped noses and dried eyes, did laundry and cleaned house, laughed as we built facilities, and cried before the Lord as I buried babies. I fed the hungry by candlelight and nursed the sick back to health. I moved people into their new homes and helped decorate their dreams with furniture, appliances, and cars. I did needlepoint and painted anything that didn't move, often while counseling, but I knew I did none of this in my own strength.

How could I, physically challenged myself, have lifted Wayne? It was because God gave me strength. How could I have answered any need? It was because God gave me wisdom and the necessary provision. How could I have motivated anyone to give of his or her time, his or her talents, and his or her resources? It was because God anointed my mouth! How could I have found an Eddie to walk out this dream with me, or a Bessie who volunteered at the Emporium six days a week for ten years and the other countless volunteers? *Because God gave me favor.* How could I have walked with no discernable leg muscles through five countries, dining at just the right establishments? B*ecause God directed my path,* helping me put one foot in front of the other? How could I have loved the unlovely with all of my heart? *Because the love of God had been shed abroad in my heart.* How could I have been crowned a queen, or eaten with a baron, or shared my life with the rich and famous? *Because God said, our gift would make room for us.* This was never more obvious to me than now.

I whispered in prayer, "Father, help me get up; I need a strong arm. Lord, give me the desire to live, help me lead my children to wholeness in you. Breathe, oh Lord, on the vision you have given me and show me if I've missed your plan for my life. Restore my joy, Lord. Amen."

Everywhere we went, we saw Wayne—at home, in the yard, on every corner. When we had a visitor, he was the subject of every conversation. I had a stirring on the inside that we were to prepare to move, but where to and for what purpose? I did what I knew to do; every day, getting up, doing the daily work, but now it was hard. I was tired by midday, and I noticed that no one was laughing much in our house. One night while I was doing a load of laundry, Jacob, who'd been in bed for hours, came running in crying, "Mommy, I need to ask my daddy a question," tears pouring from his eyes and his sobs deep.

I started to cry and said, "Ask me, baby. Maybe I can answer it for you," praying that I could.

"Why did Daddy always want a blue-eyed blonde?" he asked so seriously that I nearly laughed but knew it was important to him.

"Because your daddy had one, my precious boy; he had me."

He looked shocked at the answer as if I didn't get it or something. I smiled then and told him. "One day your brothers will explain it better. Now go back to bed." Then I added one more thing to my prayers, "Lord, I want to hear my children laugh from their toes again."

Before Wayne went to heaven, we'd dreamed together of expanding Jacob's House. Our philosophy was always to accept whomever God sent into our sanctuary of hope and healing. We made covenant with the children that they would stay with us until their parents were able again to provide a home or until the child "picked" just the right new parents. Together we envisioned a property in the country with two houses as children's homes and small handicap accessible log cabins. We saw a beautiful property with ponds, gardens, and horses. There would be cottage industries, which would provide vocational training, and produce marketable products, which would help sustain Jacob's House.

I knew the difference Jacob's House had made for so many children over the past years and that I must continue serving God in this way. I thought about Jason, while being home schooled; he studied math and science with Roger, another quadriplegic who lived with us. Jason would feed Roger lunch, and Roger helped Jason with his school lessons. One night, at the dinner table, we were talking about blood covenant that the kids were studying in Bible class.

Jason said, "I get covenant. It's how we live."

"Explain that, Jason," I asked.

"Well, Roger can't feed himself, so I feed him. I can't learn math or science without a teacher (looking at me and grinning), so he does for me what I can't do for myself. The Bible talks about farmers needing protection and warriors needing food. We're no different. We need each other. You and Wayne didn't give birth to us, but you give us everything we need. You go to court with us and to school functions. You teach us and provide for us. You love us even when we screw up. That's covenant, right? Jesus gave His life so we could have life, and be in His family calling God Father. He loves us, even when we screw up, too…I hope."

I smiled. "You're right about that."

―――――――――――

Jason summed up my vision in his explanation of covenant. That is what Jacob's House was always meant to be. Remembering that conversation with Jason made me determined to continue looking for that place of safety for our children. No matter what I knew, or how hard I looked, I couldn't find the property of our vision, nor could I rally support; in fact, every door was closing around me.

Late one night I was looking on the internet for properties in our area, and I noticed Branson, Missouri's zip code on a CD cover lying on my desk. On a lark, I put the 65616 in the search box. *Boom!* A window opened to a beautiful Victorian bed and breakfast that was for sale. I knew Billye Brim and Faith Life Church were in Branson. Wow, both ministries were within fifteen miles of the B & B. Branson, it's time for a visit.

It was Easter weekend when we first visited Branson. We attended Sunday morning service at Faith Life Church. The youth of the church were providing special music, and Haley said, "Mommy, I am supposed to be up there with them."

"I believe that, honey," I answered, knowing in my heart we were moving to Branson.

When we returned to Texas, we put our house on the market and started packing. Jeremiah was very nervous, thinking that his birth mom may come to get him before we moved. I had talked to his mother, telling her when we were leaving and where we were going. She agreed that he should go, as she still wasn't ready to care for Jeremiah.

It only took ninety days to sell the house. We loaded big trucks and said our good-byes around town. We were getting ready to get in the van when Jeremiah said, "Mommy, you better look in that big truck first thing when you get to Branson because that's where I'll be."

"Jeremiah, we don't lie, and we don't hide. You'll be in the van with the rest of us when we get to Branson."

Like the animals heading to the Ark, we were heading to our "place called there," not knowing a soul, having no reputation and no monthly support save one little country church, the Word of God Fellowship, and one faithful prayer partner, Lady Bobbie. We were leaving behind my mother, Brian, Ron, Noreen, and my granddaughter, Brittney, as well as our children in Louisiana, putting too many miles between us for weekend visits.

Many of my friends had asked if it was hard to leave everything behind, and I was to think long and hard about that over the months. We were now on mountains instead of flat lands. Jacob asked me why the people in Branson built everything on a slant, and I laughed, "Because we are on a mountain silly." We had trees with leaves that changed into the most beautiful colors before falling, which astounded us. We attended Faith Life Church, and God brought us friends on the very first day. We formed a local board for Jacob's House, but I couldn't write grants or raise partners until I knew the way God wanted me to proceed.

I still wasn't where I needed to be, "celebrating life," nor was my personal joy level very high. It was time for the Branson Victory Campaign with the Copeland's, and I was looking for a spiritual breakthrough. On the last night of the meeting as the children and I were leaving the church, Jacob screamed, "Look, Mom, there's Miss Gloria and my daddy!"

Turning, I saw Jacob looking into an almost life-size poster with a picture of Wayne being prayed for by Gloria Copeland. That picture was taken in 1999 and then used in Gloria's healing book a few years later. It was in magazines every once in a while over the years, but now it was 2005. I knew there were millions of pictures their graphics department could choose from, but this one just kept coming back.

"Can I have this, Mom? I want this poster," he said.

"I'll check on it for you, Jacob, but now let's go home."

As I took his hand, I remembered the day that picture was taken. The wheelchairs were placed in a special section during healing school on Saturday morning, and after Gloria laid hands on those standing in line, she would walk to the wheelchair section touching and praying on her way. Months before the picture was taken, I'd been listening to a series by Leroy Thompson. Leroy spoke on covenant, and something rose up in me (in the middle of the night). I was wearing earphones but talking back to the tape recorder aloud, and it woke Wayne.

"Who you got out there with you, Momma?" He laughed.

"It's just me, Jesus, and Brother Leroy," I answered, knowing he was ready to be rolled over. As I stepped into the bedroom, I said, "Wayne Robichaux, I have a covenant with God and He has promised me peace, as in 'nothing missing and nothing broken.'" I pointed at him and said, "Father, I am one with this man, he's broken, and I believe I receive him whole."

Wayne loved it when a spiritual boldness came over me. But I guess he figured he needed someone even bolder than I to speak to his body. He was chomping at the bit, waiting for Gloria to pray for him. She walked to the end of the row in front of us and then started to leave. I noticed a man who was walking with her turn her around and point at us. She moved to Wayne, laid one hand on his shoulder, the other on his head, and prayed.

As she moved past us, she turned back, pointing at Wayne and said, "Nothing missing, nothing broken."

Tears of joy ran down my face, and Wayne's eyes were huge as he looked at me.

"She must have heard you and Leroy." He grinned.

Three years later, we ordered Gloria's book, *Words that Heal,* to sell at Treasured Possessions. As I looked through the book, I was surprised to see the same picture as the one on the poster but more surprised to see the words on the page next to it, "Shalom, nothing missing, nothing broken."

All the way to the car, Jacob was telling everyone about his daddy's picture on the poster in the church. He just knew we were in the right place at the right time, and so did I, in my heart.

You can know many things in your heart and in faith believe that you receive, but it is the *time test* that is tough. Things were dry; it was time to press in. Money was tight; it was time to press in. We missed our family, but we had to press in and press on. I felt I was doing nothing for the kingdom of God and compared to all the ministry activity I was used to in Texas, it seemed true. I surely did have my answer now to the question. Was it hard to *leave* everything? The answer was no, because I knew that I knew I was called, but it was definitely hard to *stay*. It was hard, but now I knew God was still holding my hand.

It had taken me two years to adjust to getting up in the morning on my own. Wayne had been my alarm clock and my first thought after saying, "Good morning, Lord." I missed him saying, "Fret not thyself, Momma. Come lie on my chest and breathe like this." I missed talking things over with a grownup, one who was totally committed to our life; and most of all I missed being held.

Jacob would come to me, saying, "You look beautiful, Mom." Then he would add, "My dad told you that every day, didn't he, Mom? I remember."

"I remember, too," I answered. I remembered how Wayne would say, "Your momma is faithful. Every time you call her, she will answer you, she'll never leave you." I had no idea he would have such a short time to teach his children to love and respect their mates. They did remember the love, and I thanked God for the example he was to them as a husband and Father.

———————

Haley came home from school one afternoon and said, crying, "Mommy, I forgot my daddy's name."

I picked her up and dried her eyes, "No, baby girl, you didn't. You called him Daddy; others called him Wayne."

She gave me a big smile and said, "That's right. Thanks, Mommy," hugging my neck.

———————

It was our habit every morning as I drove them to school to pray aloud and tell God we were thankful for all things. It was a good time for me as a mother to hear my children's hearts and make corrections on things they may have misunderstood. It was also when they called out the names of our friends and family in prayer.

Haley would generally start. "Father, I am thankful for the Herberts and the Kirkland's and all our friends in Texas, Lady Bobbie, and Ms. Lynn. I am thankful for my grandma and brothers Brian and Ronnie and Noreen and Brittney and all the babies that live in their house and for our family in Louisiana, Jade and Geraldine and Cherie and Josh and other family. I don't know their names right now. I am thankful that Jeremiah won't cuss today and that Jacob will finish all his school work and not hide his assignments and—"

I would say, "Honey, you can't tattle in prayer. You can only confess for yourself and be thankful for your brothers."

"Oh," she would say and then go on. "Thank you for the flowers and the trees that give us oxygen and all the animals and that all our puppies have a good home and are healthy and for this wonderful day and that Mommy would get us a daddy."

Then Jeremiah would start. "I am thankful for my family, for Mom and Jacob and Haley and me. Lord, for Grandma Nelson and for Ronnie, Noreen, Brittney, and Brian and for our friends in church and our friends in Texas and that they will all come and see us. Thank you for Uncle Durm, Kalamity Falls, and that he likes to play with us in the pool and takes us to eat when he comes to visit. Thank you for our school and our teachers and that we will be a major blessing to them. Thank you that we won't get in trouble today and that I won't be in time out and for the car and our food and our house to live in and our church and the boat I am going to buy Mommy when I get bigger with a kitchen and big bedroom and a bathroom and…"

"Good job, honey. Let's move on," I would prompt as we were nearing the school.

Jacob would sit up straight after listening to their prayers. "Lord, I thank you for our president, and I pray for him and Ms. Laura and their children and their pets and for the president's cabinet that they are making good decisions for our country. Thank you that our military is protected and that they are listening to the Holy Spirit and are quick to do what He says, like duck. Thank you for our church and our church family, Mr. Curt and Ms. Kathy and big Jake, Mr. Ron and Ms. Claudia, for all the ministers of the gospel all over the world who tell everyone about Jesus. Thank you for our teachers in youth and children's church; for the God Experience and for Mr. Greg and Ms. Victoria and that it will bring millions of people to Jesus. I thank you for Kalamity Falls, and Uncle Durm, and that he'll teach children about You and their parents will learn, too, and that he will sell a lot of houses and buildings and make movies about Kalamity Falls. Thank you for the Thera-Plex that will help many people and for Treasured Possessions that Mommy will have fun painting. Thank you, that we'll find our country property to build Jacob's House and help a lot of children. Thank you that the puppy that died is with Daddy in heaven. Thank you that Mom will get married again and be happy, and we will have a daddy. Thank you that you are the multiplier of seed sown and we have lots of good seed in the ground, Lord, so we thank you for a good harvest, in Jesus name we pray, Amen."

On the drive home, I would think about the prayers and how grateful I was that my children spoke to the Lord and were not ashamed to pray aloud. "Lord, I'm thankful for the children you have appointed to me and that you give me the strength and wisdom to raise them up in the way they should go, but the daddy thing Lord, we can just skip that."

It was obvious to me that the children missed the "family atmosphere" and the times I'd been more available to them and not under so much pressure. The Kirkland's, friends from church, had taken the children after church on a Friday night and brought them home after church on Sunday. It was a shock to be alone. It was then that I realized I hadn't been alone in over three years, not for five minutes. "Lord, help me get back to that place of peace where I can celebrate life again, not just live it. Amen."

HIDE THIS NUGGET IN YOUR HEART

"Trust and know—I have directed you in the way of wisdom; I have led you in upright paths. *When* you walk, your steps will not be impeded; And *if* you run, you will not stumble."

–Proverbs 4

COVENANT FRIENDS

March 14, 2006, I received a phone call from Quantico, Virginia. The DNA office of the marine corps asked if I was Penny Nelson and if I knew anyone by the name of Chris Munson. At first, I thought it was a crank call, but the name was familiar in a strange sort of way.

"I know the name Munson. Why?"

"It seems he is the son of the captain of the USS *Mispillion*, and he said he met you in 1952."

"Oh, my goodness, that's true. But how did you find me?"

"We had your family on file in the DNA register because your aunt submitted a sample in case we found remains to match your father, Forest Nelson. Our contact number is for your cousin Durmond, so we called him to see if he knew where you were. He said he talked to you every day and gave me this number. I'm calling to see if you will allow us to release your contact information to Mr. Munson."

"Are you kidding?" I asked. It wasn't ten minutes before the phone rang. It was Chris. He had made it his determined purpose to find me for the reunion of the crew of the USS *Mispillion* to be held in October of that year. It seems that they had been looking for their queen for years without success, so Chris was assigned the daunting task of finding me.

"Penny, I'm telling you I found a parking place right in front of the White House; this is impossible. I'm finding everything I'm looking for lately." He laughed. "You won't believe this, but Air Force One just flew over me."

"Wave to the president for me, Chris. We pray for him every day." We laughed, we cried, and we talked on and on. He told me about the reunion and about Steve Dengler, a shipmate who had been looking for me. Then suddenly, Chris said, "Penny, would you go on the USS *Mispillion* website and write a note to the guys?"

"Sure, I will," I answered.

"That will knock them out." He chuckled.

I spent a lot of time thinking about that little note and trying to understand what was happening. I knew that my life had been changed by their love and kindness. I knew that the cruise book was tattered from me looking through it so many times over the years. I saw faces burned into my memory, but I had no idea that anyone of them ever thought of my family or me.

After I posted my note, I started getting e-mails from my brothers of the *Mispillion*. They came from all corners of the country, filling me in on their lives and asking about mine. Then the phone calls started coming, and every one of them ended in tears of joy.

My navy buddies even managed to track down some marines. One was my daddy's wingman, Dick Francisco, the marine that wrote my name on his airplane and signed letters to me, "Love, Daddy." I knew that when I asked God to help me renew my joy He would, but I never dreamed he would call out the navy and the marine corps to do it!

Chris sent a package for me by overnight mail. The card said that this item had been sitting on his desk waiting orders so it could take off. I opened the box to find a model of a "Miss Penny" airplane, which I had no idea even existed. I got packages with *Mispillion* bumper stickers, *Mispillion* hats, a *Mispillion* watch, and a copy of the *Mispillion* cruise book on CD. Since it was near Easter, a special basket of goodies came from one of my Cajun brothers and his wife to our family. Many of the men who had served on the *Mispillion* called and wrote to Mother; one sent her a model of the airplane, as well. We booked our reservation for Baton Rouge, Louisiana. We were going to the *Mispillion* reunion.

Chris and I wrote daily e-mails, sometimes several each day. We talked on the phone, and he designed a wonderful presentation board for the reunion telling our story that included many pictures. The ship's photographer, Wally Barrus, helped put it all together, and at the reunion gave us copies of the ships photo history from 1952-1954.

The children were so excited with all the commotion over the reunion, and the story of how I met these wonderful men delighted them. They told me if they had known I was a queen, they would have treated me a lot better!

One morning while I was getting the children ready for school, Jeremiah said, "Mommy, aren't you worried about going to that reunion? They're expecting a baby, and you got old."

"I'm not worried, honey, believe me. So have they."

I thought Jeremiah and Haley were too young to make the trip, and in fact, this trip was really for Mother and me. However, Jacob was ten, and I knew he would learn so much about the military, family, and friends. The Kirkland family kindly volunteered to stay at our house for the week and watch over the little ones and the dogs until we returned from our great adventure.

We had plenty of time to talk on the drive to Baton Rouge so I filled Jacob in on the lives of some of the men he would meet. There were not many from 1952, but the ones that were there were special to me. One in particular, Herman Kallam was the face that had looked at me all through the years in that cruise book, the sailor who had been frozen in time, just for me. I had asked Steve Dengler if he knew who that man in the picture was, and he started the hunt. He posted the picture from the fifties and sent it out to his mailing list, asking, "Who is this?" It was not long, and we had the answer.

But when I walked in the hotel and saw Mr. Kallam standing there, it hit me. I was again in that same circle of blessing, the bubble. He took me in his arms, and it was as if I was dreaming. Paul Hopper, another brother in whose blue eyes I got lost, hugged me, and I told him, "Don't let go yet." Henry Stephens who had battled his health just before the reunion said he was not going to die until he saw me again. His wife told me she thought this reunion saved his life. I thought to myself, *Mine too*. The Stephen's and the Sibley's were the hosts in Baton Rouge, so this Cajun by marriage immediately adopted them as family. Dave Sibley spent hours on the telephone and e-mailing me and most importantly, praying for me, for the vision of the children's home and for our well-being. I met others who were from different service years, but they were connected to me, too. I pondered that in my heart since I had received that first phone call. I looked for my marine daddy, Dick Francisco, but he was unable to make the journey from Washington state due to deteriorating health. I was so glad we had spent so much time catching up on the phone.

During one of those long conversations, Dick said as a fighter pilot it was very tough, so when the pilots got back together after their missions each day, they put their minds on their families to forget the horror of war. They talked about their wives and kids and showed off their pictures so they were well acquainted with each other's families. He said, "When Forey was shot down, I carried a picture of you along with my own children. I had a daughter about your age, Penny, and so did some of the other guys. Your Dad was one of us, and when he went down, we found a new reason to go on. That reason was to help you."

"Dick, you guys were the reason I held on, your letters and your love," I answered him, amazed that it gave them purpose during such trying times.

"When we got the news about you getting polio, we asked permission to put your name on my plane. We took up a collection, part of it we sent to your mother to help her out, and the other part we used to buy a piece of land in South Korea for an orphanage. The last I heard, it was still open."

For a moment, I was speechless. "Dick, do you know that I have an orphanage?"

"That's what I heard, honey. We're so glad you turned out the way you did, but that isn't all. When I got home, I opened a ranch for disabled and disadvantaged children, and I have just retired from that foundation. Our slogan is 'the best thing for a child's insides is a horse on the outside.' We spoke a little longer, but the emotions left us needing time to think on all these things. Dick promised to send me information on his foundation and all the other things he had done with his life since Korea. A few days later, I received his picture and articles about his work. One article was on his being awarded the Jefferson Award, a community volunteer service award in 1991. I smiled a very big smile, as I had been a recipient of the Jefferson Award in 1993. I laughed out loud, thinking, *Like father, like daughter.*

The trip was hard for Mother—even though she still worked every day, getting to work by five in the morning, cleaning her house, and dressing like a million dollars. As Jeremiah said, "We were getting old." She caught a bug the first day, and we spent most of our time in the hotel room, but not Jacob. He hit it off with my brothers, and they took him everywhere. He played with gators on a swamp tour, went on the USS *Kidd*, saw the WWII museum, and enjoyed his time with the men—honorable, loving men.

Mother was so happy to see the guys from our past and to tell the story and remember the goodness the men had shown us. It was wonderful to say thank you to those strangers who were now dear friends. She was showing pictures of Daddy and Jon and his family. I thought as I watched her that she was happy to show them that she had been entrusted to care for me and with their help, she'd accomplished her mission, just as they had.

The days passed far too quickly, and it was time to say good-bye. Jacob cried, and I think he called Chris on the cell phone twenty times before Chris boarded his plane. Jacob didn't want to let go of any of his new friends, and I saw a difference in him from being around men—these men.

"Mom, can we go to the reunion next year?"

"We'll try, Son, but no promises yet," I answered. "Remember, honey, just because we said good-bye today doesn't mean you'll never see Mr. Clyde or Chris or Mr. Paul again. Also, when we come to Louisiana the next time, we can visit Mr. Dave and Mr. Henry. And don't forget Harry and Carol are going to meet us in Branson next week."

We talked about all the things he had learned. I reminded him to do his homework as he was missing school to take the trip.

He read to me from his school history book about American wars and smiled, saying, "Mom, this is stuff I saw at that museum and things I heard about there. I know that freedom is not free, Mom. It cost you and Grandma a lot, and I know it was hard on you, like my dad being in heaven is hard on me; but it's good to be free, isn't it?"

"Yes, darling, it's very good to be free."

We'd been so engrossed in the conversation that we missed our turn and found ourselves on a two-lane country highway.

"You know, Jacob, I had my first car when I was your age."

"I know, Mom. Grandma told me about it before you did."

"Well, here we are in the middle of nowhere. Would you like to learn to drive?" I asked.

"You bet!" he shouted.

Our van was fitted with hand controls, so it was easy to slide my seat back and put Jacob on the seat with me. He could steer the wheel and work the pedals while I had access to the controls. He did a great job. Jake had concentrated so hard that when he returned to his own seat, I reached over and tickled him. He was stiff and very serious about driving, so repeatedly I found another place where he was ticklish. He wiggled and giggled, and then without warning, he laughed aloud, from his toes... "Thank you, Lord," I whispered.

"Do you know what I want to be when I grow up, Mom?" he asked.

"No, honey, I don't. What do you want to be?"

"Well, first, I think I'll marry a blue-eyed blonde like Daddy did..." He giggled. "...and then we are going to help a lot of people. I think I'll have about eleven houses. I want a restaurant; it will be beautiful with candles and flowers on all the tables, and I'm going to cook some of our favorite recipes. I'll have a lot of animals and a lot of children, and I'll probably preach some, too."

Then he asked, "Do kids have to move out when they turn eighteen?"

"No, Jacob. Some kids are still in school and others are working but not able to support themselves yet. There's no rule. Everyone matures at a different pace. Why, honey? Did you think I was gonna kick you out at eighteen?"

"No, but I'm thinking when I get married I'll probably still live with you."

Now I was laughing. "Somehow I think you'll change your mind and want to live in one of those eleven houses with your wife, but you don't have to decide right now. Dream on, Son... reach high...have big God dreams because your greatest days are just ahead."

"Do you think you will ever get married again, Mom?"

"No, honey, I don't think so; and after all, who would want a funny family like ours?"

"Well, the kids and I want a daddy."

"Jacob, you need to be thankful for all the daddies who share their lives with us, like Mr. Darrell and Mr. Curt."

"I am thankful, Mom, but we want a daddy of our own," he said, and then he just got quiet.

The daddy subject was fresh in my heart, too. After all the weekend brought to mind, all the prayers I had prayed as a child for my daddy and all the special men who had stood in the gap for me during the years, I realized Jacob was right; every child wants a daddy of their own, and every child needs one.

HIDE THIS NUGGET IN YOUR HEART

Jesus said, "Mark my words, no one who sacrifices houses, brothers, sisters, mother, father, children, land—whatever—because of me, and the Message—will lose out. They'll get it all back, but multiplied many times in homes, brothers, sisters, mothers, children, and land—but also in troubles. Then the bonus of eternal life."

Mark 10:30, The Message

SAME VISION, SAME HEART

Life was moving on, and I thought we were all doing better emotionally, at last. We were busy with the things of life (the cares of life as spoken of in Mark 4) and most of everyday was work. We just weren't spontaneous any more, nor did we laugh much. We just pressed on with a smile that didn't quite make it to our eyes. I realized my life was a bit boring as a teenager might say; it was reflected in my clothes and my routines. As an artist, I would say my life had become colorless. I was doing all the right things—ironing the clothes, cleaning the house, cooking and shopping and driving the same old route to school, to work, and to church, then home again.

Haley said one day, "We are the go to school, go to work, go to church family." I spent a lot of time with friends trying to ignite a passion in them for good things. Somewhere, in the back of my mind, I had settled into the thought that God would let me finish raising these last little ones and I could retire quietly, or should I say, *be put out to pasture*. Parts of the vision God had given me years earlier seemed so far away and unattainable. The bed and breakfast idea had fallen through when I moved to Branson and the country property was just an out of reach vision. I did know, however, to wait on God. I was not released any more than I was inspired. I kept looking, trying, working, and believing I was in the right place, but it was getting harder and harder to stay.

My cousin Durm had been calling me and praying over me since Wayne moved to heaven and had included me in his prayer group by e-mail. One day I asked him about a man he'd put on the prayer request, saying, "Durm, what's this guy's name on the e-mail, and what am I praying for—his health, wealth, peace, or what?"

"I don't know," he answered. "He's a guy that sits at a round table in the morning, has a cup of something, and reads with a big dog. He's your husband."

"My, what?"

"Husband, that's what God told me to do. Pray for him; he's your husband."

I quickly changed the subject.

One afternoon a friend came for a treatment on my exercise equipment, and I asked her, "Patty, do you think God would answer my children's prayer for a daddy without—like talking to me about it?"

She laughed and asked, "Why do you ask?"

I told her about the kids praying daily for a daddy. Then I told her about what Durm said. "How long ago did Durm say God told him to pray for your husband?"

"I don't know, maybe a couple of months, why?"

"About two months ago, God told me to pray for your husband."

It got very quiet in the house.

One Sunday morning, Tina, a beautiful young woman who sang at church and whose husband, Eric, taught my kids in children's church, sat down beside me, and said, "I need to talk to you, Ms. Penny."

She had a funny look on her face, and I turned to hear what she wanted to talk about, when suddenly she got up and said, "I'll be right back." She was acting a bit odd.

When Tina returned she said, "My brother-in-law Dan loves kids, he's a Rhema graduate, a cabinet maker, he has his own business, and he is my best friend. He loves to fish and camp and..."

I interrupted her and said, "Tina, I don't have any children available for adoption right now, but when I find the right property, I'll be glad to interview him," thinking she thought one of the kids was available.

"Oh, no. You see, he wants to get married. Didn't I mention he's my ex-brother-in-law.?"

I nearly fell over. "*Today?*" I answered, laughing nervously.

"Well, no, but I've been talking to him about you for several months because he is your age, and the women he dates thinks he's crazy for wanting children. I told him I thought you probably had the same problem with men your age, and well, he's coming here to meet you today. Did I mention he's good looking?"

I smiled at her and told her I was not looking to remarry. Then I kind of laughed and said, "But the kids have been praying for a daddy, so if he wants to take them fishing sometime that'd be great."

I don't remember much about the service that day. When it was over, I walked to the front where I met the kids. Tina was there, along with other friends of ours, and she introduced me to Dan. We spoke for a minute and then I gathered up the kids and we left.

As I pulled into the garage at home, my cell phone rang, and Kathy said, "Penny, this guy came from Tulsa to meet you and wanted to take you to lunch. Where are you?"

"I'm at home," I answered, "and no one mentioned lunch."

"Well, we are at the Pasta House, so get over here."

The Pasta House was just a short distance from our house. I told her I would walk the dogs and then meet them. We had a great time together, and I really enjoyed Dan. He was easy to be with and fun to talk to, and handsome just as Tina said, with the clearest blue eyes I'd ever seen. As we finished the meal and the wait staff was ready for us to clear out, Jacob stood up and shook Dan's hand saying, "You're going to make a great dad." I wanted to disappear or make him disappear, but I just smiled and thanked Dan for lunch.

Dan and I started e-mailing, and soon it was almost daily or we would talk on the phone. I really loved his ability to communicate. We shared many views and values and laughed about our past. We talked about our adult children and what they were doing with their lives. We talked about how we felt about small children and their needs. Dan was a "big brother," a Rhema ranger working with teens, planning and implementing campouts and other ranger projects. We talked about our dreams, the things that had hurt us or set us back. We both preferred humor to complaining, and we both loved God with all our hearts. It was during one these conversations that I learned Dan had a big black dog, and he sat at his round kitchen table every morning— drinking coffee and reading his Bible.

One of my friends, Rebecca who had been taking treatments with me on the exercise unit had a Victorian clothing store. Her gift was to bring out the best in any woman. One night she came to my house for a treatment and had a big bag of clothes with her. She said, "If there's something in there you like and it fits you, it's yours." My friend Patty was there, so she helped me try on the different garments. It was like Christmas. Each outfit I picked had a price tag on it to cut off and give to her for her records. As I did, I realized that it had been nearly seventeen years since I had purchased clothes for myself. My mother had brought me new outfits (the tags were off) or friends donated their beautiful clothes to me. I had little need for this kind of wardrobe at the homeless shelter. These clothes were colorful and bright, sexy girl things reminding me of my thirteenth birthday party at the Riviera Hotel in Palm Springs. That was the beginning of a second metamorphosis taking place in my life, a breath of fresh air; the celebration of life was returning.

Dan called to let me know he was coming for a visit and would like to take the kids and me out to dinner.

"Where would you like to go?" he asked.

I didn't care, but Dan and Jacob both liked Mexican food, so that determined our big evening.

I enjoyed all the e-mails and conversations with Dan, but being on a "date" was a bit tough for me. The kids thought it was great and could hardly contain their enthusiasm. Branson is full of entertainers, and there are few places in town where there isn't a show of some kind. This restaurant was the same. A one-man show was starting, and we found ourselves delighted and singing along at the table. One song would be about Texas, and then the next about Tulsa. We laughed at the coincidence. Then he sang an old song from the sixties, which the kids started singing right along with us.

"How did you know the words to that song?" I asked them.

"*Shrek 2.*" They laughed. Who couldn't love a guy that sings aloud on the first date? We went to a park, and Dan crawled through a big tunnel with the kids while I laughed at his spunk and enjoyed watching the kids enjoy him.

As the months passed, I realized how much I had missed talking to a man who was not related to me. I enjoyed his conversations, and the way he looked at things. I liked it that he prayed for me and that he shared his thoughts on things that concerned me. I loved to laugh with him at the end of a tough day, putting everything in perspective; and I enjoyed encouraging him and sharing with him.

I noticed in the kids daily thank you prayers, they were really honing in on Dan. "Thank you, Lord, that Dan is going to marry our mom…" When Dan would come to town, Haley and Jeremiah would grab him by the legs and say, "Are you going to marry Mom?"

We were never alone, and I sensed that Dan wasn't very romantic. So, when he came to town for the New Year's celebration, I was a little surprised that he held my hand as we stopped at a market to grab a bag of cookies we promised to bring the children. The night was wonderful, the entertainment great. We ate, sang, and prayed.

A few days later, Dan wrote me an e-mail that said in part, "I'm not trying to be mushy, but you really had it going on…that face and that hair…I noticed."

I wrote back that I was a woman and "mushy" is good, and it was about time.

Dan and I were both interested in each other, but distance and our age sure made it easy to drag along, making little progress. We would get closer, the kids would push harder, and yet committing to change was not getting any easier. By now though, we knew one day we'd be together, but it just wasn't convenient. On more than one occasion, Dan would call about a property he had seen online or say things like, "Look for some land with a big old house on it and a building for my shop." Or he'd call about something he saw for sale in the Branson area.

Every February we had Vision Sunday at our church. Vision Sunday is a time we write our vision for the following year. First, we were to consider what we want to do for the kingdom of God, next addressing debt resolution and finally what we desire personally and as a family. This particular year I added, "Lord, I want a formal marriage proposal." I didn't want to rock along with a casual understanding. I wanted my children to get on with their lives today and not put their future happiness on a daddy that may not materialize.

I forgot all about that item on my vision list and then months passed by. Dan and I were e-mailing each other and the subject of commitment and marriage came up. He then told me about a list he had written in 2001, after hearing a sermon on being specific with God. This list had ten things he desired in a wife, and he said he had hoped God would take notice. In his e-mail, he mentioned that I met all ten and then listed about five. I laughed and wrote back that I'd never been on anyone's top ten list, much less ten out of ten. The five he listed did fit me. They included loving God with all my heart and loving children.

One night, I told Dan about a client of mine who mentioned a ranch that was coming on the market. I was told the owner was moving to Texas and selling the ranch so I would need to contact him quickly.

Dan said, "Penny, you need to call them now."

In the two years I'd known Dan, I had never heard the tone he used that night. He had a surety in his voice that confirmed I needed to make the call. I tried but didn't make contact with the owners.

My girlfriend Victoria called about her husband, Greg's upcoming birthday and mentioned that when she asked him what he wanted to do, he said he wanted to take my kids and me to an amusement park, Celebration City. They had taken my children to other venues and the kids had so much fun. Since

I couldn't walk through amusement parks or stand up to other physical outings, they provided much needed entertainment and memory making that my children needed. Victoria said, "Greg, I don't think Penny will enjoy that; it would be too much walking."

Greg said, "Well, I want her to enjoy seeing her kids have fun, not just hearing about it. We can get her one of those electric carts."

I laughed and said, "Victoria, I will do it for Greg because I love him, and it is his birthday." Greg's birthday is on July Fourth, so we had the day off, and all I needed to do was relax, put on my make up, and go.

Later that morning, I had the strangest feeling I should call my friend Curt and tell him I was thinking about him and praying for him as he studied for the bar exam. I mentioned I was having trouble getting in touch with a ministry regarding their ranch that was for sale.

Curt said, "The man that built my house is part of that ministry in some way, and he just gave me his cell number yesterday. Call him. I bet he'll know how to contact the owners."

Within an hour, I was on the phone with the principals of the ministry that owned the ranch. I asked if it would be possible to see the property, as I was interested in it. We laughed when I said I had no money, but if they were able to carry the note as I'd done with all the properties I owned in Texas, I wanted to talk. I was given directions to the ranch for a meeting that was scheduled for Sunday afternoon. I called Dan and asked him if he wanted to see the land when I went. He said he woould try to make it in on Sunday. We were both excited about the possibilities.

From the moment we met at Celebration City, Greg and I were locked in regarding the vision, the land, the future, and things we both had in our hearts to do with hurting people. I was excited as I had longed for someone with zeal to stimulate me again, and Greg was just the right man. Victoria kept the children in check and let us carry on all evening, setting a plan to meet on the land after church. Greg and I are both passionate about God and the vision He has given each of us. We were friends and partners in our visions, his The God Experience, and mine, Jacob's House.

Saturday morning I knew I needed to locate the ranch so that everyone could follow me the next day and not waste time getting lost. The kids and I got in the car and headed out. On the way, I called Dan and told him I was going to find the land and I would call him if it were worth his time to drive from Tulsa, as many properties I looked at left him cold. I'll never forget the moment I turned onto the land, and my eyes beheld the exact vision I had written in a grant in 2004 describing our country property right down to the two ponds, two houses, and horses. I hit the brakes and sat staring while Jacob threw the car door open and ran toward the house on the hill.

I couldn't drive another inch. I picked up the phone and called Dan. "I found it," I said, and then Dan did something he'd never done before. He asked if he could ramble a minute. I was the rambler in this relationship so I just said, "Go ahead."

He told me about eighty acres he owned with a gentle hill on the left and a gentle hill on the right with a valley between and a ridgeline of trees. He said he always saw a two-story house on the hill and asked if I knew what that house was for.

"What?" I asked.

"A children's home," he answered. Each point that Dan described I was seeing through my windshield.

"Dan," I said, "I'm looking at your property."

Dan answered, "I sold that property when I divorced. I'll see you in the morning.

My heart and mind were full from just thinking about what I had seen the day before. While doing my hair for church, the Lord impressed on the inside of me that we needed a bunkhouse. "Okay, Lord," I said, finishing up. Dan arrived early and rode with us to church.

The morning thank you prayer began as usual, and Jeremiah was praying about Dan marrying his mom when Haley came over the seat, looking him in the eye, and said, "What's taking you so long, Dan, to ask my mom to marry you? She is beau-ti-ful, and you two are good together. She'll only marry a Christian, and you are one; and you like kids, and she has some...so what's the holdup?"

I smiled at him and said, "Do you feel any pressure?"

He laughed.

"Well," I reminded him, "you only hear this on occasion. I have heard it for the two years we've dated."

During service that morning, one of the pastors said there were people who knew they were supposed to marry in the congregation, and they needed to step up and step out. The scripture used for the sermon was marked in my Bible with a heart. It was the promise I received years earlier, Psalm 113. Dan was sharing my Bible and saw the note about barren woman, happy homemaker, and I had penned in the margin "Jacob's House beginning." I felt the heat on my neck, and Dan just looked at me with an odd smile. Two hours later, we were standing on the land knowing that we had found our country property. It was all there; our big house, another beautiful log home, a mobile home, and a large shop on seventy-one lush acres.

We met a young boy who was living there who would soon need a new home, and we both knew that he was to be a part of our family, if only for a season. I had no idea how God was going to bring this about, but I did know without a doubt, that it was everything I'd seen in a vision in 2004. We walked the land, explored the houses and the shop, and marveled at the beautiful horses. The kids ran as hard as they could and let us know they didn't want to leave.

We had been there long enough, and yet Greg hadn't shown up, so I called him to let him know we were leaving. He had fallen asleep so we agreed to meet early in the week and have a look around together. As Dan and I drove away from the property, Dan said, "You know, on the way from Tulsa this morning, the Lord said we needed a bunkhouse."

"What?" I laughed. "He told me the same thing." This made us even more certain that we were on the right track.

Monday, I got news that my mother was ill and I was needed in Houston. I called Greg to ask him to contact the pastor who lived on the land and tell him we were interested in the property. I said, "Greg, let him know I'm not a nut, and I really want to talk about the land, but my mother needs me in Texas, and I have to leave."

I was going to give him directions to the ranch when I heard him say, "I'm walking on the land right now, Penny."

I was sure that he could do whatever needed to be done to put us in the running for the property. There were other interested parties and all of them had the means to purchase the land, but I knew it was ours and I knew Greg was the one to help me.

Rita and her husband, Paul, were partners to Jacob's House, and she'd taken a video camera with her to the property on that first visit. She made a movie of that historic day. I was very glad to have it to show family and friends in Texas who'd known the vision for years and were now able to see it with their own eyes. The excitement was unbelievable, but the pressure in Texas to establish my mother in an assisted-living environment was intense, and trying to help her sell her business was frustrating. After years of vibrant good health, my mother was deteriorating physically and having memory problems. The woman who was so independent now needed help, but hated giving in to receiving that help. It took nearly two weeks to tie up all the loose ends and return to Branson.

During my absence, Greg and another friend of ours, Paul, negotiated a purchase agreement, and we were working daily to bring it to pass. I was on the run day and night in meetings. The kids and I took the young boy from the ranch as a foster placement. We moved our medical equipment to the ranch while we were preparing to close on the property, storing the furniture and boxes from the business.

I'd pick up my messages late at night and find that Dan had been in Branson and hadn't connected with me. We talked, and he would tell me he was at Tina's but had to leave early the next morning. This happened on more than one occasion, when finally he said, "Penny, I've been coming to town because I felt I needed to formally propose to you. I have waited and waited because I couldn't see how to get everything moved to Branson. We both have mothers who need us and homes, businesses, and I didn't want to be a weekend dad. I want to wake up the kids and make them breakfast. I want to drive them to the bus stop and be home when they eat dinner. I want to read them bedtime stories and tuck them in and pray with them every night. But the last thing I wanted was to ask you to marry me on the phone. Penny, will you marry me?"

I was not hesitant at all and answered, "Yes, Dan, I will marry you." Then I apologized, laughing, and told him about my vision list and wanting a formal proposal. "I guess we'll have to seal this with a kiss the next time you make it to Branson."

We visited a bit longer, discussed our schedules, and said good night. Climbing into bed and talking to the Lord, I said, "Wow, when you get ready to do something, Lord, you sure do know how to spice it up."

The next visit to town (which was quick) Dan did seal the deal with a kiss, and he brought me something... a letter he had written in 2004. It's wonderful to serve a loving God who never forgets your dreams, answers your prayers, and will bring you the desires of your heart if you just hang on.

DAN'S WRITING

I want to write some things down that are on my mind and some of the desires of my heart. Going back as a child and growing up in a family with parents that I know loved me very much but struggled with very little money. In the fifties, the attitude of the people in little Pentecostal churches was "Lord, you keep them humble and we will keep them poor." A good offering was ten dollars and a bag of groceries. I remember one time in North Florida, we were conducting a tent revival, and the crowds were so small you could count them on one hand. There was an older gentleman that had been coming to the meeting, and one night after service, he told my dad that he wanted to give us some food from his freezer. That was fine with us, as we needed groceries. I was driving by this time, so Dad let me take the van down the road to the old gentleman's house. He loaded me down with all kinds of stuff out of his freezer, the only problem it was all so badly freezer burned, as much as we tried, the food was not edible. It had been in the freezer so long that it was black and dried out. However, God always saw us through. This reminds me of another time years earlier, I was only a little tike about four, and Dad was the pastor of a little Assembly of God mission Church in Walsenburg, Colorado. The church was meeting in an old storefront on Main Street and had three families attending, one of the those families lived on a struggling cattle ranch fifty miles from town so they could only come to church twice a month. We were living in a little eighteen-foot trailer that my parents bought with the money they had from the sale of their farm that started them out in ministry. One day Mom had done her best fixing supper with what she had, and called us to the table. After Dad said the blessing over the food, I said "Mom, all I want for supper is a piece of bread and jelly." She realized that she hadn't bought any bread earlier that day when she was buying food for dinner and had spent all that she had, which meant she couldn't go across the street to buy a loaf of bread. Mom was true to her faith and did not complain but said a little prayer under her breath thanking God for supplying the desire of her little boy. At that very moment, the property owner who lived on the property knocked on the door, and there in her hands was a loaf of homemade bread, hot just out of the oven and just in time for supper. What an awesome Heavenly Father we serve. These are just two of the many stories of how God has provided, proving His love. All through the years growing up I missed having someone to play with my parents were unable to have more children, so I loved it when I found someone my age while on the road. For the most part, I was never any trouble for my parents; I really wanted to please them. I stayed in the ministry with my parents until two years after I married, when it was obvious that I needed to stay home and raise my growing family, as the offerings were not sufficient to support two families.

I enjoyed every day traveling and working for the Lord. I enjoyed having a wife at my side learning how to raise our son, David, and soon we were blessed with a little girl we named Sandy. I was the happiest I had ever been in my life, two kids and a wife to love and provide for. There are many fond memories of those days with kids in the yard and a wife that made me happy just being there by my side sharing every moment of life and making the best of every experience, hoping to grow old together. Now the children have become adults with lives of their own and my wife found someone else to love. Letting her go was the hardest thing I have ever done.

This brings me to the present (2004), and I still have dreams that have not fully happened. I have a strong desire to have a place to call my own, real earth under my feet not some borrowed piece of land and a real roof over my head instead of a tent or trailer that has seen too many highway miles that is too cold in the winter and unbearably hot in the summer. I long for a house in the country where there is room to work and play and land enough that playing children don't bother a neighbor, a place with trees for the children to climb and a big garden with all kinds of good things to eat. A place that always has room for friends to stop by and spend a night or two and a wife that loves to make it a home to come home to, with a wife who is happy with the simple things in life. A wife with a pleasant smile and an encouraging word, who enjoys being at my side free to enjoy her womanhood as God designed loving her husband and basking in his love for her. Is this a dream or can it be true? I thank God for giving me the desires of my heart as promised in His Word.

This is my statement of faith and my prayer: Thank you, Heavenly Father, for the wife you are giving me. I pray that you take good care of her for me until the time comes when I can take care of her. That you be there for her, providing, caring, protecting and loving her like you love me. Until that time, I will be patient, thanking you daily for the blessings you have given me. My future is bright because you are the light that brightens my day and the hope that is in my heart. Thank you for a bride that loves you most of all and loves me as only a godly woman can love her man. Thank you, Lord, for I know that you are able and that you are willing and present to meet our every need as a loving Father. Thank you for answering my prayers. Amen.

Daniel Koontz

As I finished his writing, I was amazed at the timing, 2004 was the same year I had seen as in a vision the land for Jacob's House and had described it in the grant I was writing in Texas. As I reread Dan's writing, I realized we had a similar dream at the same time, and now nine weeks after walking on the land and entering the initial negotiations, we took possession. I started praying, "Lord, help me to be all that Dan needs to love him and bless him beyond what he can ask, think, or dream.

We decided to have a big party and invited many people who had supported us and other friends and family members. We called it a "partner roundup." We ate wonderful food and were very entertained with good music and the mood of celebration.

Dan took the microphone from one of the singers. I was a bit surprised as Dan isn't much for speaking to large crowds, but he is a one-on-one kind of guy. He began talking about the amazing acquisition of the land, the wonderful people who were surrounding us, and thanking those who had put the plan together. He shared a little of our history, and I was thinking, "Wow, he is pretty good at this and even a bit funny." He spoke about his desire to remarry and that he'd been looking for the right women for years. He said, "I looked high," and then looking down at me said, "and I looked low before I found, Penny." Everyone laughed and I did, too. Then he said, "Penny, right here in front of your friends and family, and some of mine, I want to formally ask you to be my wife. Will you marry me?" I was undone.

Several of our guests being preachers said, "Let's do it now!"

Later, as the guests were leaving, Dan and I sat on the front porch with Greg and Victoria. Dan handed Greg a sheet of paper to look at. "I wrote this in church in 2001, Greg, describing the women I wanted for my wife. What do you think?"

In a minute, Greg smiled big and said, "Sounds like you found her."

Now that it was official, it was time to plan the wedding. We thought we would have a handful of friends on the land and a very small ceremony; however, the plans began to grow and grow. We had little time to put the wedding together, but our friends managed to do a remarkable job. They coordinated the wedding and a "Hootenanny" for Jacob's House on the very same day. Things were so busy, really too busy to stop and think about what was happening and how God was answering so many prayers; putting together a celebration we could not have imagined.

I wanted Mother to be with us for the wedding, but she was too frail to make the trip. She said she would be ready to move to Branson when the weather was warmer. Noreen and Ronnie had two "fragile" toddlers both in foster care and were unable to take them out of state to attend. Lady Bobbie and Frank said they'd be able to come for the wedding and so could Maria, my long-time friend and bookkeeper for the Garden and Jacob's House. Bessie had just recovered from cancer but was coming with Maria, making the wedding an extraordinary event.

Chris Munson called to say he'd be by my side, and he had a surprise for me. I had spoken to Dick Francisco, my father's wingman. He called to tell me he wouldn't be strong enough to come for the wedding and would soon be moving into a nursing home. I was struck in my heart with that information, knowing my mother was facing that, too, as both were in their nineties. Mother was diagnosed with dementia and had become as frail as a little bird. Dick teased me and said he was checking the guy out that wanted to marry me. Laughing, he said, "That's what Italian daddies do." I was lost in thought after hanging up. Chris was sending a model of Dick's plane the "Miss Penny" for a ceremony the marines were arranging to honor Dick. We were coming full circle—Dick, Mother, and me. A few days later, I received a check for Jacob's House and one for me, personally. They were signed Dick Francisco in red, the note that came with them said, "Love, Daddy." It was becoming very clear to me that God was up to something big.

HIDE THIS NUGGET IN YOUR HEART

Follow the dream giver.

ONE VISION,
ONE HEART

November 22, 2008, was the date of our wedding. My Yorkie, Juliette, started having puppies just after midnight and needed my help. She averaged three puppies in each litter, but she delivered her sixth puppy after dawn on our wedding day. I was physically exhausted, and when I looked in the mirror, it showed.

People started dropping by to participate in the hootenanny and couldn't resist a little personal time with me, either for instruction or introduction. We had been busy all day with our guests and the hootenanny, and before we knew, it was time to go to the church. We were counting the heads of children, giving the Houston guests directions to the church, and packing the car arriving at the last minute.

One of the photographers said, "Come with me to the bride's room for some pictures." I hated having my picture taken on a good day, but I'd been up all night and worked outside on the ranch all day. There was no way I could get excited about pictures.

It wasn't long and the pastor came in to have a prayer with me and to tell me that when the music started the double doors would open for me to walk through. I was nervous but not alone; my strength was right on cue. Chris Munson, the captain's son of the *Mispillion* was there, but that was not all. His surprise was that three other crewmembers that spanned the years the ship was in service were there with him as the father of the bride.

Cheyenne, Dan's little brother (from the Big Brothers and Sisters program) shared his big brother's special day as he, Brian, Jacob, and Keirsten lit the many candles that brought a wonderful glow to the altar where Dan and I would make our promises to each other.

The music started, and we went through the double doors moving into position at the altar. Dan, so handsome standing there smiling; Jeremiah and Haley, grinning from ear to ear (they tasted victory); Becky, ever strong, smiling, and I know praying for me under her breath; and Ray, Dan's best man and childhood friend watching my approach. A million thoughts rushed through my mind, and then I heard, "Who gives this bride in marriage?"

Chris answered, "The crew of the USS *Mispillion* standing in for her father, a United States Marine, do give her in marriage."

Clete, the officiating minister, invited all clergy present to come forward and join in prayer with us. It seemed half of the room moved forward. My daughter-in-law Michelle said to Brian, "Is that all your mother knows is preachers? We're surrounded."

Becky's husband Darrell spoke a blessing over all of our family. Our family of the present, our families of the past, our family of the future, a blessing over all the children God would bring to our home; children who we would make covenant with for their forever home, that forever in their hearts, they have a home at Jacob's House.

We truly drew together as a family as we received communion served by our friends Bruce and Donna, creating a sacred memory especially for Jacob as communion had always signified an important family time for him.

Dan and I were fascinated as, with the eye of a master, Mo orchestrated like a beautiful dance the capturing of each inspired snapshot. Without a word, he imparted his vision of a precious moment, a happy laugh, a sweet smile, the joy of the day to David and Jennifer as their God-given talents created photographs to be prized for a lifetime.

In slow motion, I remembered saying good-bye to Daddy as a little girl. I remembered the years of loving and being loved by my military friends who stood in the gap for my father, giving support to my mother, and now fifty-five years later were still watching over me. I could hear my father God saying, "I send my word forth, it goes where I send it—it does what I send it to do and it does not return to me without accomplishing what I sent it to do" (Isaiah 55:11 paraphrased).

I was blessed with the double just like in the book of Job, and I felt the wind of the Spirit blowing on my vision again. I was in that circle of love that only God could provide. I was taking hold of the strong arm I had prayed for as I reached for Dan's hand, and I could hear my cousin Durm as he prayed over me the first night I slept on the land, "Thank you, Jesus, that my cousin is sleeping in her dream and dreaming in her sleep."

Great it is to dream the dream,

When you stand in youth by the starry stream;

But a greater thing is to fight life through,

And say at the end, "The dream is true!"

—John Osteen
Written by Edwin Markham

AFTERWORD

Today, Dan, Penny, Jacob, Jeremiah, and Haley share the "bigger dream" of ministering to children and their families who find themselves in compromised situations, currently unable to sustain a stable home. There are many reasons families have difficulties, and it is a refreshing option to find help at Jacob's House, where love comes first and questions are asked second.

The children come with full disclosure of their past and of their family history, but enter into Jacob's House with a clean slate, allowed to write their own future. The outcome of each child's experience is a choice they make individually to do the hard work required to develop into a loving, mature, productive person. The children are led by example, learning right from wrong, experiencing through trial and error the merit of wise decisions and appropriate behavior.

Jacob's House makes covenant with every child, that they will always find a safe haven there. From the smallest infant to the older teenagers, there is a forever refuge where love is freely given and valuable life instruction is meted out to develop the whole person. It is the philosophy of Jacob's House to bring healing to the entire family whether they are together or apart, purposing to maintain a healthy parent-child relationship when possible.

Jacob's house is nestled in the Ozark Hills outside of Branson, Missouri, on Thunder Ranch. The children can run on the seventy-one acres of trees and valleys, play in the creek with tadpoles and crawfish, tramp the land filled with horses, cattle and chickens that produce the family's daily egg supply (golden nugget happy eggs). After completing their responsibilities of school, homework, helping siblings, and doing personal chores, the children enjoy the freedom of childhood.

Their mission statement is "at Jacobs's house we are protecting children, preparing parents and prospering families."

There is a second home on the property where love abounds through another giving family who share their lives and shoulder the joint responsibility for those God has placed in the care of Jacob's House.

Plans in developing the dream include expanding into the care of disabled children. Sunshine House, a specially equipped home, is on the table as the next stage of the dream. Sunshine House will have the atmosphere of a cozy home not an institution, as "brothers and sisters" work and play together, attempting to meet each other's needs on an emotional and physical level as they are guided by loving "parents." Proceeds from *I Thought You Had a Bigger Dream* will help make Jacob's House debt free and finance the future building projects.

The family matriarch, Sally Nelson, though not infallible, lived a dynamic life, continuing in business until age eighty-nine, rising early, serving her clients, and enjoying every day. Over time it became apparent that not only was there a slow physical decline but a noticeable onset of dementia. In February 2009, Penny moved Sally to her home in Branson. Sally, in her own bigger-than-life style pitched in to help. To Penny, the unthinkable happened, as Sally was no longer able to function in her formidable fashion. After a short hospital stay, the doctor advised that around-the-clock care would be required. Penny found a lovely nursing home for her mother. The facility was right up Sally's alley, clean with a beautiful dining room. Who knew that in Sally's mind, she was keeping everyone on their toes, making sure all work was done in excellence as she "oversees" the staff, ensuring a successful enterprise. The staff at the nursing home is glad to play along as Miss Sally helps throughout the day. Sally is content and at peace which gives Penny peace. Penny says, "When you look at Mother in just the right light, she still casts a mighty big shadow." When recently asked if she was ready to go to heaven, Sally's quick response was "Hell yes, I'm ready."

The Koontz family has the support of a large blended family including six daughters, seven sons, nine grandchildren, and four great-grandchildren. Brian and wife, Michelle, reside in the Branson area. Brian has his own style of ministry, getting into the trenches as his path crosses the wayward one, offering whatever he has at hand, materially, emotionally and spiritually in attempt to meet the need. Ronnie and Noreen remain in Texas caring for little children in their home, giving amazing love to each, trusting God in meeting special needs, always ready to do all they are able.

Legacy is the driving force behind this family. While blood-lines zigzag in every direction, heart-lines are strong and commitment to each other is commendable. The message is the same whether to a child born of blood or a child born of the heart. "You are beautifully and wonderfully made, loved beyond measure, created to live a full abundant life. You can fulfill your individual purpose and plan. You have the choice. Choose you this day whom you will serve….." (Joshua 24:15, KJV).

In reviewing the book with the children, they asked Penny if they were in the story. She explained that as they are part of the family, they have their part in the story. She posed the questions to them, including her two fourth graders, "What legacy will you choose? Will you do what Grandpa Blatnik did who took the little he had with only a fourth grade education and fashioned a wonderful life for himself and his family through hard work and resolve?"

Will you choose the legacy of Jesus who told us when we take him as Savior, old things pass away, *behold*, all things are new?

Therefore if any person is [in-grafted] in Christ (the Messiah) he is a new creation (a new creature altogether); the old [previous moral and spiritual condition] has passed away. Behold, the fresh and new has come!

2 Corinthians 5:17 (Amplified Bible)

Will you leave those things of the past behind and choose to be part of His forever family? In doing so, you will be a person who looks outside your own basic needs and comforts, rising to a higher plane to do all you are capable of through the God-given gifts and graces you discover within yourself.

The purpose of telling the story of this everyday family is to prove, encourage, and inspire; to prove that endurance pays off, that hope yields success and love never fails; to encourage those who feel their circumstances insurmountable to keep on keeping on, knowing there is help available and a sure reward for not giving up; to inspire the one feeling the tug, hearing the call, to yield to the joy of serving.

As an old adage goes, "the same flame that melts butter makes steel strong." A person's reaction to the *flame* (the added stress, a tragedy, or adversity) determines the outcome. Will it make you or break you?

It is Penny's belief there should be a Jacob's House in every community by any name; a safe haven for every child. Do you have a vision? Do you hear the call to be a people-lover? Do you have a bigger dream? Share it with us. We would love to hear from you.

Penny can be contacted at penny@jacobshouse.org, or found online at www.pennyrobichauxkoontz.com. For those interested in learning more about Jacob's House, you are encouraged to visit the website at www.jacobshouse.org

Sally and Forey, May 1947, "Apple Blossom Time"

Penny at 1 year, a perfect match to the pickle jar

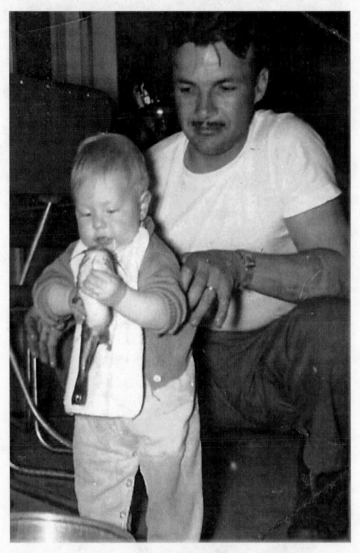

Penny and Daddy Forey, future outdoor pals

Penny at 2 ½ years below deer head rack made by Forey

Sally and Forey washing their car, always playful with a touch of mischief

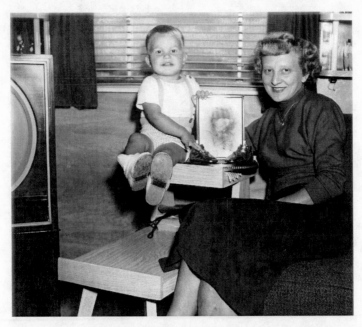

Jon and Sally, taken by newspaper reporter in 1952

Captain Munson of the Mispillion with the Nelsons

H.D. Kallam, the picture from the Cruise book burned in Penny's memory

Captain Munson and sons John and Chris (behind chair) with Penny at the electromyogram dedication

Penny said, "Go win the war, and bring my daddy home," Mrs. Neff looking on

Brother Jon in karate uniform with trophy

Brother Jon the marine, like father, like son

Penny in ANU

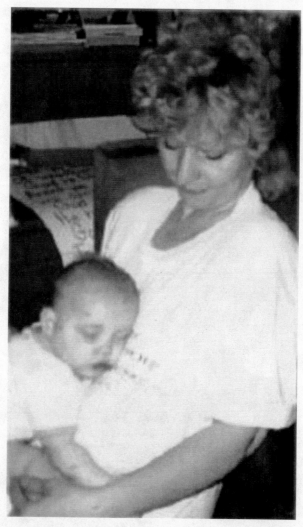

Penny and a baby, the beginning of The Garden and Jacob's house, 1991

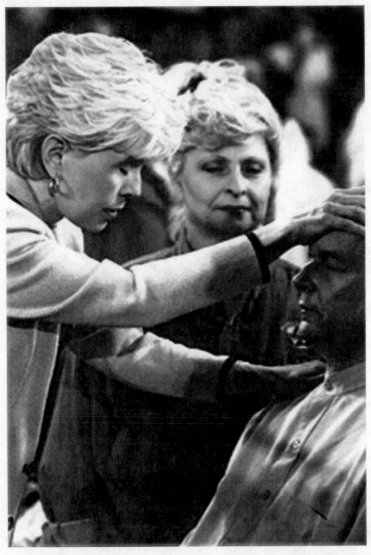

Gloria Copeland praying for Wayne Robichaux and Penny, 1999, Texas

Sally (on left) delights in showing the Navy men she accomplished her mission

H.D. Kallam and Penny, 54 years later, bless be the tie that binds

Mispillion "brothers" share the day with light hearts and good laughs

Dan and Penny on their wedding day, November 22, 2008

Jacob's House kids having fun at the creek

Jacob's House, a home for all seasons

ABOUT THE AUTHOR

Penny is an artist, teacher, motivational speaker, and business-woman who traveled the United States and launched businesses internationally in the health and fitness industry.

She established a homeless shelter in Rosenberg, Texas, and received the Jefferson Award in 1993 for public and community service.

Penny is the founder of Jacob's House, a children's home that operates outside the established norms but inside a circle of love, laughter, and discipline, providing a unique environment for the children.

Penny's desire is to inspire her readers to have a bigger dream regardless of what is against them, to prove everyone has what it takes inside to make a difference for themselves and their community. She demonstrates that if we'll respond to that deeper call to get up and go again, our bigger dream is waiting for us!